THE GROWTH AND STRUCTURE
OF ELIZABETHAN COMEDY

THE GROWTH
AND STRUCTURE OF
ELIZABETHAN
COMEDY

M. C. Bradbrook, LITT.D.

MISTRESS OF GIRTON COLLEGE
AND PROFESSOR OF ENGLISH LITERATURE,
UNIVERSITY OF CAMBRIDGE

New Edition

1973
CHATTO & WINDUS
LONDON

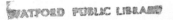

PUBLISHED BY
Chatto & Windus Ltd.
42 William IV Street
London WC2N 4DF

*

Clarke, Irwin & Co. Ltd.
Toronto

First Published 1955
Reprinted 1961 and 1962
New edition with additional
Chapter 12, 1973

ISBN 0 7011 0559 3

© M. C. Bradbrook 1955
Chapter 12 © M. C. Bradbrook 1973

Printed in Great Britain by
Redwood Press Limited
Trowbridge, Wiltshire

To

IAN AND NORAH

A TRIBUTE TO
AN INHERITANCE

CONTENTS

*

CONTENTS

PREFACE

*

This book, which attempts to trace the chronological development of Elizabethan comedy whilst distinguishing its characteristic forms, was begun in the summer of 1953 and finished in the summer of 1954. That I was enabled to complete it during the convalescence of an illness must be ascribed to the skill of Dr. Bernard Armitage; to him my most grateful thanks are due.

In the later stages of writing, I profited by recent work of Professor Alfred Harbage and Miss Madeleine Doran; in the tables especially I have relied upon Professor Harbage's work. Many friends have lent interest and encouragement; the most heartening has been that of Otakar Voçadlo, sometime Professor of English at the Charles University, Prague, whose devotion to Shakespearean studies is an inspiration to his pupils and friends.

A fully documented study by Marvin T. Herrick, *Comic Theory in the Sixteenth Century* (Urbana, 1950), did not come my way till too late, but happily it appears to support the general conclusions of Chapter III.

The Secretary of Girton College and her clerk, Miss Helen Smith, gave valuable help in the preparation of the MS.

The dedication acknowledges something of my obligation to those who bear the principal responsibility for the appearance of this work.

M. C. BRADBROOK

Cambridge, December 1954

PART I

THE MAKINGS OF ELIZABETHAN
DRAMA

CHAPTER I

INTRODUCTION

1. The Development of Drama

THE development of Elizabethan and Jacobean drama cannot readily be plotted. Too many factors are involved. The older historians, such as F. E. Schelling,[1] attempted some classification through the subject-matter of the plays, but only in the most general way. Recently writers have devoted themselves to special forms, such as Revenge Tragedy, the English History Play and the Court Masque,[2] which depend on a new understanding of the poetic principles underlying dramatic composition. This is largely due to a revival of interest in rhetoric, the pivot of the higher education in Elizabethan times.[3] Studies both of drama and of non-dramatic poetry have been written on the basis of rhetorical form, by which the special 'kinds' of poetry were distinguished.

At the same time, studies in stage history have revealed more of the popular ties of Elizabethan playwriting, its close connexion with seasonal festivals, with the lively tradition of mumming, with city pageantry and revels.[4] This tradition naturally predominates in comedy, the popular domestic tragedy, with its roots in homily and balladry, being a relatively minor 'kind'.

Comedy has received comparatively little attention from critics, perhaps because its ingredients are more varied and its lines of development less obvious than those of the well-marked forms of tragedy and history. Yet comedies outnumber tragedies on the Elizabethan stage by nearly three to one. Sweet and bitter comedy, romantic and satiric comedy, or Shakespearean and Jonsonian comedy have all been used as terms of description for the two main divisions, of which the first may be said to be characteristically Elizabethan, and the second Jacobean.[5]

In the following chapters I have tried to trace the evolution and the interaction of these two comic forms. Behind

3

ELIZABETHAN COMEDY

Elizabethan drama there lay at least two modes of acting—
first, the tradition of the revels, whether courtly or popular,
and all that these implied of intimate collaboration between
actors and audience. The general relation of actors and
audience is a subject which has become increasingly promi-
nent in Elizabethan studies. The form of the playhouses, at
one time the chief concern of stage historians, is now seen to
be important chiefly for the collaboration which it induced
between audience and players.[6]

Second, the learned tradition of rhetorical and satiric
drama upon moral themes, built up in the schools and universities, found expression in an even more intimate private
presentation; but the order and formality of such composi-
tions were in sharpest contrast to the shapeless stories of
the popular drama, based often upon the rambling medieval
romantic tale. When these two traditions coalesced, the great
age of Elizabethan drama began. The main literary tradition in England as elsewhere was a narrative one, inherited
from the later Middle Ages. The first problem confronting
dramatic poets was that of transforming narrative material
and traditions into dramatic form.[7] Not only the stories, but
the organization of the stories, was based on narrative. In the
miracle plays narrative technique had ruled the dialogue.

Classical theory enlarged less on comedy than tragedy, but
the plays of the ancient comic theatre were widely known.
The precepts of classical writers were refashioned by critics
of the Renaissance to conform with their own presupposi-
tions: Italian critics evolved a rigid set of prescriptions for
the writing of plays, which were little calculated to help the
practising dramatist. At the same time, the whole bias of
education was towards a somewhat naïve belief in the efficacy
of such formulæ.[8]

Hence the popular playwrights were confronted with a
second problem. The right way of making comedies, as indicated for example by learned friends of the Sidneys, was not
likely to be compatible with public entertainment. Yet some
deference to the rules of art must be achieved if drama was
to attract noble patronage, and the shapeless popular tradition was in need of organization. The learned tradition was
equally in need of flexibility.

4

Fortunately in England, as also in Spain, the strength of native taste was sufficiently powerful to counteract the great prestige of neo-classic form. Literary development was retarded in England by comparison with that of France and Italy; the provincial and outlying position of the country on the fringe of Europe had sheltered it from too rapid an infusion of the new learning. Hence a real amalgamation between native art and the learned tradition was possible, and in the drama, a form where the demands of the unlearned made themselves most clearly felt, it was achieved.

Even such early sixteenth century plays as those of John Heywood show this very special fusion of popular vigour and classic organization. The plays of Lyly were the first successful attempts to transplant and modify Italian eloquence and to make a drama both courtly and pungent. He gave the English drama shape. At the same time, Peele, working in the more indigenous forms, raised them to the level of conscious though simple art.

Shakespeare finally evolved a stable form of Elizabethan comedy, first modelling himself with some strictness upon learned example, and then rejecting the over-ingenious and over-planned pattern of his earliest attempts for a more popular style. His strength alone was capable of welding the two traditions firmly together, and his rejection of simple learning in favour of complex nature was a decisive step. Between *The Comedy of Errors* and *The Merchant of Venice* there is as great a distance as between *Titus Andronicus* and *Romeo and Juliet*. The development in each case is from a prescribed formula towards organic freedom of growth.[9]

Shakespeare remained in the eyes of his contemporaries a popular writer. His art was personal to himself, although his dramatic language, both verse and prose, laid the foundations for the Jacobean comic writers who succeeded him. It was through the speech of his characters that Shakespeare distinguished without dividing them; and this speech was based on the diction of common life. For him, plays belonged to an oral tradition: they sprang from the special conditions of the Elizabethan public theatre, and were designed to appeal in the greatest possible variety of ways to the widest possible audience.

The untutored and 'Elizabethan quality' of Shakespeare's art[10] was replaced by the conscious and deliberately planned work of Ben Jonson. He absorbed the work of Shakespeare, but, like a cuckoo in the nest, supplanted his fostering elder. Jonson's art was more imitable than Shakespeare's; it did not depend so much upon special insight as upon general standards of decorum, order and hard work. Nevertheless, Jonson was bold in his readiness to modify classical precept, he admired the native tradition, and the form which he evolved was as far removed from the pedantic as it was from the spontaneous.

The War of the Theatres represents the first clash between the older and the newer forms of playwriting. Shakespeare and Dekker stood for the old, and Jonson for the new. Although the traditionalists appear to have triumphed on this occasion, the history of comedy in the seventeenth century is the history of their slow retreat before the advance of Jonsonian art. Dekker and Thomas Heywood, who represented the oral way of writing, gradually sank to a spectacular melodrama, as their plays became more and more dissociated from those of the wits; and as the audience lost its old homogeneity and split up into the noisy 'prentices at the Red Bull and the fine gallants at the New Blackfriars, the possibility of a truly inclusive dramatic form gradually disappeared. Fletcher and Chapman wrote for a sophisticated but narrow group; moreover, they wrote not only for the actor but the reader of books also. Finally, in some of the courtly revels, Jonson recalled almost nostalgically the simpler forms of his youth, as the living tradition disintegrated, and the older form perished.[11]

ii. Drama and Society

It has been frequently observed that the comedy of Jonson and Fletcher is closely linked with that of the Restoration theatre, where their plays were often revived. Comedy, unlike tragedy, modified and survived. Yet the especial greatness of the plays written in the last decade of Elizabeth's reign and the first decade of James's was dependent on conditions essentially transient—upon the momentary fusion of the popular and learned traditions, the temporary interaction of two modes which were not permanently compatible with each other.

Out of this tension, the greater Elizabethan and Jacobean comedies were bred. Theatrical and rhetorical, organized and spontaneous, artificial and natural, they reflected a way of life and of speech which were likewise of the hour. Formal manners and violent passions, gravity and brutality, jest and dignity might be exemplified in the lives of the great from Sir Thomas More to Sir Walter Ralegh; these virtues did not equally belong to the generation of Strafford and Laud, Pym and Milton.

The critic cannot hope to recreate the Elizabethan point of view for the modern reader. A work of art, once committed to publication, stands in independence of its author. In the custody of the generations which transmit it, it may acquire a patina of meanings which formed no part of the original design.[12] Yet this very tradition, being partly formed by the works of art themselves, will not develop irresponsibly; and eccentricities of misinterpretation can always be corrected by an appeal to the general understanding, and, where it is ascertainable, to the original intent.

In this book, I have attempted to recover something of the original point of view from which these comedies were written, not in order to impose a new valuation of them, but to make them more intelligible and more accessible. Understanding, which is no substitute for insight, may recover some measure of prestige for those unformulated, traditional elements of the drama which give it vitality and by which alone it lives. Such comedy should not be read in terms merely verbal; it should be imagined as a living, complex, transitory performance. Many Elizabethan plays which appear shapeless on the printed page acquire complete integrity in the theatre. Middleton's *Changeling* is the outstanding example in tragedy;[13] comedy is in general of a far lower vitality when transplanted to the study, and this perhaps may account for the comparative neglect of it by literary historians. Even in the theatre, it is impossible now to re-establish the atmosphere of the older drama. The Elizabethan audience, rowdy, vocal, sometimes dangerous, far more conscious of its unity, far better acquainted and more unified than the modern audience, was also prepared to be instructed and edified. It came with a very definite set of moral expectations, with which both players and playwrights were familiar. Neither the manners nor the morals of the original audience can be recaptured.

Lesser writers accepted the conditions of the theatre; greater writers transformed and thus transmitted them. Among the great, Ben Jonson and Shakespeare stand so far above all competitors that they may well be called the creators of English drama. They were friends and rivals; their contemporaries and successors were aware of the fact, and throughout the seventeenth century they were contrasted. But whereas 'Shakespeare's magic could not copied be', Jonson provided the succeeding age with a model which was only too acceptable. His influence might be compared with that of Milton on the subsequent writers of heroic verse. The 'Chinese wall' which he built against barbarism remained to divide Elizabethan from all subsequent drama; after Jonson nothing was quite the same again.[14]

His return in old age to the forms of an earlier day is none the less proof of the power which they had for him. He himself, if not, like his sovereign, 'mere English', was rooted in the life of the City, and his crowded stages as hospitable as Shakespeare's to all sorts and conditions of men. Jonson's comedies include however the odd rather than the ordinary, and the idiosyncratic rather than the typical character. Shakespeare's characters 'are not modified by the customs of particular places . . . by the peculiarities of studies or professions . . . or by accidents of transient fashions' as Jonson's are. 'In the writings of other poets a character is too often an individual: in those of Shakespeare it is commonly a species.'[15]

In this, too, Shakespeare relied upon older traditions and native models. English poetry had already known, in Chaucer, a writer whose eye for the 'genuine progeny of common humanity' went with a temper both sympathetic and ironic. The connexions between Chaucer and Shakespeare are not of the kind to be readily and easily demonstrated—unlike Spenser, Shakespeare did not make the mistake of trying to use a Chaucerian vocabulary. But the poet whom

Deschamps had called 'the very God of Love in England' was the readiest model for 'sweet Master Shakespeare' whose reputation depended upon *Romeo and Juliet* and *The Merchant of Venice*. In Chaucer's young Squire—

> 'Embroudered was he, as it were a meede
> Al ful of fresshe floures, whyte and reede.
> Syngynge he was, or flóytgynge, al the day;
> He was as fressh as is the month of May—'

may be seen the original of Master Fenton, the wooer of sweet Anne Page—

> '. . . he capers, he dances, he has eyes of youth, he writes verses, he speaks holiday, he smells April and May . . .'   3.2.

or of Orlando himself. The creator of Harry Bailly and the Wyf of Bath would certainly have recognized in the creator of Falstaff his true heir and successor.

When Jonson wrote of the greenwood, as he did in *The Sad Shepherd*, he produced lovely poetry but indifferent drama. He was a Cockney, and his rogues' gallery was based not only on reading but also on observation. Shakespeare saw all large towns, ancient and modern, as if they were London; each had a tidal river and a populace of small tradesmen, and even in Italy the south suburbs held an Elephant Inn.[16] Jonson on the other hand first set *Every Man in his Humour* in Italy, then in the revised version moved it to London and added local colour. Such immediate reflexion of 'the time's form and pressure' in Elizabethan and Jacobean comedy is the origin of its success and the guarantee of its continuing life; for this comedy of character depended upon social relationships, and the delineation of men in society. Both Shakespeare and Jonson themselves enjoyed that kindled fellowship which is the special glory of the theatre.

Modern sympathy with primitive art and with the symbolic rather than the logical structure of poetry make it easier to accept the form of a writer like Dekker as a genuine alternative to Jonson's. The surviving relics of popular art have in this generation recovered their significance for a wide public.[17] Among literary critics there is a new appreciation of such asyndetic form as that of *Piers Plowman*.[18] Modern

9

poets themselves have learnt from such sources; on the other hand, they have rehabilitated the art of rhetoric, which often, especially in the later plays of Yeats and Eliot, determines their dramatic structure. The conditions for an understanding of Elizabethan comedy are therefore at present unusually favourable; and even the possibility of stage revivals may now be entertained.

In the early chapters it has not been possible to separate the rise of comedy from general dramatic development, nor were the divisions between the kinds rigidly adhered to even by the learned Elizabethan. To trace lines of development consistently, strict chronological order must also be abandoned, though a general perspective has been maintained. The separate consideration given to the works of Shakespeare bears no relation to their intrinsic interest; they have been considered only in so far as they illustrate the work of other writers, or determine the course of literary development.

Since it has survived in considerable quantity, satiric comedy may also appear to receive less than its due. It is more easily read than popular comedy, since it was designed as literature; the great names of Jonson and Middleton are associated with it; and it is directly ancestral to Restoration comedy, and so to the modern theatre. To taste the full savour of the greatest Elizabethan comedy it is necessary however to recover something of that manifold inheritance in which satire was only an ingredient.[19]

CHAPTER II

POPULAR DRAMA: THE TRAFFIQUE OF THE STAGE

1. Medieval Drama

DRAMA is the co-operative creation of author, actors and audience. It exists, when completely realized, in a mutual relationship between these three, an intercourse from which it issues and on which it depends. Criticism which is embodied in production, like that response of the audience which kindles and transforms the actors, is too evanescent to be captured or repeated, for all performances are different; yet it is only in such moments that the special richness, the living fullness of drama is displayed.

Ancient drama, and the medieval English drama in part, were Acts of Faith, directed to a God who might be both subject and audience of the play. A ritual, bringing down to bare board self-subsistent and eternal truths, required that actors, playwrights and musicians should be anonymous: an individual style would be inappropriate. Nevertheless the nativity might be set on a Yorkshire moor, for here, as everywhere, Incarnation was daily re-enacted. To the modern eye, the tradesman who portrayed a story suitable to his trade may have been indulging in a primitive form of advertisement: to the pious of his day, he might be offering his skill in the fashion of Our Lady's Tumbler. The *governing intention* is the most difficult aspect of meaning to establish, indeed some modern critics would deny the possibility of doing so.

Physical traffic on the lurching waggons ceased before Shakespeare's boyhood: he might have seen a Coventry Hock Tuesday play. The memory of these performances at least would be with the first generation of his audience. When he wrote a cycle of secular history plays, depicting the Fall and Redemption of the English monarchy, Shakespeare was adapting the forms of the old Faith to the glory of the new state, as any good Protestant would do. With the fall of Richard II, the Garden of England is despoiled. With the casting out of the diabolic Richard III, and the triumph of the angelically supported Henry, the ghosts are led out of hell and the curse is annealed. A divine comedy is re-enacted in political terms. In this history cycle the whole over-arching design does not preclude a large liberty in develop-ing individual plays. The relation of the parts to the whole is a matter of consequences and echoes, not of a single story. Falstaff and Mak the sheep-stealer are equally irrelevant in one sense, equally necessary in another. Shakespeare's one individual creation of dramatic form, the secular history cycle, has its roots in the oldest and strongest of the popular dramatic traditions, and the transition had in fact been made by the people themselves, as in the Coventry play of English and Danes, 'their old storial show', which was revived for the Queen in 1575, and led by the celebrated tradesman-player, Captain Cox.

Here too the permanent validity of the action would come home to all spectators. This was the history of their own land, and a lively mirror of dangers still apprehended as present. Queen Elizabeth's portrait was often drawn en-closed in the red rose and the white: the blood of these kings ran in her veins. When she appeared in person, in such plays as *England's Joy, When you see me, you know me,* and *The Whore of Babylon*,[1] the story of her early troubles developed into the legend of a Protestant saint, guarded by angels, miraculously delivered, and divinely strengthened and ad-monished. The familiar patterns of medieval hagiology glorified the Protestant Virgin who may have inherited through meekness, but who did not find it a virtue com-patible with sovereignty.

II. The Public Stages: Actors and Audience

The continuity of medieval and Elizabethan drama does not need to be stressed; and this continuity is not merely a literary tradition. The Elizabethan theatre, though it prob-ably did not allow the actor to be completely surrounded by his audience, as did the old pageant waggon trundling through the streets, owed as much to triumphs, and to street theatres, as it did to the structure of the innyard. The audience were brought into the play by direct address, by being invited to join in song or prayer or to bestow applause: and the actors may have used the yard, and yard alleys, for entries and exits.[2] The wooden boards set up on barrels in a country town for a one-night stand must have left the player rather in the position of a modern orator on his soap box. Investigation of the history of provincial companies in Elizabethan England has shown how extensive were their activities, which, from the end of the fifteenth century to the Civil War, 'covered the land like lace'.[3] Dozens of small and obscure bands of players are known only from town records, which mention the payment of ten shillings for a night's entertainment, or the bestowal of ale and sugar as payment in kind. Four or five men with a cart of costumes and a drum and trumpet to proclaim their approach might prove worthy rivals to the town waits, who were still surviving as late as 1612, when Heywood wrote in his *Apology for Actors*:

> 'To this day, in divers places of England, there be towns that hold the privilege of their fairs and charters by yearly stage plays, as Manningtree in Suffolk (sic), Kendal in the North and others'[4]

Local players would combine their function with some other trade; the professional actors were largely recruited from among the artisans and might in their wills describe themselves as tilers, vintners or glaziers. The high degree of professional organization which characterized the leading London stage companies in the fifteen-nineties was akin to that of the gilds who had so persistently opposed this establishment; and they had of course their 'prentices, the boys who played women's parts, as well as their hired men. By contrast, in *Histriomastix* (1599), a beard-maker, a fiddle-string maker, a peddler and a down-at-heels poet are shown illegally incorporating themselves as country players:

Incle: This Peace breeds such plenty, trades serve no turns.
Belch: The more fools we to follow them.
Posthaste: Let's make up a company of players,
    For we can all sing and say,
    And so (with practice) soon may learn to play . . .
Incle: What parts would best become us sir I pray?
Belch: Faith, to play Rogues till we be bound for running away.

1.3.

Calling a scrivener to draw up articles, they give the 'obligatories' condition' as 'politician players', and invent a patron for themselves.[5]

Thus while the position of the leading actors gradually became prosperous and secure, so that they wrote themselves gentlemen, such poor strollers with forged licence and a repertory of three or four shabby plays were little better than the Rogues and Vagabonds the Statute declared them to be. The audience varied in like manner. That same play which was studied by courtiers and performed before the Queen might on another day be acted before 'the very scum, rascality and baggage of the people, thieves, cutpurses, shifters, cozeners: briefly, an unclean generation and spawn of vipers'.[6] Most Elizabethans, if not all, were trained listeners. They attended the law-courts as a recreation: they heard sermons by the hour: their education lay largely in the practice of disputation, which Sir Humphrey Gilbert thought necessary even for those who intended to engage only in practical affairs.[7]

To compensate for their lofty position, the leading London companies must have developed a special familiarity with their audience. The casual customer of the modern box office drawn from a London of nine millions is quite without identity; but the Elizabethan actor and the rest of the audience would be acquainted not only with the Lords in their rooms over the stage or their stools upon it, but also with any notable wag in the twopenny gallery or among the groundlings whose interruptions had made him familiar.

Appeals to the audience, soliloquies and asides directed towards them, and sudden allusions to familiar scenes or everyday events—those anachronisms which worry the solitary reader—would be varied according to the nature of the listeners. Actors might turn towards the principal spectator, might interpolate a few lines or reword a scene. The barometer of feeling, fluctuating freely, might be met by the practised player with almost extempore adaptation. Insistent calls for the clown might bring him on. At Shrovetide, when 'prentices were out for a frolic, the audience might call for their favourite play:

'sometimes *Tamburlaine*, sometimes *Jugurth* or *the Jew of Malta*, and sometimes parts of all these, and at last, none of the three taking, they were forced to undress and put off their habits and conclude the day with *The Merry Milkmaids*. . . . And unless this were done, and the popular humour satisfied, as sometimes it so fortuned, that the players were refractory, the benches, the tiles, the laths, the stones, oranges, apples, nuts flew about most liberally, as there were mechanics of all professions who fell everyone to his trade.' [8]

In the Prologue to *The New Inn*, Jonson himself hints at such a possibility even in the private theatre, when he compares the author to a cook dressing plays and promises that

> 'Every dish
> Be serv'd in i' the time and to your wish'

but fears, when the expectation grows too loud,

> 'That the nice stomach would have this or that,
> And being ask'd or urg'd, it knows not what.'

A Puritan preacher might intervene with a denunciation as Zeal-of-the-Land Busy broke up the puppet show at Bartholomew Fair, or as Bunch and Mistress Flowerdew interrupt at Blackfriars in Randolph's *Muses' Looking Glass*. More congenial interference is parodied in *The Knight of the Burning Pestle*, where the citizen and his wife thrust their favourite 'prentice in to play a part. At the end of Act IV of *The Staple of News*, the four good gossips who have come to see the play decide how it shall end, like the audience at the conclusion of *The Beggar's Opera*. The courtly auditor would jeer and interrupt and draw attention to himself, for he went to see and to be seen: censurers of the play would become so vocal that in the Induction to *Bartholomew Fair* Ben Jonson drew up a form of agreement with them, licensing them to judge at more or less length according to the price of their seats. The actors on the other hand might use not only the standing room of the 'yard' but the groundlings themselves as part of a crowd. [9]

III. Courtly, Popular and Academic Plays

The great headstreams of Elizabethan drama are not without hidden springs: courtly plays are recorded or sometimes published, as are those which took place in the Universities and Inns of Court; but the existence of a popular romantic drama from the middle of the fifteenth century onwards can only be inferred from occasional hints, such as the play of Sir Eglamour performed at St. Albans, and the one on 'a knight named Florens' given at Bermondsey in 1447. York saw a drama on Joly Wat and Malkyn in 1447, and a pageant of Christmas and the twelve months was performed at Norwich a few years earlier.[10] Lincoln, Hitchin, Coventry had plays. All great households might act at the festivals of Christmas, Easter and Whitsun: country-folk would put on a Whitsun pastoral and a play of St. George at Christmas. Mumming and masquing, in the hands of rustics or courtly amateurs, grew perhaps from ballads on Maid Marian and Robin Hood, or the strife of Holly and Ivy and the Flower and the Leaf. In their College Halls, students staged Latin and English *ludae* on some academic argument such as might have formed the basis of a disputation in the schools that very morning. Frequently their plays turned on topical matters of a social or political interest which could not have been put upon public stages. *Wisdom* and *Wit and Science*, *Like Will to Like* and *The Longer thou Livest the more Fool thou Art* are at once extremely coarse and extremely moral: scenes of good advice and of gay riot are mingled in an attempt to provide both doctrine and mirth. The young lawyers or clerics often framed their plays as debates between four or more disputants. Arguments were in themselves exhilarating, especially the fallacious arguments of the Vices. Plays staged in a crowded Hall with the actors elbowing their way to the dais and coming on through the audience could only be given with the participation of the bystanders. Cries of 'Room' come chiefly from the comic characters, as they push the spectators back and indulge in a little horseplay to cover the change of costume for a doubled part. The spectators might on the other hand be swept into the action, given a coat to hold or deprived of a hat, appealed to with great deference or ribald impoliteness—the extremes of courtesy from prologue and epilogue, the extremes of discourtesy from the clowns, who would refer pointedly to their stinking breath, feeble wits and unprepossessing appearance. Nicholas Newfangle in *Like Will to Like* nicknames individuals:

'How say you, woman, you that stand in the angle,
  Were you never acquainted with Nichol Newfangle?'

he cries on his entrance: and when the cutpurse and pickpocket enter, he admonishes:

'See to your purses, my masters, and be ruled by me,
For knaves are abroad, therefore beware.
Ye are warned: and ye take not heed, I do not care.
How sayest thou, Wat Waghalter? is that a true thing?'[11]

Sometimes a stooge was planted in the audience, and according to the well-known story of Sir Thomas More, sometimes
a gifted member of it would improvise a part for himself,
and graduate actor on the spot. When the common actors
came to play at court, there must have been similar crowding
up to the stage, as the play scenes of *Hamlet* imply. It appears
that an arena stage—i.e. one completely encircled by the
audience—was used at Whitehall. In *Love's Labour's Lost*
and *Midsummer Night's Dream*, the amateur actors are mercilessly baited, whereas in Middleton's *A Mad World, My
Masters* and *The Mayor of Queenborough* the 'players' turn the
tables on the stage audience.[12]

Courtly shows might range from a fully independent
drama, transplanted from the public boards at the Queen's
request, to a masque or device in which players had minor
parts. Frequently the Queen would be drawn into the action,
being required to receive a gift, judge a contest, guess a
riddle or name a 'ship'. The gap between art and ordinary
life narrowed here, not by an allegorical shadowing of real
events, but rather by the culmination of the action in the
present moment, the present situation.[13]

In her frequent progresses the sovereign brought something of the courtly activity into the countryside. In the
Cotswolds, Elizabeth saw the local sports: the pageants at
great houses linked on naturally to festivals both public and
private—at wakes, fairs and great weddings—so that a whole
network of dramatic activities joined the common life and the
stage. With the founding of the great companies of the last
years of Elizabeth's reign, a degree of specialization grew
up: the Admiral's may have excelled in heavy tragedy, the
Children certainly specialized in witty satire and fantastic

horrors: the Chamberlain's was a general utility company, and it is clear that they succeeded in pleasing a wider variety of people than most theatres. Some attempt has recently been made to distinguish the expensive, fashionable private theatres in which the Children played as 'the theatre of a coterie' where Italianate plots, risqué personalities, and salacious epigrams were purveyed; while the public theatres showed genial and honest characters, in comedies that were cleanly and tragedies that were noble, ruled by traditional virtues.[14] In general it may be hazarded that the public theatres evolved from the old gild play, the civic procession and the public show: while the private theatres reproduced the conditions of courtly and university acting and would draw their audiences from the classes who had been accustomed to such performances. However this may be, Shakespeare could rely upon his audience for an imaginative response, as the bold appeal at the beginning of the third act of *Henry V* makes plain.

> 'Play with your fancies and in them behold
> Upon the hempen tackle, ship boys climbing;
> Hear the shrill whistle which doth order give
> To sounds confused: behold the threaden sails. . . .
> Work, work your thoughts and therein see a siege. . . .' [15]

This is not, like Ben Jonson's prologue to *Every Man in his Humour*, an ironic underlining of the public stage's imperfections, which would be very poor tactics, but an appeal for sympathy. The events to be depicted were part of English history, of a great victory, which was for the audience a living part of themselves, in which perhaps they saw the reflexions of a recent expedition. Such appeals recall the moments in pantomime when the audience are invited to join in the songs, or the moment in *Peter Pan* in which they are asked to save the life of Tinker Bell by clapping their hands. Appeals for applause at the end of a play are often made by characters who step out of their roles to speak the epilogue. Those moments when the characters directly address the audience are usually either at the beginning, the end or the climax; that is, at the time when sympathetic contact is most necessary.

In listening to soliloquy, an audience feel in particularly

close *rapprochement* with the speaker; but an aside also might not rebuff them by recalling that this was 'only a play': it might, on the contrary, imply that they were, in the French sense, assisting at it. The various levels of conventionalism and realism in an Elizabethan play are not evidence of an audience's detachment, in Dr. Johnson's sense: 'The truth is, that the spectators are always in their senses and know from the first act to the last, that the stage is only a stage, and that the players are only players. They come to hear a certain number of lines recited with just gesture and elegant modulation'.[16] Dr. Johnson gave demonstrative proof, by the composition of *Irene*, that he had no notion of the nature of theatrical illusion. *If challenged*, any spectator would be capable of detachment and would know Johnson's facts; but this is quite different from being constantly and consciously aware of them. Instead of stressing the artifice of the moment, Choruses were a recognition of the degree to which the audience were involved. The Elizabethans were not the dupes of theatrical naturalism, but their power of sharing a group-response was highly developed, their threshold of emotional reaction low, and their taste, though varied, was relatively unsophisticated. When Cassius looks forward to the acting of the lofty scene of Cæsar's death upon the stage, his speech underlines the most ritualistic moment in the play—that in which the conspirators wash themselves in Cæsar's blood. It transmutes the stagey qualities of dramatic climax: the audience are drawn into the original event, as the audience at a gild play might be drawn in.[17] When the boy Cleopatra parodied his own 'squeaking' greatness in the death scene, he must have spoken with especial mellifluousness: it was a positive challenge to the audience to detach themselves if they could. In one of the Children of Paul's plays, the ironic exclusiveness of the private playhouse is underlined:

Sir Edward: I saw the Children of Paul's last night,
And troth they pleased me pretty pretty well:
The Apes in time will do it handsomely.
Planet: I' faith, I like the audience that frequenteth there
With much applause: a man shall not be chokt
With the stench of garlic nor be pasted
To the balmy jacket of a beer brewer.[1]

The Prologue, spoken by the Tire-man, says that the poet has published 'the Booke' and the children will have to extemporize. Although Jonson began the practice of bringing on the little actors in their own persons with the Induction to *Cynthia's Revels*, where three of the Children of the Revels fight to speak the prologue, actors soon transferred it to the Globe, and Burbage appears with Sly and Lewin in the Induction to *The Malcontent*. The fool occupied a special place in the building up of this sympathy, and in *Greene's Tu Quoque*, the actor Greene, who gave the play its title and who played the foolish Bubble, is invited to 'go see a play at the Globe'.

> *Bubble:* I care not, any whether so the clown have a part: for i' faith I am nobody without a fool.
> *Geraldine:* Why, then we'll go to the Red Bull: they say Greene's a good clown.
> *Bubble:* Greene! Greene's an ass!
> *Scattergood:* Wherefore do you say so?
> *Bubble:* Indeed, I ha' no reason: for they say he is as like me as ever he can look.

Only the star actor, even in the Elizabethan theatre, could be sure enough of his public to be entrusted with such lines.

The crowded little London of the later sixteenth and early seventeenth centuries formed a single community,[19] and although the City Council, actuated perhaps as much by dislike of the financial implications of the new amusement industry as by their Puritan tenets, had done their best to keep out the harlotry players, they were hemmed in on all sides. To the northeast, in the marshes of Shoreditch, stood the old Theatre of the Burbages, and the Curtain: north of Cripplegate, Henslowe eventually built the Fortune playhouse. To the northwest, in the Priory at Clerkenwell, the hard-working Master of the Revels, Tilney, presided over an immense collection of properties and costumes; and here in the evening, after their performances at the public theatres, the actors would trudge to rehearse the shows they put on before Royalty at the great festivals. In Clerkenwell too the Red Bull theatre was built in 1604, after the players had been driven out by the plague to tour for a year, and many of the actors lived in the parish. Inside the City itself there were private playhouses within the liberties; and parish halls, then as now, were used for amateur theatricals.[20]

Southwest of London in the city of Westminster and the Temple, more amateur playacting flourished under royal and legal patronage, but often with the players' advice and collaboration. Across the water was the Globe Theatre, together with the Swan, the Rose, and the Bear Garden: here too was an actors' colony, and St. Saviour's, now Southwark Cathedral, was the actors' church of the day. Henslowe was at one time churchwarden, and Alleyn vestryman.

Within this little world, the city comedy of Jacobean times found its material. Dekker at times openly glorified the tradesman, while the wit of his *Westward Ho!* and *Northward Ho!* is directed against the citizens, but the scheme of these plays is based on exact local topography. In spite of the Aretine satire and cosmopolitan flavourings of Marston, Middleton and the other followers of Jonson, they were reflecting that same world which Greene and Dekker had described in coney-catching pamphlets. It is only with the drama of Chapman and Fletcher that an impersonal scene and characters merely literary appear.

iv. The Oral Tradition

Within an oceanic tide of sympathy, irony and delight, Elizabethan plays had their only being. Books were one thing, plays were another. The modern audience may go to see a play which they already know on the printed page; a film may draw a demand for 'the book of the film'. The difference which the printed text makes to an audience is small compared with the difference for the poet between composing for the ear and composing for the eye.

The integrity of an Elizabethan play was less stable than that of printed literature. There is some evidence that the Italian habit of extemporizing comedy was not quite unknown. In *The Travails of Three English Brothers*, Will Kempe is brought on the stage, and offers to extemporize 'a merriment' with an Italian team consisting of 'Harleken' and his wife. Hamlet's objection to gags from the clown is matched by his 'Come, let's have a play extempore'; and Cleopatra's

'The quick comedians
Extemporally will stage us'

seems to refer to the kind of command performance which might involve vamping an old play, as Shakespeare is said to have vamped *The Merry Wives* in a fortnight. A play a month was the normal ouput of some of his contemporaries. The speed with which the bill was changed, and the readiness with which successful pieces were copied must have meant that hasty work was taken for granted. When four or five poets were engaged on a single work, the various plots, loosely connected through a central moral, might be picked up from old plays.[21] 'The old Jeronimo as it was first acted' was so popular that the play was altered without any attempt to disguise the relation of the old and the new, but a new title and a few new lines might enable players to put forward botchers' work as a new play.

In the sixteenth century, literature and especially poetry was still predominantly an oral art. Ballads, songs and the courtly romance, sonnets and above all plays, were written to be transmitted through speech. The printing press, established in England some eighty years before the beginning of Elizabeth's reign, had not killed the older tradition of poetry, the spoken tradition which Chaucer had used, and which lingered on particularly at the two social extremes. In the Court, verses recited for a special occasion and directed to a particular person were discarded when their hour was past; while the broadside or popular song, cheaply printed and sold by peddlers, was only a means of implanting its material in the longer-lived memories of the country folk. Even Shakespeare's First Folio, handsome and dignified as it was, bore the marks of 'spoken words which had strayed on to the page' in its typography and lay-out, as a recent technical analysis has made clear.[22]

Authors, especially the nobility, made little attempt to claim their work as their own, in spite of the poet's habit of promising immortality to a patron or a mistress. The Elizabethan is the last age in which any large body of anonymous literature survives. Fifty years later only the scurrilous, the politically dangerous or the very ephemeral was so likely to go unfathered.

Even printing did not stabilize the plays. There were perhaps alternative versions of others than *The Spanish Tragedy* and *Hamlet, Every Man in his Humour* and 'York and Lancaster's long jars'. It is not reasonable to expect that a play should remain on the boards for thirty years without modification. The life of Shakespeare's plays, as of his lesser contemporaries', must have been fluid, amorphous, not unlike the life of a ballad. On the other hand, theatrical tradition included much that was not in the text—details of production such as alternate ways of doubling parts, business and effects, songs.

With Ben Jonson's publication of his plays in folio in 1616, the dignity of plays was asserted. There was much ribald comment at his raising common stage plays to the status of Works. Frequently in his prologues he appeals to those who come to listen as against those who come to see.

Seven years later, Shakespeare's friends claimed for him what he had never attempted to claim for himself, and the First Folio, his 'Monument', marked the end of the oral tradition. 'Our first duty as critics is to examine the words of which the play is composed, then the total effect which this combination of words produces in our minds' is the observation of a twentieth century critic. It could never have been made in Shakespeare's working'life.

Although retaining traces, in more ways than one, of the oral tradition behind it,[23] the Folio was a completely different thing from the flimsy little quartos: it was printing on the grand scale reserved for religious, legal and educational works. The very existence of the Bad Quartos shows how uncritical were the simple public who bought them. The cheap little twopenny or sixpenny books which appeared from Wynkyn de Worde's day onward, most of which have been thumbed out of existence, prove a taste for entertainment on the part of the humble. Even if a good many stage plays were printed—and it is on the whole probable that the majority were not [24]—they were composed in the manner determined by the players, and thought of primarily, like sermons and law-pleading, as oratory. Just as the older form of publishing with the help of a patron was still considered the most natural way to produce a dignified work, though it was really a survival from the age of manuscripts, so the status of print gave to popular works the means for transmission to the popular memory. Yet even the ballads as sold by Autolycus and learned by the clowns, cheaply printed though they were, must have hastened the death of pure oral literature. Romance, lyric and ballad, the great body of popular composition was vanishing before these ephemeral baggage books; the tradition passed, for a brief moment, to the popular stages. These late sixteenth century works stand in relation to the older verbally transmitted forms as Burns's songs to the folk-songs of Scotland. From the middle of the fifteenth century, it is probable that a popular romantic drama existed, closely related to ballads and festival games. But only fragmentary remains survived, compared with the bulk of moralities. The proportion recalls the slender handful of medieval secular lyrics compared with the quantities of sacred lyric. *Sir Clyomon and Sir Clamydes*, *Common Conditions* and *The Cobbler's Prophecy* indicate the kind of plays upon knights and monsters, fairy adventures and magic wonders, wishing wells, princesses and dragons of which those two extremely successful works, *Mucedorus* and *Pericles*, were the descendants. Some of these were among the most applauded plays of the time, and a debased version of *Mucedorus* was still being played in Shropshire villages in the early nineteenth century.[25] This is the kind of play which the mechanicals of *A Midsummer Night's Dream* think of: Bottom wants either to play a tyrant or a lover and Flute hopes Thisbe is 'a wandering knight'.

In publishing his Plays, Ben Jonson selected and rewrote those which he wished to preserve and left out his hackwork, such as *The Fall of Mortimer*. In his lines of praise for Shakespeare, he courageously claimed for his fellow the standing of a classic, and the right to literature's immortality. This was a reckless proof of his 'love for the man', which some would have held not to fall short of idolatry. Ben Jonson's own followers claimed even more for their master:

'The Greeks and Romans, denizen'd by thee
Are both made richer in thy poetry.'

Meanwhile Puritan clergy were fulminating that players' stuff received worthier printing than the word of God. There should perhaps have been sumptuary laws for the works of the mind, restricting certain garb to certain classes.

Occasionally the learned dramatist, a Chapman or a Daniel, or one of the Countess of Pembroke's circle, might publish a drama which was never intended for the stage. It is not for these works that the Elizabethan drama is remembered. In its 'divine fluidity' of rhythm and form, in its inclusiveness, its vigour and its myriad facets, no less than in its roughness, violence and bawdry, it remains the product of the boards, the mirror and offspring of the times. These playwrights knew the freedom of improvising, the enchantment of disembodied speech. There is no substitute for its lightness and flexibility.

When, in the course of the eighteenth century, the traffic of the stage was finally reduced to a one-way stream, the language had already undergone those restricting limitations which are suggested by popular dictionaries, uniform spelling and a standard pronunciation. 'It is not lack of character or lack of action and suspense, or imperfect realization of character, or lack of anything that is called "theatre" that makes early nineteenth-century drama so lifeless: it is primarily that their rhythm of speech is something that we cannot associate with any human being except a poetry reciter.' [26]

Yet 'There's no acting without an audience': as Sir Godfrey Tearle said on turning down a film contract, 'the public gives to the actor its warmth and responsiveness'. Sir Lewis Casson has observed that an audience should be like a football crowd, so engaged that they make involuntary sympathetic gestures, and become part of the scene. When the actor interprets for the audience, and the audience responds, stimulating the actor, the final event belongs exclusively to neither of them.

To the natural advantages of the Elizabethan audience must be added those supplied by education. For the educational system was also very largely an oral affair. The dispute, the lecture with commentary, the *viva voce* examination predominated; reading and writing occupied correspondingly less time. The grounding was firmly intellectual and moral: 'religion and good literature' were the requirements of more than one pious founder: [27] but for recreation and entertainment, playacting was allowed to take its part. The drama of the schools not only gave to the later Elizabethan stage literary models, but it also formed the habits of actors and audience. As cautionary tale and recreation the *utile* and the *dulce* combined in these plays, in the way suggested by Philip Sidney, himself no great adherent of pure learning:

> '. . . the child is often brought to take most wholesome things by hiding them in such other as have a pleasant taste: which if one should begin to tell them the nature of aloes or rhubarb they should receive, would sooner take their physic at their ears than at their mouth.'

THE LEARNED TRADITION 1560–1580: THE LANGUAGE OF COMEDY AND THE DRAMA OF THE SCHOOLS

1. Early Elizabethan Theories of Comedy

TO define comedy as the opposite of tragedy has always been a temptation to critics, for definitions of tragedy are more easily made, especially since Aristotle began by making them. In the Middle Ages, when tragedy disclosed the fall of great men from prosperity to adversity, comedy showed the happy issue out of initial difficulties. The medieval grammarians—Donatus in particular, whose essay was known even to schoolboys—were concerned above all to evolve a clear and precise antithesis between the two forms.

Tragedy being concerned with the great, remained primarily the imitation of an action seen from outside: comedy, revealing more familiar humbler persons, tended more and more to become the imitation of fixed types.[1] The basis of action was the contrast of such characters with each other, which led to comedy of situation or of manners according to the depth of realization. In an age when the predominant form was narrative, recited to an audience many if not most of whom would be illiterate, Chaucer's *The Monk's Tales* and *Troilus and Criseyde* were accepted as tragedies. They would at least be known to most of their auditors in dramatic readings.

Although the critics of the renaissance inherited many of the preconceptions of the later Middle Ages, they recovered a sense of the dramatic and the terms tragedy and comedy were generally used with reference to plays. Tragedy was sometimes loosely applied, rather in the manner of the modern journalist, to any violent action ending with physical death. It was still generally agreed that tragedy dealt with the downfall of great men, was based upon historical events, and that it revealed passions, and was consequently written in a lofty style: comedy depicted ordinary people but was not based on history, it revealed the fixed basis of temperament, manners and sentiments, and its style was varied.

For the entire sixteenth century, comedy was most readily defined by the learned not in terms of its own form and structure, but in terms of its effect upon the audience. The ultimate authority was Plato in the *Laws*, where comedy was seen as either satirical or farcical:

> 'It is necessary also to consider and recognize ugly thoughts and persons and those which are intended to produce laughter in comedy. ... For serious things cannot be understood without laughable things. And for this very reason, he should learn them both, in order that he may not in ignorance do or say anything which is ridiculous and out of place—he should command slaves and hired strangers to imitate such things, and should never take any serious interest in them himself. ...'
>
> vii. 816.

Comedy as a species of cautionary tale might justifiably deal with the scurrilous and the criminal: but in general it was restricted only to follies and treated of 'no weighty matters', as Ascham observed. Sir Thomas Elyot, like Plato, saw comedy from the pedagogue's point of view, recommending Terence or Plautus as:

> '... an interlude wherein the common vices of men and women are apparently declared in personages ... a mirror of man's life, wherein evil is not taught but discovered: to the intent that men beholding the promptness of youth unto vice, the snares of harlots and bawds laid for young minds, the deceit of servants, the changes of fortune contrary to men's expectations, they being thereof warned may prepare themselves to resist or prevent occasion.'

Thomas Wilson, the author of the influential *Art of Rhetoric* (1553)—which Shakespeare himself was to read—saw all laughter as derisive.

> 'The occasion of laughter and the mean that maketh us merry ... is the fondness, the filthiness, the deformity and all such evil behaviour as we see to be in other. ... Sometimes we laugh at a man's body, that is not well proportioned, and laugh at his coun-

tenance if it be not either comely by nature, or else he through folly cannot well see it. For if his talk be fond, a merry man can want no matter to hit him home, ye may be assured.' pp. 135–136

He went on to describe the various ways in which a man may be abashed by queries, jests, sneers and direct ridicule. Thomas Lodge declared that comedy will 'reprehend'— yet 'delightfully'. Harrington defended comedy as making 'vice scorned, and not embraced', Puttenham because it 'tends altogether to the good amendment of men by discipline and example', while the well-known passage in Sidney's *Defence of Poesie* echoes Plato.

'Comedy is an imitation of the common errors of our life, which he representeth in the most ridiculous and scornful sort that may be; so as it is impossible that any beholder can be content to be such a one. Now, as in Geometry, the oblique must be known as well as the right, and in Arithmetick the odd as well as the even, so in the actions of our life who seeth not the filthiness of evil wanteth a great foil to perceive the beauty of virtue.'

This was naturally somewhat dangerous doctrine, as without due heed to Plato's caveat, it could be used as the justification for a plentiful course of wild oats. It is indeed so used in Shakespeare's *King Henry IV*, where Prince Hal's wildness is excused as a comedy in which he has cast himself for the role of hero.

'The prince but studies his companions
Like a strange tongue wherein, to gain the language,
'Tis needful that the most immodest word
Be looked upon and learned: which once attained,
Your highness knows, comes to no further use
But to be known and hated. So, like gross terms,
The prince will in the perfectness of time
Cast off his followers.'

4.4.68–75.

Those Puritans who disapproved of plays on ethical grounds could query which way the learning would be taken as did Gosson, Stubbes and Northbrooke.[2]

' If you will learn how to be false and deceive your husbands . . . how to ravish, how to beguile, how to betray, to flatter, lie, swear,

foreswear . . . murder . . . poison . . . rebel . . . to consume treasure prodigally . . . to be idle, to blaspheme. . .' etc.,
go to the play. As Sidney notes,

'They say the comedies rather teach than reprehend amorous conceits.'

The defence often merely took the form of reassertion, but the more subtle apologists shifted their ground from ethics to medicine. Nicholas Udall, though a schoolmaster, aimed only at amusement, and comedy was generally recognized as physic for the mind and body. The Prologue to his *Ralph Roister Doister*, 1541, proclaims

'Nothing more commendable for a man's recreation
Than mirth which is used in an honest fashion.
For mirth prolongeth life and causeth health.
Mirth recreates our spirits and voydeth pensiveness.'

The author of *Jack Jugler* (1553)—a short one-act play for schoolboys, based on *Amphitryon*—aims no further:

'To make at seasons convenient pastime, mirth and game,
As now he hath done this matter not worth an oyster shell:
Except perchance it shall fortune to make you laugh well,
And for that purpose only this maker did it write.'

Udall's recipe of 'mirth mixed with sadness' is echoed by Ulpian Fulwell, the author of *Like Will to Like* (1568), who also provided a mixture, explaining 'mirth for sadness is a sauce most sweet'. A mixed form may produce a more powerful moral effect, as Whetstone observes, 'for by the reward of the good, the good are encouraged in well-doing: and with the scourge of the lewd, the lewd are feared from evil attempts'.[3] The defence in general, however, was conducted by subverting moral arguments rather than by meeting them. Comedy continued because the public was determined to have it; nor did learned and satiric comedy evoke the support commanded by plays of revelry and adventure, which flourished with all the faults that Whetstone, Sidney and Jonson deplored.

'Your Englishman first grounds his works on impossibilities: then in three hours he runs through the world, marries, gets children, makes children men, murders monsters, and brings Gods from heaven and fetcheth devils from hell.'[4]

30

This description, which remains exact though irrelevant as applied to the later popular plays of Dekker, Heywood or Haughton, was justly applied to early works such as *The Cobbler's Prophecy*.

In a passage which follows his denunciation of 'gross absurdities' of story and treatment, Sidney comes nearer to the description of comedy as it was actually to evolve than in his formal definition of it.

> 'But our comedians think there is no delight without laughter' which is very wrong. . . . Nay, rather, in themselves they have as it were a kind of contrariety: for delight we scarcely do but in things that have a conveniency to ourselves or to the general nature, laughter almost ever cometh of things most disproportioned both to ourselves and to nature. Delight hath a joy in it, either permanent or present. Laughter hath only a scornful tickling. For example we are ravished with delight to see a fair woman and yet are far from being moved to laughter. We laugh at deformed creatures, wherein certainly we cannot delight. We delight in good chances, we laugh at mischances: we delight to hear the happiness of our friends, and country, at which he were worthy to be laughed at, that would laugh.'

His illustration of Hercules 'painted with his great beard and furious countenance, in woman's attire, spinning at Omphale's commandment' forecasts all later comedy which depends upon the mockery of transformed lovers, from Alexander sighing for Campaspe to Benedick shaving his beard. By *delight* Sidney seems to mean a complete surrender to sympathy, in which the spectator utterly loses himself in the joy of what he contemplates. Delight is the opposite of the mocking ironic laughter of Plato and of Wilson. Between these two extremes of irony and sympathy, the best Elizabethan comedy resides: sweet and bitter fooling was easily distinguished,[5] but in the plays of Shakespeare the impulse towards identification and the impulse towards judgement might be simultaneously evoked—for example in *The Merchant of Venice*.

Comedy which aimed at giving 'an imitation of life, a mirror of manners and an image of truth'[6] was designed directly to promote noble deeds and the pursuit of virtue. The drama's especial power in compelling sympathy implied that 'in this most excellent work it was the most excellent workman'. Drama involved the spectator more completely than any other kind of poetry and therefore its action was decisive. Stories of thieves and murderers who had been brought to confess by seeing their deeds enacted were a commonplace of the day.

Since medieval definitions of comedy had depended on their antithesis with tragedy, comedy was all that tragedy was not. Such a dialectic mode of thought was perhaps inevitable in a scholastic age. It was not pursued in England, where theoretic criticism of the drama is very scanty; and the main concern of the later sixteenth century was with the general means of persuasion: that is, with the language itself. The drama was attacked and defended on ethical grounds, but before Ben Jonson there was little technical analysis of how it worked. To examine the critical evolution of comic writing is therefore to examine the general theory of rhetoric as applied to comedy.

Rhetoric was the whole art of using language to delight and compel the hearer's assent. Originally a school discipline, it became in this period something new—the study not of classical forms but of the rapidly shifting forms of the English language itself. Though based on classical rhetoric, the English *Arts of Rhetoric* were concerned with the immediate solution of an urgent practical problem.

ii. General Theories of Language

The speed of development within the English language during this period produced many perplexing problems of usage. At the same time that the language was changing with extreme rapidity, it was also being employed in new ways, particularly in education and literature.

The quite peculiar badness of much early Tudor poetry needs to be recollected. It was not merely dull and monotonous, like Lydgate: it was frankly monstrous. This resulted from experiments, carried on in a language which was changing too rapidly for such experiments to be fully controlled. Fantastic importations ranged from inkhorn Latinisms and quantitative metre to Petrarchan conceits and all the courtly flourishes which went with sonneteering, Italianate manners and foreign attire. In 1584 John Soowthern, a servant of the Earl of Oxford, translated Ronsard into a kind of pidgin French, in which English words are given French stresses.

> 'Though I wish to have your favour, which is such
> That it is but for Gods, think you my Audace,
> Like his that in your stead, did a cloud embrace,
> Or his that was a harte, by seeing so much.
> Or would you else, because of my hautaine thought,
> That I might augment the sepulchres of Thrace,
> Or that I were as the giant Briareas:
> Or paid like the waggoner so evily taught. . . .'[7]

In his *Art of Rhetoric* Wilson gives an example of inkhorn terms in a letter from a Lincolnshire man, asking a servant of the Lord Chancellor to procure a benefice for him.

> 'Pondering, expending and revoluting with myself, your ingent affability and ingenious capacity for mundane affairs: I cannot but celebrate, and extol your magnifical dexterity above all other. For how could you have adopted such illustrate prerogative, and dominical superiority, if the fecundity of your ingenie had not been so fertile and wonderful pregnant.'   p. 163.

In the midst of such encumbered stuff, the drama flourished in familiar and humble guise. It was conservative in its language, an element making for stability. Comic interludes were lustily coarse, and even the most learned translators of Plautus were as vulgarly and vigorously given to their mother tongue as the country clown.

In learned circles it was, up to the eighties, a question whether English was fit to be used at all for any but practical everyday affairs. Wilson, Cheke and Ascham preached a return to Chaucerian, and even Saxon vocabulary: Spenser, a dutiful son of Cambridge, endeavoured in *The Shepherds Calendar* to comply. Passionate national feeling, such as that upholding the Welsh and Irish languages today, ensured the triumph of English—not through the prescriptions of the grammarians but through the performance of the poets. Quite suddenly, towards the end of the fifteen-eighties, apologies for the rude, barbarous, base, vile, barren and 'misorned' vulgar tongue gave way to triumph.[8]

It was, however, not the triumph of nationalist purists 'By the eighties, the Saxon shield-wall had everywhere given way and the foreigners were swarming through the breaches. Coinage now became rampant'.[8a] Confidence in the English language led to a general taste for gorgeousness. The late Elizabethan rhetoricians such as Peacham, France, Puttenham and Day were ready to set out plans, after the poets had begun to practise: Sidney and Spenser were acclaimed not for the literary merits of their works but for the general service they had performed to the language. In complete and irresistible force, the literary movement swept past the reforming rhetoricians, who now found themselves derided pedants. In the sixties, Ascham, Cheke and Wilson had led the way: but Gabriel Harvey, the donnish friend of Spenser, emerged in the nineties as Harvey the ludicrous opponent of Tom Nashe. Parody of the schemes and tropes, parody of sonneteering, parody of the older tragic style and of Euphuism in comedy testify to a complete emancipation on the part of writers from the leading-strings of academic discipline.

The changes in the language were apparent to all. Hence the large amount of time which is given to word-games in comedy is not merely a learned habit or a stage trick; it is a way of dealing with a real social issue; the problem of the English language was part of the general problem of the new secular education.[9] The working man tried to follow in the steps of the learned: in the days when inkhorn terms were still popular, Wilson tells one or two stories of Dogberry in real life, adopting a learned speech as Shakespeare's Dogberry did.

'When I was in Cambridge and student in the King's College, there came a man out of town with a pint of wine in a pottle pot, to welcome the Provost of that house, that lately came from the court. And because he would bestow his present like a clerk, dwelling among the scholars: he made humble his three courtesies and said in this manner. Cha good even my good Lord, and well might your Lordship vare, understanding that your Lordship was come, and knowing that you are a worshipful Pilate and keeps abhominable house: I thought it my duty to come incantivante, and bring you a pottle of wine, which I beseech your Lordship to take in good worth.   p. 164.

In the early years of the next century it was generally acknowledged that English could look after itself, and even the chorus of praise and triumph died down. Heywood the dramatist ascribed much of the improvement to the practice of the stage: [10]

> 'Our English tongue, which hath been the most harsh uneven and broken language of the world . . . is now by this secondary means of playing, continually refined, every writer striving in himself to add a new flourish unto it; so that in process from the most rude and unpolisht tongue it is grown to a most perfect and composed language, and many excellent works and elaborate poems written in the same: that many Nations grow enamoured of our tongue (before despiséd). . . . Thus you see to what excellency our refined English is brought, that in these days we are ashamed of that Euphony and eloquence which within these sixty years the best tongues in the land were proud to pronounce.'

The *Apology for Actors* is special pleading, perhaps, but in the rapid discarding by the players themselves of their earlier habits there ·is additional evidence that the experimental period quickly passed away. Wilson described the Dogberry of King's in 1553: Shakespeare was still finding him a useful type more than forty years later: but by 1614, in the Induction to *Bartholomew Fair*, Jonson classes Dogberry with the Vice riding in on the Devil's back in 'master Tarleton's time' as thoroughly archaic.

> 'You should ha' seen him ha' come and ha' been cozen'd in the cloth quarter, so finely! and Adams, the rogue, ha' leaped and capered upon him, and ha' dealt his vermin about, as though they had cost him nothing: and then a substantial watch to ha' stolen in upon 'hem, and taken 'hem away, with mistaking words, as the fashion is in the stage practice.'

The development of learned comedy passes through three phases which roughly correspond to a general development of the language itself. First comes the practical work of schoolmasters and students of language, in academic plays which are half disputes and half farce, but where the drama is closely related to educational ends, linguistic or moral. Then in the eighties comes the period of innovation and experiment by poets in general, represented in comedy by the virtuosity of Lyly. Finally the free work of the nineties, when the 'high style' of the eloquent is both practised and mocked, when instead of following a single prescription, dramatists were able to produce special effects for a special audience. The Parnassus plays, acted at St. John's College, Cambridge, in 1598–1601 and packed with dramatic criticism, including a personal appearance of Burbage, are linked with the new satiric drama, and represent a third stage in learned comedy.

The general emancipation of writers is very hard to reconstruct with imaginative sympathy. Stern and simple rules of what had always been, the illogical powers of custom and prejudice had to be sapped; although many of the literary disputes take an outwardly logical form, this is profoundly irrelevant to the real issue, which was worked out far below the level of conscious debate. Thus the opponents and defenders of English, or of stage plays, tend always to take up a moral attitude, to stigmatize their antagonists as obscurantist, lewd, profane, full of ostentatious desire for glory or corrupting insinuations. Every issue assumes an ethical cast: for Cheke, to reform spelling was only to return the poor misused letters of the alphabet to the right and fitting roles which they were divinely ordained to fulfil. The moral iniquity of silent medial consonants, the treacherous falseness of synonyms and the wasteful indulgence in unsounded final E were almost to be counted among the deadly sins. Jonson and Marston import into their later literary quarrel a powerful note of moral self-righteousness.

III. The Drama of the Schools

Although they girded at pedants, the great Elizabethans had behind them a generation of great teachers. Ben Jonson dedicated his first play to his old master Camden, with a noble acknowledgement of his debt; Shakespeare laughed at schoolmasters, but he may have been one himself. In the

freedom of their experiments and their amazing capacity for
assimilation, the men of the later sixteenth century were no
bad advertisement for the educational system that produced
them.

The extent to which that education was based on exercises
in language has recently been very fully shown.[11] The syllabus aimed at a grounding in the Latin tongue, which involved the young in years of construing, of writing themes
and epistles and eventually in declamation. Debate or ques-
tion-and-answer was the staple mode of instruction. The
dramatists all show the effects of this highly organized system
of mental drill, one of the most forcible ever evolved. It was
part of the system in many schools to train the boys in playacting. Mulcaster at Merchant Taylors' put his boys to the
stage to teach them 'good behaviour and audacity' and Udall
pursued the same policy at Eton and Westminster.

The Plautine comedies of the mid-century, *Ralph Roister
Doister* and its livelier successor, *Gammer Gurton's Needle*, belong to Eton and Christ's College respectively. In these two
plays there is no starch and no moralizing. Hodge's torn
breeches and the fisticuffs of the two dames are in the same
tradition as the jokes of the interludes: the songs of Ralph
Roister Doister are such as might be heard in any tavern.
Gammer Gurton is full of such idioms as 'Too bad' and 'Stick
to it' and sown thick with bywords and proverbs. School
plays of the Prodigal Child, popularized by Erasmus, were
grafted naturally on the tradition of the English moral play
and prepared the way for full drama, but they remain themselves allied to declamation and to *exemplum*. The boys were
acting parts which held the mirror a little too close to Nature;
admonition or the art of persuasion was too frankly displayed.
The characters debate or quarrel in set fashion: they do not
escape into a dramatic world where speech and action may
move freely. Judicial, deliberative and demonstrative speech
(the three divisions of rhetoric) postulate a speaker persuad-
ing an audience, not a group of actors and spectators collaborating in a work of art. Didactic intention may be as clear
in drama as in oratory, the relations between actors and audience may be as close; but the sturdy proclamation of moral
commonplaces should not be so relentless.[12]

The range of the boy actor—and the university student as
well as the schoolboy might be included here—readily en-
compassed only lyric and farce. Their plays have some
variety of style, some attempt to vary the speech according to
the type of character, but perhaps such a tremendous tirade
as that of Hypocrisy in *Lusty Juventus*, which stands out so
sharply from the rest in scale and in power of writing, was
intended for a special professional speaker. Schoolboys
would be trained from their study of Plautus to appreciate
variety of style, and the cultivation of such variety would be
one of the fruits of their acting. High, mean and low styles
were as distinct in speech as in singing. In *Like Will to Like*,
the evil and the good characters have very different vocabularies. Their speeches will serve to show the rough distinction between the tumbling couplets of the Vices and the
stately quatrains of the Virtues, which would give the young
performers practice in variety, while spreading wholesome
doctrine.

> *Newfangle:* What old acquaintance, small remembrance?
> Welcome to town, with a very vengeance!
> Now welcome, Tom Collier, give me thy hand,
> As very a knave as any in England!
> *Collier:* By mass, god-a-marsy, my vrend Nichol!
> *Newfangle:* By God, and welcome, gentle Tom Lickhole!

> *God's Promises:* I am God's Promise which is a thing eterne,
> And nothing more surer than His promise may be:
> A sure foundation to such as will learn
> God's precepts to observe: then must they needs see
> Honour in this world, and at last a crown of glory;
> Ever in joy and mirth and never to be sorry.

Provincial performers probably clung to such plays long after
the public stages had developed more complex forms,[13] and
school drama continued into the seventeenth century. In
Jonson's *The Staple of News*, which is his version of *The
Prodigal Child* in Caroline terms, the gossips of the Induction
complain that their children are taught nothing but playacting.

> 'They make all their scholars playboys! Is't not a fine sight to see
> all our children made interluders? Do we pay our money for this?

we send them to learn their grammar and their Terence and they learn their playbooks! . . . I hope Zeal-of-the-Land-Busy and my gossip Rabbi Troubletruth will start up and see we shall have painful good ministers to keep school and catechize our youth and not teach them to speak plays, and act fables of false news, in this manner, to the supervexation of town and country, with a wannion!'

It was a schoolmaster writing for the choristers of St. Paul's Cathedral School who first devised for himself a distinct and individual comic form, and who propounded a practical as distinct from a text-book theory of comedy. The work of John Lyly, if designed for fashion, is rooted in the Schools. In his Prologues he follows the tradition of Udall in seeing his plays as recreation; but he also submits them to the judgement of the audience. For the audience had changed its character: the court was patron and arbiter, and the players, with the author, were not improving their equals but soliciting applause of their betters. Lyly is not striving to impose a meaning, but invites a variety of interpretation. The plays signify 'what you will' and should be taken 'as you like it'. The audience's demands, however various, will all be met. These players, though still schoolboys, are now professionals; their motto 'Placere cupio', 'We hope to please you.'

'At our exercises, Soldiers call for Tragedies, their object is blood: Courtiers for Comedies, their subject is love: Countrymen for Pastoral, Shepherds are their saints . . . what heretofore hath been served in several dishes for a feast, is now minced in a charger for a Gallimaufrey. If we present a mingle-mangle, our fault is to be excused, because the whole world is become an hodge-podge.'

Prologue to *Midas*.

The learned Lyly defies the theorists, Sidney included, and claims his right to mingle the kinds. On the other hand, the unity and consistency of his style and temper exceed those of any other Elizabethan writer. His rhetorical artificial patterns of alliteration, antitheses and simile have an almost steely strength, and on the surface, his plays would appear to have far less variety than the academic drama. The smooth enamel of his style, the formal grouping of his characters and

39

the simplicity of his action are stiffened by further restraints which he proudly acknowledges:

> 'Our intent was at this time to move inward delight, not outward lightness (did he remember Sidney's words?) to breed, if it might be, soft smiling, not loud laughing. . . . We have endeavoured to be as far from unseemly speeches to make your ears glow as we hope you will be from unkind reports to make our cheeks blush.'
>
> Prologue to *Sapho and Phao*.

There remained the possibility of various interpretations of his deceptively simple comedy. Here disagreement among the spectators still persists—which is clearly what Lyly designed. He avoids a final significance: and draws the audience within the circle of the play by inviting them to complete it with their judgement.[14] He presents an open field for their 'exercises', only making plain that there is room for all, and that he has 'mixed mirth with counsel and discipline with delight'. Lyly's humility, that of the true artist, is the natural consequence of his own unwavering sense of design. Each spectator may adapt the work to suit his own imagination. Constantly in his prologues he uses the image of a dream. Dreams are at once private and messages from beyond the world, free from the logic of daytime existence, and yet a commentary upon it, open to many interpretations.

There is irony therefore in the apparently guileless words of the Prologue to *Sapho and Phao* at court, addressed to the Queen:

> 'We all, and I on knee for all, entreat that your Highness imagine yourself to be in a deep dream, that staying the conclusion, in your rising your Majesty vouchsafe but to say, *And so you awaked.*'

The prologue to *Endimion* varies the metaphor:

> 'We must tell you a tale of the Man in the Moon . . . we hope in our time none will apply pastimes, because they are fancies. . . . We present neither Comedy, nor Tragedy, nor story, nor anything. . . .'

In the last and most subtle of his plays, Lyly returns to his original claim:

> 'Remember all is but a Poet's dream.'
>
> Prologue to *The Woman in The Moon*.

These phrases invite attention to the literary complexities of the plays, which are the means of engaging the audience. Lyly had broken with the old moral allegory; his plays would have satisfied that Italianate Lord who in *Histriomastix* laughed at Sir Oliver Owlet's men, with their traditional repertory of *Mother Gurton's Needle*, a tragedy, and *The Devil and Dives*, a comedy.[15] When their play of *Troilus and Cressida* relapses into 'a roaring devil with the Vice on his back and Iniquity in one hand and Juventus in the other'—the traditional themes of cautionary tales for schoolboys—Owlet's men are dismissed and Lord Landulpho comments:

> 'I blush in your behalf at this base trash.
> In honour of our Italy we sport
> As if a synod of the holy Gods
> Came to triumph within our theatres
> (Always commending English courtesy) . . .'

Such were the triumphs and such the Gods of Lyly's comedy. It was idealistic but secular. Virtue might be mirrored, but moralizing was inappropriate. The mirror of manners was no longer contained in the schools, but in the court. There was no need of moral instruction when the audience was composed of patrons who must be models of all the virtues and when it might even include the Phoenix of her age.

In Lyly's drama the actors were servants of the audience, as they had been for Plato. But their function was not to move laughter and contempt: it was to present the Gods in triumph. In Lyly's works the Italianate style was truly made a denizen of the stage and such awkward efforts as *Two Italian Gentlemen* (1584) for ever outmoded.[16] His style took the literary world of his day by storm; and his achievement was more than a personal one. He provided a basis upon which others could build; later, his work might be parodied, his stiff patterns broken up, but the results remained. Security, stability and easiness had been achieved, and the particular linguistic problems which vexed the previous generation could not re-occur. The English tongue was now capable of eloquence, and their language was to the generation that followed 'our nation's best glory'.

CHAPTER IV

THE DECORUM OF THE SCENE

1. The Kinds of Comedy and the Garment of Style

HOWEVER liberal his attitude towards the authority of the ancients, the Elizabethan playwright could not escape the fixed habits of thought which dominated his age. It is by now a commonplace that decorum governed converse: in real life there was a wide variety of speech, and formal address, as that of parents to children, or children to parents, scholar to patron, or even condemned criminal to the surrounding crowd; each conformed to a set pattern.[1] This formal quality of language was not only the result of rhetorical education and a general belief in social order and degree: it rested on a very deep belief in the necessary connexion between word and action. This was an age of incantation and spells, of blessing and curses, an age in which the word 'spoken with power' would inevitably produce effects which might be cataclysmic. The word spoken with power was a word spoken according to a recognized formula. The right word would call up the Devil: the right word would call down God upon the altar in the form of bread and wine— or at least the question whether it would do so or not was central in all the great religious conflicts of the time.[2]

Hence it is not surprising that literary criticism was haunted by a search for definitions, and that it was generally felt that the right rhetorical prescriptions must ensure a successful work of art. The critics produced endlessly and hopefully their pedantic formulations, unworkable models, mechanical repetitions of ancient precept unconsciously distorted and misapplied. If the word of power were really spoken, it was thought, then the achievement must follow, as the night the day. The many unfortunate attempts at heroic poems are the chief monument to this reverence for prescription.

Elizabethan drama, like the popular dream of Spain, escaped from the tyranny of rhetoric most completely because

42

of the demands of the popular audience.[3] When eventually it was partly recaptured for learning by Jonson it had absorbed all that was best in the popular tradition. And of all the dramatic kinds, comedy was the least controlled, and was allowed, even by classical precept, the greatest variety of style.

None the less, comedy had its own conventions. There was no such dominant form as the Revenge play gave to tragedy; rather, the formal variety of speech which the habits of society had fixed was enjoined upon the writer of comedy by the rhetoricians. Quintillian, the most influential of all, had said that comedy resembled *ethos*, or the set definition of a fixed personality, as distinct from tragedy which resembled *pathos*, a mood or phase of feeling; and set descriptions of persons (*ethopæia*) had always required an appropriate language, specially adapted to set that person forth. The person, however, was not an individual in the modern sense, but a representative of a particular social group. Each of Chaucer's pilgrims, the perfect specimen of his own kind, was defined in this way, both in his choice of a tale and the manner in which he told it. Such conformity, or decorum, implied in comedy not the uniform grandeur of tragic speech, but a collection of verbal contrasts, artfully disposed to set each other off.

Traditionally, society was divided into the three regions of Court, Country and City, and the comedy for each had its own decorum, though the pure specimen of each kind is the exception rather than the rule.[4] Those plays which, like Lyly's, were directed to the public of the sonnet and the masque, relied on the small group, with its strong corporate sense of 'who's in, who's out', a group at once polite and dangerous, sophisticated and brutal. In this world, comedy resided upon the surface, picturing manners and compliments.

Those simple stories of adventure, wandering knights, marvels and true love which drew on the popular tradition had their roots in the country. Such stories were outmoded even in Chaucer's day, and he ironically gives one such old wives' tale to himself on the Canterbury pilgrimage: the tale of Sir Thopas,

> 'White was his face as payndemayn,
> His lippes rede as rose. . . '

which is cut short in disgust by the Host of the Tabard Inn. Though the original medieval romances survive in greater quantity than any but scholars would desire, many more have perished, along with much other secular literature of the oral tradition. Chaucer's own tales of Patient Grissel and Constance of Rome were used by the popular dramatists: Dekker's play on Grissel remains, his drama of Constance is lost.[5] Many of these stories, by Elizabethan times, had developed a strong infusion of local patriotism, whether London or provincial. Gog and Magog, Simon Eyre and Dick Whittington and other City worthies find place beside Hob the Tanner of Tamworth, Tom Stroud the yeoman of Norfolk and Marley the Brewer of Dunstable; they are often connected with the more popular monarchs, Henry V, the Edwards, Henry VIII. The stories of Deloney and the ballads of Elderton furnished other tales. Above all, the wild youth of England's princes or the overseas exploits of London 'prentices fed the young citizens' dreams of greatness. Each of the livery companies had its own legends, as Lord Mayors' pageants suggest. They might include atrocities or pathos, but these elements were softened down in the general atmosphere of fellowship and success. The City cherished its stories as a club or team cherishes its legends today; Munday, Dekker, Heywood and other purveyors of such plays worked within clearly defined social limits.

City comedy as such, that is to say the kind of play which was popular in the private playhouses within the city limits, was very largely satiric, and often at the expense of popular drama. Stories of broken gallants, spendthrift knights, erring city wives, knaveries of coney-catchers and hypocrisies of Puritans introduced the respectable gildsman either as rogue outmanœuvred or as cheated gull. Foreign courtesans, fantastic humorists and bitter clowns added spice to the dish. Such plays were addressed to the young 'termers', many of whom were nobles or squires' sons, whose ambitions were to cheat usurers, despoil tradesmen and outwit bawds. To these young men, the gentlemen of the Inns of Court, Jonson dedicated his first satiric play;[6] and during the early years of the seventeenth century, satiric comedy largely replaced courtly allegory except at courtly revels proper. The most popular theme is the successful marriage hunt for the prize of a rich widow; a spendthrift succeeds, while his rivals are married off to courtesans by some deceiving trick. To this kind belongs the main work of Middleton and Marston. The connexion with classical comedy is obvious; the differences equally clear.

Each kind of play, like a suit of clothes designed for a special employment or a song adapted for a particular occasion, evolved its own decorum. Characters, incidents and language had to meet very definite expectations. While the audience demanded novelty in the bill, they wanted conformity to the pattern. The garment of style identified the plays as being each of its particular kind, and these were by no means the set classical kinds.

The specific style for princes, for lovers, for clowns was fixed. Even Bottom the Weaver could distinguish between 'Ercles' vein, a tyrant's vein' and a lover's, which was 'more condoling'. Decorum required that lovers, gentle or simple, speak in verse and the comic characters in prose; Shakespeare in his subtler comedy deliberately flouts it. Falstaff's opening lines:

'Now, Hal, what time o' day is it, Lad?'

was as indecorous a mode of addressing the heir apparent of England as Prince Hamlet's opening aside:

'A little more than kin and less than kind'

was indecorous towards his uncle, stepfather and king. His letter to Ophelia, opening in a decorous manner 'To the celestial and my soul's idol, the most beautified Ophelia' becomes suddenly tender, familiar, ironical—in the personal accent of wit and pain.

The formal love-letter was especially open to parody; and the strength of any firmly established convention may be tested by the recognition which such parody affords. The great popularity of the Revenge play, of which *Hamlet* is an example, had led, long before Shakespeare's rewriting, to burlesque of the ghost, the revenger, the mad scene and the most quotable lines of earlier *Hamlets*. As early as 1592, when Queen Elizabeth visited Rycote, she was given, in the course of an entertainment by Lyly, a letter supposedly intended for 'the Lady Squemish' from her servant, a soldier. The ancient trick of delivering the letter to the wrong person brought it about that some Launce or Costard addressed her Majesty thus:

> 'Oft have you told me that I know not what love is, and oft have I told you that this it is, which makes the head ache, and the heart too: the eyes jealous and the ears too: the liver black and the spleen too: the veins shrink and the purse too. . . . You object that I have many Mistresses: I answer that you have ten times as many Servants, and if you should pick a quarrel, why should I not bring my Mistresses into the field against your Servants. . . . Let me have my love answered and you shall find me faithful: in which, if you make delays, I cannot be patient: the wind calls me away, and with the wind, shall my affections. . . .'[7]

This, if a genuine blunder, would not have been committed to print; but coming at the end of a long string of compliments, it ironically depreciated the rustic simplicity of the whole entertainment, and invited a self-satisfying display of Tudor graciousness; but probably only such intimate friends as Elizabeth's 'good Crow' could have risked such a trick. The blunt style of the soldier's wooing depends on its contrast with the conventional court love-letter.

Lyly's own *Mother Bombie* and Peele's *Old Wives' Tale* were not parodies but slightly ironic refashioning of the popular play for a particular effect. The straightforward courtly pastoral, 'as smooth and soft as cream', might be exemplified from Peele's 'diploma piece' *The Arraignement of Paris*, a metropolitan tribute especially designed to do honour to Elizabeth. The pleasures of humble life, in contrast to the cares of Majesty, provide a subtle compliment.[8]

> 'Contentment is my wealth;
> A shell of salt will serve a shepherd swain,
> A slender banquet in a homely scrip,
> And water running from the silver spring.
> For arms, they dread no foes that sit so low;
> A thorn can keep the wind from off my back,
> A sheepcote thatched a shepherd's palace hight.
> Of tragic Muses shepherds con no skill:
> Enough is them, if Cupid be displeased,
> To sing his praise on slender oaten pipe.'   4.1.

Some ten years later, both Shakespeare and Jonson were mocking the courtly world of Lyly and Peele. In *Cynthia's Revels* and in *As You Like It* it is surveyed through a diminishing perspective glass. Its elegance and artifice is set in contrast with a newer embittered style, through the introduction of Crites and Jacques. Mockery in one mood produces Corin's:

'You told me you salute not at the court but you kiss your hands: that courtesy would be uncleanly if courtiers were shepherds ... we are still handling our ewes, and their fells, you know, are greasy ...'

in another Silvius, the literary shepherd's:

'If thou rememberest not the slightest folly
That ever love did make thee run into,
Thou hast not loved:
Or if thou hast not sat as I do now,
Wearying thy hearer in thy mistress' praise
Thou hast not loved.'

2.5.

Cynthia's Revels (1598) belongs to the War of the Theatres, which allowed each side to define by parody the shortcoming of their opponents. Here are to be found some of the best definitions of sweet and bitter comedy, the old and the new. Jonson lumped together Dekker's folk-tales and Marston's old-fashioned academic coinage of strange words as outmoded. In *The Return from Parnassus*, the unemployed scholars, after trying popular journalism and the public theatre, resign themselves to the life of real shepherds, with tarbox and scrip, on the Kentish hills.

Jonson worked out his theory by parody. In *Eastward Ho!* —partly by him—the old plays on Prodigals are mocked with a straight face. *The Tale of a Tub* as written uses simple jests

'from old records
Of antique proverbs drawn from Whitsun lords,
And their authorities, at wakes and ales,
With country precedents and old wives' tales'

to make 'a ridiculous play' aimed at putting Inigo Jones in his place. In *The Devil is an Ass* and *The Magnetic Lady* the old moral play is recalled with a mixture of irony and affection such as colours the courtly masques.[9] *The Staple of News* is another prodigal play. Such critical refashioning is far from the cruder attacks of the War of the Theatres. Here both sides became violent—though part of the quarrel was also played to the gallery in the manner of a medieval poets' scolding match. In *The Whipping of the Satire*, John Weever addresses the writers of such plays, probably with his eye on Jonson:

> 'Experience, the looking glass of fools,
> Shows much contention, little good affords,
> And ye might learn this at the grammar schools,
> *That man is wise, that speaks few things or words. . .*
> Leave that ambition, that led you away
> To censure men and their misgovernment,
> Judging the world before the latter day,
> As though ye would the Son of God prevent. . . .'

The stinging quality of the city comedy and its contempt for the honest trademan, its 'stabbing similes' and pungent use of the low style are found as readily in Jonson's opponent in the War of the Theatres, Marston.

> 'I have it, I'll gargalize my throat with this vintner and when I have done with him, spit him out, I'll shark, conscience does not repine; were I to bite an honest gentleman, a poor grogaran poet, or a penurious parson that had but ten pigs' tails in a twelve month and for want of learning had but one good stool in a fortnight, I were damned beyond the works of supererogation; but to wring the withers of my gouty, barmed, spiggod-frigging jumbler of elements, Mulligrub, I hold it lawful as sheep-shearing, taking eggs from hens, caudels from asses or buttered shrimps from horses, they make no use of them, were not provided for them.'
>
> The Dutch Courtesan, 3.1.

In spite of criticism, the popular plays continued. The famous parody by Beaumont, *The Knight of the Burning Pestle* (1611), shows them relatively unaltered more than a decade after the War was over. Monsters—but the same old monsters: virtuous 'prentices, cut to the stock pattern: startling adventures, but all of a familiar type. The fool, the conjuror and even the devil might put in an appearance, but, everything ended happily and virtue always triumphed.

A year after this, in 1612, Heywood, Dekker's successor

as a popular writer, one not without learning, defined the object of comedy in a manner which would have satisfied Udall, but must have infuriated Ben Jonson:

> 'mingled with sportful accidents, to recreate such as of themselves are wholly devoted to melancholy, which corrupts the blood: or to refresh such weary spirits as are tired with labour, or study, to moderate the cares and heaviness of the mind that they may return to their trades and faculties with more zeal and earnestness, after some small soft and pleasant retirement.' [10]

ii. The Development of Style

The development of Elizabethan comedy is very largely the development of its language. Twenty years before Lyly, in 1564, an earlier Master of singing boys, Richard Edwards, had composed for performance in his own college of Christ Church before the Queen *Damon and Pithias*, wherein the Prologue sets out a theory of decorum.

> 'In comedies the greatest skill is this, rightly to touch
> All things to the quick: and eke to frame each person so,
> That by his common talk you may his nature rightly know.
> A roister ought not preach, that were too strange to hear,
> But as from virtue he doth swerve, so ought his words appear:
> The old man is sober, the young man rash, the lover triumphing
> in joys,
> The matron grave, the harlot wild and full of wanton toys.
> Withal in one course they in no wise do agree,
> So correspondent to their kind their speeches ought to be.
> Which speeches well pronounced, with action lively fram'd,
> If this offend the lookers on, let Horace then be blamed,
> Which hath our author taught at school, from whom he doth
> not swerve,
> 'In all such kinds of exercise decorum to observe.'

The theory is impeccable, but the practice in this case hardly corresponds: for though the characters range from Dionysus the King and the two faithful friends to Gronno the Hangman, and Grim the Collier of Croydon, with the Nine Muses appearing to lament 'with yellow rented hairs':

> 'Alas, what hap hast thou, poor Pythias, now to die!
> Woe worth the man which for his death hath given us cause to
> cry!'

their language is quite indistinguishable. In other plays of the same period there may be considerable variety;[11] but until Lyly the distinction is largely metrical—and the Vice or the tragic hero may interchangeably be given trotting octo-syllabics or tumbling fourteeners.

The norm in Lyly is the courtly speech of Euphuized gentlewomen. His plays are among other things conversational models. There is also a great variety of jargon which appears for its comic effect: in *Gallathea* the jargon of alchemists—which Chaucer before him and Jonson after him found equally fascinating. Here, too, there are seamen's terms, and huntsmen's terms in *Midas*. The proverbs of rustic fools at quarterstaff are set against the rapier-wit of the quarrelsome pageboys. Delicate songs are mixed with boisterous jests; 'variety' was a rhetorical requirement of which Lyly was conscious, for he praised the sonnets of Thomas Watson precisely for this quality. Such artifice did not allow much development, and the long set tirade which appears in *Campaspe* and *Midas* is only a little less formal than the language of the earlier *Sapho and Phao* and *Endimion*; but in his latest plays, Lyly moved nearer to the diction of common life.[12]

In tragedy, Marlowe had imposed a like consistency. The language of drama seems to have remained always a degree more formal than that of lyric. Sidney, who objected that courtiers spoke a better language than scholars, had earlier introduced into *Astrophel and Stella* that 'ironia' or quizzical self-depreciation which Shakespeare alone could recapture for the drama. And Shakespeare himself began in a style as formal as Lyly or Marlowe. His early plays, *Titus Andronicus, Henry VI* and *Richard III, The Comedy of Errors* and *Two Gentlemen of Verona*, are heavily rhetorical, and make some parade of both fashion and learning. Classical atrocities and Senecan style link *Titus Andronicus* with the grave and lofty *Rape of Lucrece*, a poem which won the praise of Gabriel Harvey. *The Comedy of Errors* was a Gray's Inn play, modelled directly on Plautus' *Menaechmi*. The classic setting, with its three 'houses', the bewildering symmetry of the reduplicated twins harmonize with the quibbles and cross-talk, which is at times (as in the dialogue on Time and Hair between Antipholus and Dromio of Syracuse in Act II) even more pedantic than Lyly. It is also, however, a great deal more improper than Lyly, and this reflects the current taste of the young men who enjoyed the poems of Donne, and whom Shakespeare was later to depict in Mercutio. In doubling the twins, Shakespeare improved Plautus. This is a characteristically florid Elizabethan device; they liked adjectives in pairs, clauses in antithesis, and Lyly always provided at least two of everything.[13] Backchat, horseplay and exceptionally skilful intrigue are further embellished in *Two Gentlemen of Verona* by an elegant picture of courtly manners; but some of the wit combats—those between the clowns, and those between Valentine and Thurio—have the same quick, shallow dexterity as *The Comedy of Errors*. In *The Taming of the Shrew*, a play near to Italian comedy,[14] the subplot keeps to this same level, but the main plot and the Induction belong to a different style. Here the true Shakespearean art of depicting characters begins to develop; and though the play can be staged as knockabout farce, it has also other possibilities, which are perhaps first disclosed when Petruchio, at the end of his first bout of wit with Kate—a flashing exchange —becomes exceedingly broad-spoken; with a prompt snub, the lady prepares to leave him. He apologizes:

> Nay, come again,
> Good Kate: I am a gentleman.
> *Kath:* That I'll try. (She strikes him.)

This of course gives him his opportunity to deflate the whole situation.

> *Petruchio:* I swear I'll cuff you if you strike again. 2.1.

Petruchio's wooing, the comic counterpart of Richard III's wooing of Lady Anne, depends, like his, upon the unexpected quality of the lover's speeches; far from being 'condoling' they are of a calculated impudence which, baffling all prepared defences, in an assumption of plain bluntness backed by a slight display of force, carries Petruchio onwards to the triumphant and uncontradicted exit line:

> 'Kiss me, Kate, we will be married o' Sunday.'[15]

Both Petruchio and Richard III, like the author of the Epistle at Rycote, are soldiers. Here already is the voice of Hotspur, whose love of honour enchanted the London 'prentices, but whose scorn for the mincing terms of courtiers or the magic mumblings and threats of Glendower sprang from his own military speech and Northcountry manners.

Perhaps the most significant moment in the development of English drama was that in which Shakespeare turned an ironic glance upon the rhetoric of both the schools and the courtier, threw his energies into developing 'what public means with public manners breeds' and, defying prescription, achieved his own style. He was not long enslaved to the pretty uses of epiphora or the four separate kinds of pun.[16] This does not mean that his rhetorical training was abandoned; only that he had digested it. The same development can be seen in Chaucer, from the elaborate pattern of *The Compleynt of Anelida* to the effortless ease of *Troilus and Criseyde*; and perhaps it was in the *Sonnets* that Shakespeare first developed the new tone of voice. Here he defied a very strongly established convention, in protesting himself a 'plain true-speaking friend' who can mention the faults as well as the beauties of his lord, or woo his mistress by discommending her.[17] Rhetoricians themselves had, even in Chaucer's day, recognized the power of

'un sens naturel, d'où vient que, même sans penser à la théorie, le génie des ecrivains applique les règles d'instinct et fait spontanément des trouvailles heureuses.' [18]

All Chaucer's disclaimers of his own art, all his protests of 'lewdness', like Shakespeare's of his 'simplicity', may be read as the hall-mark of complete mastery.

The decline of schemes and figures in favour of emotional rhetoric can be traced in many kinds of Elizabethan literature, even in religious controversy, where the earlier disputants aimed at logical refutation of their opponents in the manner of the Schools, and with the appropriate flourishes. The school of Louvain was replaced by the dexterous and impassioned propaganda of Parsons and the emotional appeal of Southwell; the Protestant champion, Bishop Jewel, delivered at Oxford an *Oration against Rhetoric*. Later, the scandalous invective of the Marprelate controversy, in which the Archbishop of Canterbury engaged graceless Thomas

Nashe as defender of orthodoxy, rose to such heights that by comparison the War of the Theatres sounds tame.

There are two reasons for Shakespeare's rejection of formal schemes and tropes, and the patterned language of his early plays. The first is that he was himself an actor; with Heywood and Jonson, the only actor-playwright of the age. He knew the exact quality of speech required to hold a large mixed audience. It has recently been urged that his acting was more important to him than his plays: it was certainly the acting, and not the plays, that built his fortune, as it built Alleyn's.[19] The second reason is that during the years 1592–1594 he was, with the actors, driven out of London by the plague. His ventures into courtly literature, *Venus and Adonis* and *The Rape of Lucrece*, did not apparently reap the kind of reward that the older literary figure such as Spenser might have sought for, though they enjoyed popular success. Shakespeare returned to London to produce *Romeo and Juliet*, and that rhetorical satire upon rhetoric, *Love's Labour's Lost*. He had thrown in his lot with the rogues and vagabonds.

The best orators amongst Shakespeare's characters are those who disguise their use of the art; Richard III, Mark Antony and Iago each claim, like their author, to be a plain blunt man. The contrast between Brutus' Attic speech to the mob and Antony's Asiatic style is the contrast between school rhetoric and the true art of persuasion as learnt in the theatre itself—the art of engaging the sympathy of the spectators, bringing them into the action and allowing them to take the initiative. Antony's speech works on the crowd, as the Chorus was meant to work on the spectators of *Henry V*—it stimulates them to 'work their thoughts', and they are never more truly in Antony's power than when they rush wildly away. In the mid-nineties, when he had the stage to himself, Shakespeare accomplished the creation of his own dramatic language, partly prose, in his romantic comedies and chronicle histories. When, towards the turn of the century, Ben Jonson and Chapman appeared, they brought to the stage a new kind of dramatic rhetoric, in which delineation of Characters in the classical sense by approved Roman formula combines with a new and haughty attitude towards the audience. These two saw themselves as called to high office: the poet as *vates* or prophet. Satiric comedy was largely dependent on the critical literary sense of an educated audience. The rhetoric of Ben Jonson is a true dramatic language,[20] varied for each separate character, but always ostentatious. He enjoyed hyperbole and conscious exaggeration: the great speeches of Epicure Mammon and Volpone are exercises in bombast. He also, like Lyly, enjoyed jargon: the alchemists', the travellers', the statesmen's and the scholars' speech appealed to him through oddity. Though sometimes he confused the satirist with the critic, a curious, finely-dissected diction was the fatal Cleopatra for which he lost his critical detachment and was content to lose it. He admired Bacon's oratorical practice of the familiar style: *Discoveries* shows his almost professional concern for rhetoric: but he declared that he would as soon choose an orator for speaking in the Schools as a pilot for rowing in a pond.

Chapman, with characteristic intransigence, refused to modify the scholastic forms of rhetoric to the demands of the theatre. The tremendous encomium of the horn, at the end of *All Fools*—ninety lines of prose—or that on tobacco, in Act II of *Monsieur d'Olive*, are grand tirades in an ironic vein: in a mock funeral oration on one of Poppæa's hairs, *A Justification of a strange action of Nero*, Chapman parodied a set rhetorical exercise.

Jonson was also capable of a great set speech, but never at quite such length, and possibly his were cut in the performance.

Both Jonson and Chapman call attention to their own use of rhetoric by this exaggerated display of it: they invite the spectators to admire their virtuosity, and to follow the finer points of technique. For a young member of the Inns of Court, with a professional interest in pleading, such displays must have been especially entertaining; and these young men formed the most intelligent part of the audience, being themselves much given to the sort of dramatic amusements in which parody of formal styles predominates.

Satire was recognized as the most rhetorical kind of literature: and the Theophrastian characters, which Jonson adapts to describe the persons of *Every Man out of his Humour*, demonstrate the close link between rhetoric and social ethics.

The decorum of satire required an analytic approach to speech. Nevertheless, his first concern was to win the response of the spectators, and this controlled Jonson's artifice, though not Chapman's.

> 'A man should so deliver himself to the nature of the subject whereof he speaks, that his hearer may take knowledge of his discipline with some delight: and so apparel fair and good matter, that the studious of elegancy be not defrauded: redeem Arts from their rough and braky seats, where they lay hid, and overgrown with thorns, to a pure open and flowery light: where they may take the eye, and be taken by the hand.'
>
> *Timber; or Discoveries.*

The decorum of fools' speech, which lies in misuse of language, is Jonson's particular study. In *The Staple of News* Pennyboy Canter observes

'All the world are canters'

that is, users of thieves' jargon. Each man has his own characteristic idiom, which actually defines his character: 'No glass renders a man's form or likeness so true as his speech.' The rhetorical character of such speech is obvious to the spectators but not to the characters in the play. They are acted upon by beguilers, like Face and Volpone, whilst the spectator watching from without observes both cause and effect. Courtly affectation is satirized only in the early plays, chiefly in *Cynthia's Revels*: the widest variety of affectations are deployed in *The Alchemist*. Innuendo and suspense are maintained by the ambiguities of Tiberius' letter in *Sejanus*; but *Catiline* fails because Jonson's respect for Cicero leads him to reproduce the orations. Elsewhere he enjoys satirizing the law, as in the legal arguments of *Epicoene*.

In Jonson, the formal art of rhetoric is modified to the needs of the theatre; meanwhile theatrical hacks clung to the older fashions. At a climax, the moral of a domestic comedy may be set forth in verse of special formality, as in the bawd's praise of gold in *How a Man may choose a Good Wife from a Bad*, a passage which adumbrates those same commonplaces that Timon reflects upon in Shakespeare.

'Money can make a slavering tongue speak plain.
If he that loves thee be deformed and rich,
Accept his love: gold hides deformity.
Gold can make limping Vulcan walk upright,
Make squint eyes straight, a crabbed face look smooth,
Gilds copper noses, makes them look like gold;
Fills ages' wrinkles up, and makes a face
As old as Nestor's look as young as Cupid's.
If thou wilt arm thyself against all shifts,
Regard all men according to their gifts.' [21]   23.

The most consistently rhetorical speaking in these plays is
the clowns'; they are generally given some catchphrase.
Nicholas, the clown of Porter's *Two Angry Women of Abingdon*, in almost Jonsonian decorum, speaks all proverbs.

'Good words cost nought; ill words corrupt good manners,
Richard: for a hasty man never wants woe. And I had thought you
had been my friend: but I see all is not gold that glitters: there's
falsehood in fellowship, amicus certus in re certa cernitur: time and
truth tries all: and 'tis an old proverb, and not so old as true, bought
wit is the best: I can see daylight at a little hole: I know your mind
as well as though I were within you: tis ill halting before a cripple:
go to, you seek to quarrel, but beward of had I wist. . . .'[22] 4.3.

The lovers' parts are sometimes distinguished from each
other in popular plays, and where there are two or three
couples, the youngest will be given especial sprightliness.
The youngest brother in *The Four Prentices of London* and
The Fair Maid of the Exchange, the younger sister and her lover
in *Greene's Tu Quoque* and *Englishmen for My Money* are each
distinguished for nipping wit and volubility, a faint echo of
the gaiety of Rosaline and Berowne or Benedick and Beatrice.
In *Patient Grissel* and *The Shoemakers' Holiday*, Dekker
alternates decorously between verse for the love story and
prose for the low comedy; in *The Honest Whore* the pattern is
very complex. The blank verse of Dekker is in any case
colloquial and unemphatic. Easiness and facility marked
most of the hack writers; lesser playwrights could degenerate
into almost senseless mouthing—even allowing for the state
of the text, Armin's *Two Maids of Moreclacke* probably represents a low water mark.

The freedom with which colloquial speech was reproduced on the stage reflects a growing freedom in the general theory of writing, represented at its best by Samuel Daniel's criticism.[23] Heywood used the low style for pathos in his domestic tragedies. His prologues employ self-deprecation

'Look for no glorious state . . .'

though hinting that he is not without unexercised abilities:

'We could afford . . .
Our coarse fare, banquets: our thin water, wine;
Our brook, a sea: our bat's eyes, eagle's sight;
Our poets' dull and earthy Muse, divine.'

If the language of *The Rape of Lucrece* represents Heywood's loftier vein, his usual choice of the low style seems well judged.

The pointed and epigrammatic wit of the first satiric comedies did not long persist in favour. Although Jonson served as model to the younger playwrights, and although they relied heavily upon his plotting and on some of his characters, they did not affect his laborious, highly wrought and intricate style.

The rhetoric of Fletcher is of another sort. Throughout his plays the language is limpid, easy and based upon the ordinary speech of the gentleman. He has a few clowns but they are unimportant. As Professor Waith has shown, however,[24] his stories are often based on the dilemmas of the Roman law exercises, particularly the *Controversiae* of Seneca the Elder. Frankly preposterous series of events were predicated, in order that the pleaders should have the maximum opportunity for display. The characters of Fletcher are governed by one ruling passion—the attempt to persuade, the orator's motive. They may be apparently absorbed in love or revenge but they are really devoted to putting a case; and they are always ready at the end to abandon the position they have taken up, and reveal that they have been indulging in a trial of constancy or some other form of dissimulation. Educated young men, who were trained to defend opinions they did not hold, by way of exercise, would follow these dramatic orators with delight. The huge tirades, the sharp

exchanges and the startling reversals of Fletcher's comedies
are displayed in a style which is modelled on that of the law
courts. Frequent repetition, which works up the passions
and at the same time drives the point home: complex, paren-
thetical and involved sentences which wind up the whole
argument in a cocoon, and suspend the vital word often
through a dozen lines together: heavy underscoring of
pathos and rage—these are law tricks. The breathless rush
of one of Fletcher's great speeches is meant to sweep the
audience along, whilst they are only too likely at the end of
it to be faced with complete reversal of the whole argument.
Sophistical pleading, ingeniously strained and always
emotionally coloured, was a powerful stimulant; as a basis for
comedy it leads to farce. Debating games on fantastic
themes, trickery and the joys of a rake's progress are the
subjects best suited to this style.

PART II
NATURE AND ART AT STRIFE

CHAPTER V

ARTIFICIAL COMEDY AND POPULAR COMEDY: SHAKESPEARE'S INHERITANCE

1. Artificial Comedy: Lyly

IT is not merely because his work, alone among that of early dramatists, survives in fair quantity and in good texts, that Lyly ranks beyond the other comic authors of his day. The plays are still actable, though not often acted.[1] In his own time their significance as a foundation for other men to build upon established them with the poems of Sidney and Spenser. Lyly set a standard, and shaped a model; and his limitations were part of his achievement.

Vigour was the chief virtue of early Elizabethan comedy; what was needed was a strong infusion of order and of grace. This was Lyly's gift, and it came to him in part from the Court Revels.

> 'Instead of ending an ordinary play with a masque-like denouement, Lyly sheds his compliment over the whole piot. Instead of framing a realistic story in a masque-like induction, Lyly makes his whole action approximate to the symbolic movement of the masque. . . .' [2]

Since Lyly's plays partook of the peculiar intimacy of the Revels, he could afford coolness and the reserve of his elaborate style. In revels and masques, actors and audience were literally joint performers, for both took part in the final dances, and the chief spectators were often reflected in the slight story which served to support the spectacle and musical shows. Masque was the Elizabethan form of cabaret; the plays of Lyly, deputy master of the Children of St. Paul's, might be described as a cross between a floor show and a prize-day recitation.

The plays, however, as Professor Harbage has observed,[3]

61

are *not* masques, but were intended to give the feeling of court entertainment to a wider public—though they were written with a special eye to complimenting Elizabeth. If some of the older theories on their 'inner meaning' now appear far-fetched, there is no doubt that at least *Sapho and Phao*, *Endimion* and *Midas* had such significance. Like *Euphues*, the work on which their author's reputation was chiefly based, the plays also provided a model of elegant speech, and a mirror of manners. The appeal is to a critical and selected few. Negations and prohibitions are important; there is no fighting, no excitement and no true-love, but only wooing games. There is likewise no broad jesting; Lyly, alone among Elizabethan playwrights, observed decorum in the modern as well as the older sense.

The organization of Lyly's comedy depends on the symmetrical grouping of parts; the fable seems often a chess-play with animated chessmen. His role dictates the way in which any one character can move; none can modify, but metamorphosis, like the taking of a piece, transforms the pattern.[4] Women are turned into trees, birds, stones, monsters—ruled by the planets—constrained by the charms of a sorceress or controlled by an old wise-woman. It is a world in which the rules of movement are fixed, but the powers governing them work arbitrarily. So, in real life, a courtier's role was fixed; his fate depended on luck and the uncertain temper of the great. The debate between Concord and Discord in *The Woman in the Moon* might apply to any of the plays; it is resolved by the goddess Nature, in a truly Lucretian fashion.

> 'Your work must prove but one;
> And in yourselves, though you be different,
> Yet in my service must you well agree.
> For Nature works her will from contraries.'
> 1.1.26–9.

Breaking the pattern by metamorphosis, love potions or other charms, does not make a progressive action: it works like the shift of focus in a perspective puzzle with cubes or pyramids: any visual reading may be reversed. It is no matter which of the two girls in *Gallathea* is ultimately to be transformed into a man, and so the audience is not informed.

Interest is intellectual, not sympathetic; the plays are full of gossip, laced with spectacle; declamation pipes, but passion disappears. Lyly is a lover of phrases, or at most of postures; his efforts to be philosophical end in diatribe, encomium or backchat.

The form which he evolved is verbal; it is exquisitely phrased for youthful speakers, but not fully dramatic. Like Pygmalion's image it wants the breath of life. But variety and control in language, and order in construction, were essentials which the drama had hitherto lacked, and these Lyly supplied. Learning joins with old wives' tales; jargon and proverbs with a clear central norm of speech. The earlier plays, such as *Sapho and Phao* and *Endimion*, interlace two or three stories very loosely: the characters are hardly connected, and the plays fall into a succession of long tirades. *Midas* and *Campaspe* are Ovidian Romances in dramatic form; but the chatter of witty page-boys, riddles, jests and songs break up their monotony of style. In *Love's Metamorphosis* and *Gallathea*, which are even more Ovidian, the extraordinary predicaments of the disguised and transformed lovers produce logical dilemmas: the fable now predominates. Even the clowns of *Gallathea* and the familiar setting on the banks of Humber do not destroy the play's artifice; the pace quickens, moving towards fantasy and farce. In the last plays, *Mother Bombie* and *The Woman in the Moon*, lovers, clowns and pages are strongly contrasted in speech; the writing is richer and more varied than before. There is much more boisterous jesting: Pandora, compared with Midas, is made ridiculous by her transformation. Elegant courtly love is thrust into the background.

Lyly indeed always treats love as a disease which transforms, captivates and makes its victims absurd. Though inescapable, it is really preposterous. Even when they are taken as models of elegant speech and correct sentiment, the lovers attract no sympathy. *Endimion* and *The Woman in the Moon* are the only plays to satirize women; yet Lyly always supplies the poison and antidote, Amor and Remedium Amoris, together. In his prologues he displays a diffident irony about his own intentions and, perhaps not altogether truthfully, disclaims all purpose of bestowing a shape upon the fancies of his audience.

'Our exercises must be as your judgement is, resembling water, which is always of the same colour into what it runneth.'

In effect, the artifice and symmetry permit a wide liberty of interpretation. Oxford or Leicester will fit the role of Endimion equally well, and both have been discerned. Devotion itself in these plays, 'all breathing human passion far above', may become a symbol for the pursuit of fame or knowledge. As Petrarchan sonnet-form could be applied to education, religion or politics, so that allegory enabled the Elizabethan poet to use it as a formula for the discussion of any important intellectual issue,[5] so by the stiffness of his rhetoric and the rigidity of his fable Lyly cast a matrix, in which the audience could shape what forms they pleased. The symmetry of the sonnet form resembles the symmetry of Lyly's plays; today the effect is not one of flexibility and variety, but rather of consistency and even monotony.

Like the sonnets too, Lyly's drama relies on a façade of complete social assurance. The ultimate aim is self-mockery, achieved through invoking social standards, so inadequate as to be judged in the definition, against feelings so absurd as to be fittingly condemned even by such standards as these. The Sybil's definition of love from *Sapho and Phao* supplies an example.

'Love, fair child, is to be governed by art, as thy boat by an oar: for fancy, though it cometh by hazard, is ruled by wisdom. If my precepts may persuade (and I pray thee let them persuade) I would wish thee first to be diligent: for that women desire nothing more than to have their servants officious. Be always in sight but never slothful. Flatter, I mean lie: little things catch light minds and fancy is a worm, that feedeth first upon fennel. Imagine with thyself all to be won, otherwise my advice were as unnecessary as thy labour. . . . Be prodigal in praises and promises, beauty must have a trumpet and pride a gift. Peacocks never spread their feathers but when they are flattered, and Gods are seldom pleased if they be not bribed.'

This *obbligato* continues for another fifty lines. In its

irony and not quite trustworthy assumption of worldliness it may be compared with the attitude of Congreve's Angelica or Wilde's Mrs. Allonby.

> 'She that marries a fool, Sir Sampson, forfeits the reputation of her honesty or understanding: and she that marries a very witty man is a slave to the severity and insolent conduct of her husband. I should like a man of wit for a lover, because I would have such a one in my power; but I would no more be his wife, than his enemy. For his malice is not a more terrible consequence of his aversion, than his jealousy is of his love.'
>
> *Love for Love*, 5.2.

> 'The Ideal Man! O, the Ideal Man should talk to us as if we were goddesses and treat us as if we were children. He should refuse all our serious requests and gratify every one of our whims. He should encourage us to have caprices, and forbid us to have missions. He should always say much more than he means, and always mean much more than he says.'
>
> *A Woman of No Importance*, Act II.

The artifice of Congreve and Wilde, like that of Lyly, consists in presenting the spectator with what appears to be an authentic glimpse of an impossibly elegant world, which in its simplified outline and heightened speech makes no attempt at naturalism. This Contention between Manners and Passion is a sham fight, for Passion is present only as postulate; the informing mood is sceptical and evasive.[6]

There are later Elizabethan plays which have something of the wit and sparkle of Lyly, such as *Humour out of Breath*: there are others which have only a comparable symmetry, such as *The Wit of a Woman*:[7] but there are none which combine so gracefully an artificial form and a clear governing intention. Lyly, however, scarcely achieves full drama: the plays remain dramatic recitative. Each type of character has its appropriate speech, which is shared with the others of the group. The pages' retorts could be interchanged, as the lovers change their identity or even their sex, or as the gods turn mortal and reassume godhead. Constancy in change, unity in contrast, is the governing structural principle: yet in the final plays there is an approach towards popular form. In *Mother Bombie*, the setting is Rochester, and there is good store of homely proverbs: the play is cut to the English Plautine pattern of *Gammer Gurton's Needle* rather than the Italian Plautine of *The Comedy of Errors*. All the characters are countrified, and the theme is Crabbed Age and Youth.

> *Sperantus:* It is you that go about to match your girl with my boy, she being more fit for seams than for marriage, and he for a rod than a wife.
>
> *Prisius:* Her birth requires a better bridegroom than such a groom.
>
> *Sperantus:* And his bringing up another gate marriage than such a minion.
>
> *Prisius:* Marry gup! I am sure he hath no better bread than is made of wheat, nor worn finer cloth than is made of wool, nor learned better manners than are taught in schools.
>
> *Sperantus:* Nor your minx had no better grandfather than a tailor, who as I have heard was poor and proud: nor a better father than yourself, unless your wife borrowed a better to make her daughter a gentlewoman.[8]
>
> 1.3.7–20.

The play is not interrupted with shows, such as those of *Love's Metamorphosis*—Ceres' tree and the delightful Siren who is directed to 'sing with a glass in her hand and a comb'. Lyly's rhetorical artifice now concealed a powerful unifying imagination, which welded together Ovidian, Italian and English tradition. He became the dramatist's dramatist, providing a model both for the youthful Shakespeare and the youthful Jonson.[9]

Both reacted against him, but it was the kind of reaction that presupposes a debt. Long before his death Lyly's achievement was already outmoded and his best work served for a target to the younger wits: but to him in particular the words of a modern writer would apply: 'Someone said "The dead writers are remote from us because we know so much more than they did". Precisely, and they are that which we know.'[10]

II. Popular Comedy: Peele, Greene, Nashe

Lyly at last approached popular drama: the 'merriness' of 'old Mother Bombie' became almost proverbial. Meanwhile, the men's companies were putting on plays which embodied much more directly the old traditions of the romances, whether saints' lives or tales of wandering knights.[11] Peele and Greene are the two authors most definitely associated with the attempt to raise popular comedy towards a simple form of art; the one a Londoner, son of the clerk to Christ's Hospital, the other the son of a Norwich saddler, both had reached the Universities, and therefore wrote themselves gentlemen. In their comedies, a variety of experiments proclaimed that comic form was as yet but inchoate. Yet comedy, though fluid, was not amorphous. The work of these men was in a common style which makes it impossible with any confidence to assign an exact contribution to each, and the popular comedy of the eighties is best considered as a whole. The shadowy contribution of Nashe, and the yet more shadowy one of Lodge [12] still leave several plays unfathered. A number were ascribed to Shakespeare, including the most popular of all, *Mucedorus*. These were comedies belonging at the time of publication to Shakespeare's own company; they reflect, however faintly, the popular view of Shakespeare's work; and they place him, where he was placed by Webster, in the line that leads from Peele and Greene to Dekker and Heywood.

In the most shapeless and primitive of such popular plays, Greene's *Orlando Furioso*, some foreshadowings of Shakespeare may be found. Less a gallimaufrey than a farrago, this play has often been dismissed as hopelessly corrupt: yet within the popular kind it has a unity of its own— the unity of an old wives' tale. Orlando is a 'wandering knight' (2.1.638), one of the Twelve Peers of Charlemagne, and these worthies appear in the final scene, when the disguised Orlando fights with three of them before he is recognized as the man they seek. In the opening scene a parade of monarchs from the four corners of the earth appears to woo Angelica, with pompous Marlovian terms that in each case conclude with the same modest vaunt:

> 'But leaving these such glories as they be,
> I love (my Lord): let that suffice for me.'

Orlando is chosen by Angelica, as his varied conclusion hints he will be.

'But leaving these such glories as they be,
I love, my lord:
Angelica herself shall speak for me.'

His madness is induced by the wicked Sacrapant's hanging elegies and love poems upon the trees of the grove which suggest that his lady is unfaithful: it is not as close to *As You Like It* as the opening scene is to the stately wooing of the Lady of Belmont. When her rejected suitors make war upon Angelica's father, and Orlando in the disguise of a poor soldier appears to win the day and to effect Angelica's rescue as she is about to be executed at the demand of the peers of France, there seems to be a yet more distant glimpse of Posthumus and the sons of Cymbeline. The madness of Orlando, which leads to a good deal of low comedy, is finally dissolved by an unexplained Good Fairy, who appearing in the disguise of a poor old woman charms him asleep with her wand and proceeds to recite her spell in Greene's best Latin. Orlando himself breaks into Italian, but only in the height of his madness. He beats the clowns, leads an army equipped with spits and dripping pans to victory, and as a climax enters dressed like a poet, prepared to storm both heaven and hell, comparing himself to Hercules and Orpheus.

This attempt to unite old fairy tales with an Italian plot, scraps of Latin and Italian learning, Spenser and the fashionable Ariosto, is held together by stage devices, such as the procession of kings—Orlando's rivals—at the beginning, and the combats of the Twelve Peers—his companions—at the end. It has been made without any ambition to impose a general design. The natural harmony lies in the *kind*, which is the fairy-tale; [12a] in Lyly, this had been the minor ingredient and the Italianate form had predominated. Here the naïve attempt to put in something for everybody is justified only by the literal treatment of Lyly's theme—Love's Madness. This binds the play together and distinguishes it from such utterly shapeless monstrosities as *The Cobbler's Prophecy*. But it is still very close to the old romance.

The magician Sacrapant from *Orlando* mingles with *The Golden Ass* and legends of the English countryside in Peele's *Old Wives' Tale*, but here, as the title suggests, there is a greater degree of critical consciousness. The play has indeed been sometimes taken as a parody upon the kind of *Orlando Furioso*: but more modern critics have recognized its genuine 'dream quality', its 'fairy-like atmosphere of enchantments and transformations'.[13]   In his earlier court play, *The Arraignement of Paris*, Peele had experimented in the adaptation of masque to drama: here he presented a series of riddles, shows and songs, beautifully and subtly set in the humble frame of a cottage kitchen.   Three benighted revellers are sheltered by Madge, the Old Wife whose tale forms the main play.

> *Antic:* Methinks, gammer, a merry winter's tale would drive away the time trimly; come, I am sure you are not without a score.
> *Fantastic:* I'faith, gammer, a tale of an hour long were as good as a night's sleep.
> *Frolic:* Look you, gammer, of the giant and the king's daughter and I know not what: I have seen the day, when I was a little one, you might have drawn me a mile after you with such a discourse.

This is, of course, the Induction of medieval narrative adapted to dramatic form: it is the Dreamer of Chaucer's *Book of The Duchess* and *Parliament of Fowls* triplicated, with an old wife instead of a book to provide the Tale. The tone of the play is suggested by the names of the three revellers. The enchanted Well of Life, with its two golden heads rising from the water, the White Bear of England's Wood, and the dead man who rewards his benefactor like Hans Andersen's Travelling Companion are pure fairy-tale: the satire of Huanebango is directly topical: and, rarest of virtues in that age, the whole thing is brief and close-packed. Such delicate balance of diverse elements could be maintained only by a poet with some dramatic practice. Peele wrote for a wide audience: if his sympathies were with the city, for which he devised gorgeous pageants and shows, he could also celebrate the stately ceremonies of the Order of the Garter at Windsor Castle in a dream vision which is entirely in the Chaucerian mode. At the same time his name became attached to an old collection of Merry Jests, the kind which might have been used by countrified Master Silence in his wooing of sweet Ann Page at the humbler end of Windsor Town.[14]

James IV, *Friar Bacon and Friar Bungay* and *George-a-*

Greene are experiments in Comical History, of which *James IV* is much the most pretentious and least successful. The induction includes fairies and mortals, stoics and frolics; in the main play a patient wife, of the kind familiar in ballads and romances (Griselda or Constance), is subjected to severe trials before she recaptures the affections of the Scottish King. The figure of Dorothea, much praised as the first sympathetic heroine of English tragi-comedy, is a traditional one; the Machievel Ateukin, and the Merchant, Divine and Lawyer who supply the graver notes, belong to quite a different tradition and the two are not reconciled.

Friar Bacon and Friar Bungay was popular enough to evoke a second part, the fragmentary *John of Bordeaux*. It is a play of revelry among the country folk of Suffolk, with a good deal of local colour about Bungay, Fressingfield and Beccles. Prince Edward hands over his part to the Fool, while he goes wooing a country maid. They keyword of the play is 'frolic': it occurs again and again. The king and courtiers make merry in an atmosphere of curds and cream, deer-hunting and practical jokes; though Robin Hood does not appear, his spirit rules. The rival magicians conjure largely by way of entertainment: the play is full of shows. Friar Bacon's magic glass brings about the death of two Oxford scholars, whereupon he abjures magic, only to resume it in order that the Devil may carry off the Clown to hell, and the play concludes with a resounding prophecy of the birth of Queen Elizabeth.

Against this vivid and very notable medley may be set the ballad-story of *Fair Em, the Miller's daughter of Manchester*, the wretched *John a Kent and John a Cumber* of the ballad-maker Antony Munday, and the even more wretched anonymous *Wisdom of Doctor Dodypoll*, as proofs that plays of conjuring and magic are not as simple of composition as they seem. *Friar Bacon* has the charm of a mixed cottage nosegay; but in *John a Kent and John a Cumber* the bewildering succession of disguises, false spectres and actions at cross-purpose which sustain the efforts of two Welsh princes to win their brides are so breathlessly crowded upon each other, that the effect is less like a poet's dream than a drunkard's double vision.

The patriotic note is most firmly struck in *George-a-Greene the Pinner of Wakefield*, where all the characters from the centenarian Musgrove to the infant Ned-a-Barley are aflame with heroism: George-a-Greene himself conquers the rebels single-handed, fights a bout with Robin Hood and lives to feast the king, who in turn honours the Shoemakers of Bradford. In this play the characters have a solidity perfectly in keeping with the lively but well-planned action. There are a number of minor episodes, where the strength, fidelity and true love of George are shown in turn. Bettris, his love, defines her role ballad-wise in the third speech she makes:

> 'I care not for Earl nor yet for Knight,
> Nor Baron that is so bold,
> For George-a-Greene, the merry pinner,
> He hath my heart in hold.'

At the end of the play, George refuses a knighthood from the king, preferring to live a yeoman as he was born. Sturdy preference for kind hearts rather than coronets is typical of Comical History as a whole and is always endorsed by the king, who himself relaxes among his subjects, in the style that Shakespeare revives for Henry V on the field of Agincourt.

The fashion of the Comical History was now almost completed. A king or prince revelling and giving his friendship to a particular craft, or a particular town: a strong love interest and a popular hero, magic and horseplay, songs and shows. *The Shoemakers' Holiday* descends from *George-a-Greene*, as *The Merry Devil of Edmonton* does from *Friar Bacon and Friar Bungay*.

A simple definition of comedy is given in the Induction to the popular success *Mucedorus*, where the figure of Comedy is opposed by Envy, who promises in the play martial exploits, severed legs and arms and the cries of many thousands slain. It sounds indeed as if Envy had originally been Tragedy. Comedy replies:

> 'Vaunt, bloody cur, nursed up with tiger's sap. . . .
> Comedy is mild, gentle, willing for to please,
> And seeks to gain the love of all estates:
> Delighting in mirth, mixed all with lovely tales,
> And bringeth things with treble joy to pass.
> Thou . . .
>   delights in nothing but in spoyle and death.'

At the end, this Demon King owns himself defeated by the Fairy Queen, and indeed the play contains nothing more daunting than a bear, which the hero slays as easily as Shakespeare's Orlando slays his lion. Prince Mucedorus is disguised as a shepherd for this feat; in his later disguise of a hermit he slays a cannibal by a cunning device to win his faithful princess Amadine. The clown falls over bottles of hay, runs away with a pot of ale and keeps up a set of merriments, as well as making all the mistakes possible to the servant of the only villainous character in the piece. This pretty little romance, played before King James by Shakespeare's company, was printed more frequently than any other play of the time. It received additions, apparently at the time of the Poets' War, when Envy was given a poetic ally, a figure shaped in the likeness of Envy-Macilente from *Every Man Out of his Humour*—that is, Ben Jonson, the only begetter of the new satiric comedy.[15] *Mucedorus*, boldly attributed in the third Quarto of 1610 to William Shakespeare, relies simply on the ancient formula of true-love, disguise, wanderings in search of adventure, and 'such conceits as clownage keeps in pay'.

Transplanted into the hall of a great house, and exposed to the criticism of a learned audience, popular comedy dissolved into pageant. Nashe's *Summer's Last Will and Testament*, coming at the very end of this early season of comedy, is more like Spenser's procession of the months than it is like a full-fledged play. Spring with his morris dancers and songs

'Spring, the sweet spring, is the years pleasant king . . .'

may play the prodigal, but such figures as Solstice, Orion the Hunter, Bacchus and Harvest, though they appear in sequence, have none of the dramatic vitality which rules the disorder of *The Old Wives' Tale*. At far too great length, all the seasons are condemned; Summer makes his will to the sound of the dirge

'Beauty is but a flower
Which wrinkles will devour,
Brightness falls from the air,
Queens have died young and fair,

Dust hath closed Helen's eye,
I am sick, I must die,
Lord have mercy upon us,'

and goes out to the sound of a litany.

'From winter, plague and pestilence, good Lord deliver us.'

Only in the figure of Will Summers, King Henry VIII's jester, who provides the Induction, and acts as critic, can true dramatic energy be found. Will emphasizes the artificiality of the whole masque: he addresses the actors and tells them how to behave, jeers at their speeches and their roles, mocks the author and appeals even to the prompter. The voice is that of Nashe himself; it is recognizable even as he comes in, pulling on his fool's coat 'but now brought me out of the laundry'. Here can be seen the first germ of the new critical comedy that appeared only after the great interregnum, of which this play, performed in October 1592 in the seclusion of Croydon, the Archbishop of Canterbury's country house, is a sharp memento. For, at the end of summer, in September 1592, the old order of comedy had come to an end. The Council declared a state of emergency. The plague had struck London: and all theatres were closed. For two long years the players tramped the countryside, acting among the simpler audiences such versions of the London repertories as they could collect. Companies broke, plays were allowed into print; and more important, playwrights disappeared. Marlowe was killed: Greene died theatrically cursing the players: Peele had sunk into illness and was to end by piteously appealing for charity to the deaf ears of Lord Burleigh: Lyly in his poor lodging within the precincts of Saint Bartholomew's Hospital was surrounded by brawling washerwomen and plague-struck inmates: Nashe took refuge first with the Archbishop of Canterbury at Croydon, then in the Isle of Wight with the Hunsdons: and Lodge, who in a later visitation of the plague, as practising physician, was driven to protest against the quacks who battened upon misery, went for a second voyage sailing the coasts of South America with Thomas Cavendish. None of these returned to the writing of plays.

III. The Shakespearean Synthesis

The years 1592–1594 mark a crucial turning point in the history of the Elizabethan theatre. The one playwright who returned to London when at last the Council relaxed their ban was Shakespeare. At the first tentative opening performances of his company in June 1594, four plays were given: *Esther and Ashuarus*, *Hamlet*, *Titus Andronicus* and *The Taming of a Shrew*. These plays were staged far out on the Surrey side, at Newington Butts, a mile beyond Southwark, and after ten days the company departed for their summer tour of the provinces. But hardly had the company returned than theatre building began, and by now not only Henslowe, but also such respectable citizens as Francis Langley, goldsmith by trade and member of the Drapers' livery, began to invest in a splendid new building. It was named the Swan, and stood in Southwark, for in his capacity as citizen and Draper of London it behoved Francis Langley to oppose playacting. Meanwhile, under the eyes of disapproving citizens, something very like two new livery companies emerged. The Chamberlain's Men at the Theatre and Globe, the Admiral's at the Rose and the Fortune were ahead of all competitors in talent, wealth and popularity. The one company was led by Burbage, the other by Alleyn: both catered for mixed audiences of courtiers, citizens and foreign visitors. The Earl of Worcester's Men came in a very poor third.

The two leading companies offered very different conditions to playwrights. It is from the date of his association with the Chamberlain's Men that Shakespeare emerges clearly into greatness. He was their chief writer, a full shareholder; this gave him stability and security; his great series of comedies and histories followed.

These playwrights who wrote for the Admiral's Men were not in so happy a case. Henslowe, the financier, Alleyn's father-in-law, drove them hard, and they had no voice in the production. About half a dozen authors collaborated, cut down, rewrote and expanded old plays. Speed was essential. Shakespeare produced two plays a year: Dekker and Heywood each produced about one a month. Their company billed one new play almost every week. The Admiral's kept to the older, simpler style of plot based on legend, folkstory, chronicle and broadsheet. Later they became Prince Henry's Men and after his death they soon broke. The kind of tradition they represented had had its day by 1612. The King's Men, as the Chamberlain's had now become, developed new interests at their private theatre, the New Blackfriars; but with Shakespeare's retirement they too had reached the end of an era. The period 1594–1616, the most important phase in English dramatic history, is one in which the old and the new, the traditional and critical forms of drama grew into each other and through each other. This covers the span of Shakespeare's working life; it is also a period of unparalleled general fertility.

Before the interregnum, Shakespeare appears to have been the Johannes Factotum that Greene so angrily berated. His Lancastrian histories were popular enough; but some of his plays were even more artificial than Lyly's. If Egeon of *The Comedy of Errors* is to us a little too tragic for the Plautine tradition, he is no more so than the heroes of the learned Richard Edwards' *Damon and Pithias*, a play which Shakespeare evidently knew.[16] The elegance of the youthful Shakespeare's work is that of one who aspired to learning, and who inclined towards the great for patronage. After two years of trudging the roads, Shakespeare returned to sink his own interests in those of his company, and to become the poet of *A Midsummer Night's Dream* and *Romeo and Juliet*, plays of lyric beauty and low comedy wherein it is no longer possible to distinguish separate strands of the older kinds of play, for Shakespeare is here creating his own. These two plays are as original in form as his English history.[17] A tragedy which is based on the officially 'comical' and lowly subject of the loves of two private persons, and a May Game which is also artificial are hybrids. Whether Shakespeare preferred acting to playwriting, as Saladin Schmitt has suggested, or whether he kept his roots in the little Warwickshire town, where his family dwelt,[18] he remained a popular writer. If *Mucedorus* were wrongfully ascribed to him, he was capable, even at the end of his career, of refashioning that symbol of barbarity, *Pericles*, to his own ends. His

plastic mind, absorbing and transforming the whole comic
tradition as it had evolved up to that time,

'cast the kingdoms old
Into another mould.'

In Shakespeare's mature comedy—it is worth remembering
that in comedy Ben Jonson put him above the classics—he
presents 'a harmonious society in which each person's individuality is fully developed and yet is in perfect tune with
all the others'.[19] While keeping to the old principle that
comedy portrays characters, he profoundly modified it by
deepening and strengthening each separate character, developing the relations between different characters, until the
characters *became* the plot.

CHAPTER VI

CHARACTER AS PLOT
I: PROTEAN SHAPES: SHAKESPEAREAN FORM IN COMEDY

1. From Art to Nature

THE writer of good Elizabethan comedy must pass a very narrow strait between Scilla and Charybdis. These two Italian monsters were, on the one hand, the many-headed Italian criticism, legislating for all Europe,[1] which demanded for Learned Comedy (*Commedia Erudita*), in the name of the ancients, obedience to rules the ancients never knew, and which was fatal to all but the most rarified academic plays. On the other, the danger represented by professional comedy (*Commedia dell'Arte*) threatened to engulf the poet. Organized professionalism amongst the actors reached its height in the Italian troupes, who were famous all over Europe. Characters were stereotyped—the youthful lover, the boastful soldier, the cunning politician, the braggart captain; and the acting tradition confined each man to play only one such part—Harlequin, Pantaleone or the Doctor. Jests and speeches belonged to a common stock, and could be interpolated in the scenario to fit the occasion. Stream-lined and highly integrated, this drama provided the delights of expert theatrical entertainment; but poetically flesh and blood were reduced to animated puppets.

Needless to say, opinion has not been wanting that Shakespeare modelled himself upon the Commedia dell'Arte, and that his work was precisely of this kind.[2]

He was confronted with the alternatives of Italian tradition, with all its prestige and its ready models, or the shapeless native popular play, in which material designed for narrative was struggling to accommodate itself to dramatic form. Each type had its own set of incidents and of characters. For the first there was the Plautine tradition of mistakings and farce: for the second, a series of marvellous and inconsequent adventures, probably involving magic. The characters of the first kind were those descended from the Masks of ancient comedy, but modified by rhetorical 'Characters', and by medieval practice of character-drawing in debate and homily, sermon and moral play. Such were the shrew and the hen-pecked husband, the prodigal, the witty child; familiar types, worn and featureless, and each equipped with decorous speech.[3] On the other hand, a series of improbable figures embodied the simple dreams of the unlettered audience—'prentices who turned out to be princes, goosegirls wooed by fairy lovers, tradesmen wooed by the fairy queen, possessors of magic hats or invisible cloaks, magicians and giants, clever cobblers or peddlers, and wise old women.

Lyly had moved from the artificial towards the natural in the course of his playwriting; Shakespeare's movement fol-lowed Lyly's. The artificial nature of his earliest work has already been indicated.[4] His fable reproduced familiar models—Plautus, or Italian courtly wooing; the characters were symmetrically grouped; the language alternated be-tween tirades and quibbling 'sets of wit'. Clowns, as comic servants, interjected their merriments; and lovers ranted when occasion served. The development of Shakespeare's art lies basically in the development of his language, and this was neither steady nor regular. It proceeded largely through the speech of individual characters—the sudden leap ahead in Launce's soliloquy to his dog, a pure vaudeville turn, is followed by Petruchio, the Nurse in *Romeo and Juliet*, the mechanicals and fairies in *A Midsummer Night's Dream* and all the rich variety of *Love's Labour's Lost*, that artful plea in favour of Nature. This is the underlying progress; the external progress may be seen, first in a new development of the story, and secondly in a new development of individual characters. Briefly, Shakespeare tried and rejected the learned formula of farcical *imbroglio* for a more complex plan based on the medieval narrative tradition, as modified by his own dramatic sense. Within this form, comic characters took on a new power. They were not merely grouped together; they interacted and even developed each other. Their rela-tion is organic. In more than a stage sense, they feed each other. The characters of ancient comedy, and even of Lyly's comedy, were, in spite of their symmetrical grouping, quite without this vital interplay. Their disposition may be as formal as that of an Elizabethan knot garden: a quartet of fools or lovers or knaves go through the chain of a dance, or, in the later satiric comedy, a crowd of fortune-hunters pursue their prey with all the doublings and turnings of the chase.

Elaborate grouping of characters in a play of Lyly or the early Shakespeare is only a visible equivalent to the elaborate symmetry of their speech, the rhetorical figures of echo and antithesis. The young lovers reduplicate each other as their speeches cross and recross upon the meanings of a single word, while the gambols of such a clown as Mouse in *Mucedorus* are the physical equivalent of his verbal mistakings. Arabesques of action and words could not be too intricate, the matching alliteration or the matching persons too thickly clustered. In Lyly's *Gallathea* there are two Gods, two aged shepherds, four humorous artisans, three comic sons of a miller, two Goddesses, four nymphs and two leading juveniles, the children of the aged shepherds.

Metamorphosis or the changing of shape is not unknown in this earlier drama:[5] it is an obvious variant of the pattern. It affects the feelings no more than a conjuring trick. 'So now you are masculine! O dear, what a bore' is a perfectly adequate response to the vicissitudes of *A Maid's Metamorphosis*. Shakespeare never employs this device: the magic changes of the lovers in *A Midsummer Night's Dream* are his nearest approach to it. In Katherine the Shrew, and still more in the King of Navarre and his followers, he evolved a new and subtler form of metamorphosis—an interior one. Both plays are variants upon the great comic theme of Growing Up; a theme which he made his own, and which no one else attempted, although contests between Age and Youth were common enough. For in Art characters were fixed, only to be transformed by some external violence. In Shakespeare, as in Nature, they were permitted to develop.

All the characters of Shakespeare's comedies are easily to be placed by a popular audience, although their full depth is only to be appreciated by readers' or actors' study. That is to say, they can be immediately recognized, and indefinitely explored. The implications of quite a minor figure—such as the sea captain Antonio in *Twelfth Night*, with his reckless generosity and tragic moment of deception—may alter the balance of the whole play; yet his moment upon the stage is a very brief one. Much depends on the physical contrast of his roughness and Sebastian's elegance. On the other hand, even a leading figure may sink back from individuality to a role which is purely conventional, as Hellen does in *All's Well that Ends Well*. When, with a moral reflection upon his lack of moral sense, she strips off her pilgrim's weed to catch her runaway husband by a trick more worthy of him than her, she has become the puppet-figure of an overworked craftsman.

The contrast of character with character, the blend of irony and sympathy in the portrayal of romantic love, and the self-deceptions of lovers are Chaucerian qualities which, nevertheless, Shakespeare need not have learnt from any book. The art of comedy had always in addition to include a role for the low comedian. Shakespeare's early Clowns have a family likeness—Launce, Gobbo and Dromio appear for their special comic turns, but the wit of the later Court Fools is diffused through the whole play and affects all the other characters. Shakespeare uses the traditional parts of the countryman in russet (for Old Gobbo and Costard) and the comic constable (for Dogberry, Dull and Elbow): all constables were foolish by tradition as all shoemakers were witty.[6]

When about 1599 Armin replaced Kempe as the company's chief comedian, the jesters, Touchstone and Feste, appear: they are witty professionals masquerading as 'fools natural' and therefore motley is for them a species of disguise.

As separate characters became deeper, a single character takes into itself a variety of traditional parts. Falstaff, besides much else, combines in his nature at least four such roles—the braggart soldier, the parasite, the Vice and the court jester. (He is also a London Reveller, like Simon Eyre, with his jovial band of 'prentices). He is both familiar and unfamiliar; above all, unpredictable.

Shakespeare's innovations in character-drawing may be compared to the introduction of perspective in painting:

he gave the illusion of life. It was his characters which engaged the audiences of his own day; and character was, after all, the acknowledged basis of comedy.

In all this, he proceeded as a skilled craftsman, working for established players. By modern standards, no doubt, Elizabethan acting was formal; it was partly based on the gestures of the orator, though it included also such lively activities as fencing and singing.[7] The tradition of teamwork was strong in the Chamberlain's Men; but the pre-eminence of Richard Burbage was equally incontestable, and Burbage did not act in the Italian style. As Flecknoe described him, he was Protean, and threw himself into each role afresh.

> 'He was a delightful Proteus, so wholly transforming himself into his part, and putting off himself with his cloaths as he never (not so much as in the Tyring-house) assum'd himself again until the play was done.'[8]

Shakespeare too subdued himself to what he worked in; and in spite of his 'facility' it was conceded even by Ben Jonson that if he 'wanted Art' he was not entirely lacking in it. Some lines might even have cost him sweat. By stooping to the conditions of his stage, and accepting its basic features, he transformed his art until 'The art itself is nature'. His first great achievement, the articulation of the fable, was based on the scenic conditions of the Elizabethan stage; and his second, the development of a many-sided character, exploited the basic equipment of the actor; the 'varying of shapes', by costume or disguise. Both were evolved by the insight of dramatic poetry, checked by the experience of the actor.

ii. The Articulation of the Fable

Nothing could be more skilful than the refashioning of Plautus to the Italian model in *The Comedy of Errors*. It was a professional job; the Italianate setting with the three mansions of Antipholus, the courtesan and the abbess followed the fashionable model. In *The Taming of the Shrew* the subplot is equally Italianate, and even contains some of the Masks; but the simple pattern of farce is complicated by the figure of Petruchio himself, and by the Induction.

Inductions were a medieval narrative device. In nearly all of Chaucer's poems, the Induction introduces the main story by a variant upon the same theme. In *The Book of The Duchess*, the tale of the faithful lovers Ceix and Alcyone introduces the story of the bereaved John of Gaunt, told as a dream: in the *Legend of Good Women*, the poet, dreaming again, is forced to recant the defamation which he had perpetrated by drawing faithless Criseyde. He proceeds, as penance enjoined by his sovereign Queen Anne, and the God of Love, to tell 'The saints' legends of Cupid'.

(So Shakespeare at the command of an equally imperious sovereign transformed Falstaff to be the butt of Windsor housewives, in a play on the Italian model, which throughout the next century was praised as his most regular and artistically satisfying comedy.)

The method of the Induction, enclosing the main story or group of stories in a dream vision, to bring out its underlying theme, was that of the rhetorical formula, *interpretatio*: 'Let the same thing be covered in many forms: be various and yet the same.' [9]

Dramatic Inductions in early Elizabethan drama had not always fulfilled the high medieval narrative requirement. Certainly it was met by moral figures in such a play as *The Rare Triumphs of Love and Fortune*, or Comedy and Envy in *Mucedorus*. Yet in popular drama the Presentor, as the spokesman of the Induction was called, was more like the leader of a mummer's troupe: and in the plays of Peele and Greene, except for *The Old Wives' Tale*, the Induction is little more than a Prologue. In *The Taming of the Shrew* it returns to the full medieval purpose of contrasted story, and brings with it the idea of something greater: the articulated plot and subplot of later Shakespearean comedy.

Christopher Sly, the drunken tinker who appears at the beginning of this play, is picked up asleep by a certain Lord, and for a jest is ennobled, provided with a wife and entertained with the play of Katherine tamed by Petruchio. In the conclusion, which survives only in the primitive version of the play, he finds himself a poor tinker once more, but is fired by the memory of what he has seen to attempt the taming of his own shrew. Throughout the action, he has been

courting a boy who is dressed in woman's clothes and claims
to be his lady. Now, like the dreamer in a medieval poem, he
is awake:

> *Sly:* Who's this? Tapster? O Lord, sirrah, I have had
> The bravest dream tonight that ever thou
> Heardest in all thy life.
> *Tapster:* Ay, marry but you had best get you home,
> For your wife will course* you for dreaming here tonight.
> *Sly:* Will she? I know now how to tame a shrew!
> I dreamt upon it all this night till now,
> And thou hast wakened me out of the best dream
> That ever I had in my life.
> But I'll to my wife presently,
> And tame her too and if she anger me.

This is the only occasion upon which Shakespeare uses the
Induction, and that was perhaps because it gave him a hint
which made it obsolete. Sly's magical dream, the best dream
he ever had in his life, projected into the play, becomes Bottom's Dream (4.1.204 ff). Instead of a boy-bride, Bottom
acquires no less a love than the Fairy Queen herself, though
he himself wears the ass's head. By lifting the induction *into*
the play, Shakespeare produced a completely new kind of
comedy. Act I and Act V of *A Midsummer Night's Dream*,
set in the daylight, act as frame to the Dream-Visions of the
woodland. This is the formula of subsequent comedies.
Shakespeare puts the action at the beginning and the end—as
in *Love's Labour's Lost* and *As You Like It*—leaving the body
of the play to be devoted to the interplay of contrasted groups
of characters. Few would disagree with Professor Charlton
that *A Midsummer Night's Dream* is Shakespeare's first masterpiece. The disintegrator J. M. Robertson believed that it was
the only play that Shakespeare wrote entirely by himself.
Its beauty has been ascribed to many causes. Miss Welsford
relates it to the wedding masque and sees in it 'a dance of
bodies', the changes of a pavane: Mr. Pettit sees in it the first
sharp criticism of romantic love, in the character of a lover
given by Theseus and the parody of a lover sustained by
Bottom; others may find traces of a treatise on silkworms.
There is the characteristic Shakespearean virtue of pleasing

* hunt.

many, and all for different reasons: it is certainly Protean. What precarious literary basis it posseses is Chaucer's tale of Palamon and Arcite; a tale already dramatized by Richard Edwards and to be treated yet again, with the most curious blend of Chaucerian matter and Shakespearean style, in *The Two Noble Kinsmen*. The masterful swagger and exuberance of Bottom are nearer to Chaucer's Harry Baily than to any of his predecessors upon the boards: his play of Pyramus and Thisbe embodies one of *The Legends of Good Women*. Besides the presence of Titania there is a passing compliment to the more formidable Fairy Queen, who, unlike the gracious Alcestis of Chaucer's *Legend*, was no servant of Cupid. Finally it may be not altogether fanciful to recapture in the flowers and scents of the midsummer woodland some of that delicate fragrance with which Chaucer described his May Dream of the daisy; or Emily's garden 'ful of braunches grene' where

> 'She gadereth floures, party white and rede
> To make a subtil garland for hire hede,
> And as an aungel hevenyisshly she soong.'

All these details add up to far less than the total impression given by the play—the fantastic but symmetrical quartet of lovers, the mechanicals, fairies and royalty whose actions, braided in and out of each other, are finally dissolved by Puck's appeal to the audience, when the fairies, 'following darkness like a dream' return as epilogue.

> 'If we shadows have offended,
> Think but this, and all is mended,
> That you have but slumber'd here,
> While these visions did appear,
> And this weak and idle theme,
> No more yielding but a dream,
> Gentles, do not reprehend. . . .'
>
> 5.1.430–6.

This at once recalls Lyly's

> 'We all, and I on knee for all, entreat that your Highness imagine yourself to be in a deep dream, that staying the conclusion, in your rising your Majesty vouchsafe but to say *And so you awaked*.'

The dream vision was still a live poetic form, used to create an artificial distance for subjects either too intimate or too grand for the poet to approach directly—as in Lodge's *Scilla's Metamorphosis*, a wooing poem, or Peele's *Honour of the Garter*, a celebration of the installation ceremony of June 1593, which draws upon Chaucer's *House of Fame*. The medieval dream vision had enabled the poet to present the world of everyday through a light veil, with all the laws of cause and effect suspended; familiar lords, such as the Duke of Lancaster or Richard II, appear without being positively identified; Chaucer had indeed discussed the theory of dreams as if it represented for him the whole problem of consciousness and perception.[10] Shakespeare re-discovered the power of the dream to combine intimacy and a sense of æsthetic distance. In this play the courtly lovers are always kept distanced, while Bottom and his crew in one way, and the fairies in another—with their hopes of sixpence a day, and their freckled cowslips—belong to the world that is known. Queen Mab had appeared in a dream in *Romeo and Juliet*, but Puck is a household spirit of kitchen and dairy, who leads the woodland into the glimmering firelight of the royal presence chamber. The power of this play resides not in any individual part of it, but in the controlling sense of design, ordering the Protean changes of mood, quickly transposing the scene, as the unlocalized stage allowed, and yet keeping its own continuity. Here, for the first time, Shakespeare exploits the flexibility of his scene. His growing dramatic sense is displayed through the parody of primitive stage technique. (A second great dramatic advance, *Hamlet*, is similarly marked by some conscious reflexion on the art of the stage and by a play within the play.)

In *A Midsummer Night's Dream* the bare stage is clothed by the poetry of the fairies. Here is no question either of Italianate mansions, or of a neutral setting. The quick run and succession of scenes, in a place generally but not exactly constant, the boldness which exposes the sleeping Titania and the sleeping lovers to view throughout other scenes, and the dreamlike ease with which space is conquered—Puck's opening speech sets the key—belong to the great open platform of the public theatre and call for no spangles, candle-lights, or manufactured illusion.

iii. The Use of Disguise

The only characters in *A Midsummer Night's Dream* who are left much as Lyly might have depicted them are the ironically-fashioned victims of love's metamorphosis. They are transformed; but it is Bottom who is 'translated'. His change of shape is, of course, incomplete; the ass's head, familiar from rustic mumming, leaves him still very visibly Bottom the Weaver.[11]

It was in his subsequent comedies that Shakespeare explored the most potent device in his love-comedy: disguise or the varying of shapes. Here again he was faced with two traditions. The Italian comedy of travesty-doubles, of quick-change artists and of clever cheating was at the opposite extreme from the native use of disguise. In the moral play, disguise had almost always had the flavour of the supernatural; it was the special role of the Vices to disguise themselves as Virtues and to adopt their names; their unmasking ended the play.[12] 'Disguise was the old name for a masque', as Ben Jonson observed in the *Masque of Augurs*, and some of the mummers' animal masks were—and still are—intended to terrify, and to suggest the diabolic. In *The Disobedient Child*, the devil presides over the whole play: in the immensely popular *Wily Beguiled*, he appears first in the Induction 'like the Knave of Clubs' in a juggler's wide skirts, and subsequently as Robin Goodfellow; but reassumes a devil's shape to terrify the hero.

In romances and ballads, disguise is a proof and almost a badge of the lover. From Hind Horn to Fair Annie, the heroes and heroines put on mean attire, the men to test their true-love, and the women to follow theirs. Shakespeare's predecessors had used this device: Queen Dorothea, Prince Mucedorus, Prince Edward in *Friar Bacon* had all put off their royal dignity in the cause of love. In the popular drama such transformations continued, sometimes with a moral flavour added. The heroine of *The Fair Maid of Bristowe* is forced to strip off her bridal finery to adorn her husband's mistress, while the heroine of *Fortune by Land and Sea* puts off her wedding dress for serving maid's attire, to the horror of the clown:

'O, young Mistress, how comes this? Ovid's Metamorphoses could never show the like!'

Clothes, which indicated both the status and occupation of the wearer, were the Elizabethan actor's chief means of distinction. The wardrobe was, after the playhouse itself, the company's greatest capital asset, and was as magnificent as possible. In a daylight theatre, gaudily painted, gaudy clothes were the equivalent of the modern lighting system. Exotic apparel specially emphasized the leading characters; in *Satiromastix*, Dekker punishes Jonson by stripping off the melancholy black which he evidently affected, and dressing him in 'a player's cast suit of satin'. 'Disguised apparal', the quaint costume of the antic, might perhaps descend to the players from the Office of the Revels. On the other hand, the clown, as countryman, would wear russet homespun; and the fool, as Mr. Hotson has shown, did not wear a bright party-coloured suit, but a 'natural's' long coat, like a baby's petticoats, made of coarse homespun cloth, or 'motley'. When Duke Vincentio puts on a friar's rough habit, or Orlando Friscobaldo a serving-man's blue coat as disguise, they would become physically inconspicuous; when Prince Hal descends to a drawer's leather apron, his suit would merge him with the 'balmy jacket of the beer brewer' standing in the yard. There was a firm popular tradition that gaudy clothes were the sign of a fop or a gull, and that plain attire indicated honest worth.[13] From Duke Humphrey, in *Woodstock*, with his serving-man's frieze jerkin to Edgar in the old countryman's 'best 'parel' and best accent, defying Oswald, the truly noble tended to such simplicity as amounted to a disguise. This is perhaps the most subtle and paradoxical form of emphasis, the visual equivalent of that eloquent silence which Shakespeare reserves for the supreme moments of his plays.

All sections of the audience enjoyed the feats of the quick-change artist. Robert Armin wrote a comedy, in which he played the part of John-in-the-Hospital, a famous natural, doubled with that of the Fool, Touch: the story is so full of disguises for other character and lightning changes of part, that it must have been impossible to follow. A series of plays involving a quick-change artist were put on about 1599 by the Admiral's Men.[14] Shakespeare himself was highly selective about disguise. After the russet homespun and the coarse motley of country clown or courtly fool, his most constant and successful use was that of the page's doublet and hose for the heroine. Indeed three such characters— Jessica, Nerissa and Portia—appear in *The Merchant of Venice*: whilst Rosalind and Viola are the central figures in his maturest comedies. Physically, of course, it was easier for the boys who acted these parts to appear in their usual attire, but this could not have been a determining factor with the writer who created Beatrice. In taking up the part of a witty lad (Rosalind borrows the name of Jove's own page, as she takes care to point out) the ladies were assuming not only a disguise but a definite stage role: one which Lyly had first developed, but which Shakespeare had also employed, when in *Love's Labour's Lost* he invented Moth. The boy's clothes are, then, no mere masquerade; they provide a second dramatic identity which is superimposed upon the first, and interlaces with it. When Shakespeare puts his heroines into page's wearing, the two roles are sharply contrasted, giving an effect like shot silk, as the boyish wit or the feminine sensibility predominates. Both must be sustained, and this calls for acting as subtle as the professional fool's, when under the stalking horse of 'natural' folly he shoots his shafts of wit.

The paradoxical quality of the 'disguise' in both the fools' and the pages' parts is that it enlarges the original role, and also discovers its latent possibilities. When Jessica, one of the first of the pages, protests at being given the duties of a torchbearer in the masquerade:

> 'Cupid himself would blush
> To see me thus transformed to a boy. . . .
> Why, 'tis an office of discovery, love,
> And I should be obscured'
>
> 2.6.38–44.

Lorenzo promptly replies, with more wisdom than he is aware of:

> 'So are you, sweet,
> Even in the lovely garnish of a boy.'

Puns and paradoxes are the natural language of disguise such as this. To be *shadowed* with *embellishments* (*garnish* was used of stars and jewels) is true in a deeper sense of Portia in her doctor's scarlet. From the dreamy musical realm of Belmont, she comes to solve the riddle of justice at the mart of East and West; the graceful fancy of the casket scenes and the moonlight hymn to famous lovers in the conclusion are separated by strong melodrama; Portia's character is enlarged by her disguise, it 'suffers an expansion like gold to aery thinness beat'. Antonio's is deepened by the paradoxical contrast of the merchant's occupation and the contemplative's malady, a puzzle which he himself cannot solve:

'In sooth, I know not why I am so sad.'

Rosalind and Viola, in disguise for most of the play, are enabled to discover themselves more fully than Portia; Rosalind woos by paradox in the attacks on love delivered by the pert Ganymede, and Viola tells her story to the Duke under the figure of the sister who never told hers. Her subtle self-betrayal is varied by the literal disguise of Malvolio in his cross garters and yellow stockings and by the Fool's assumption of Sir Thopas's part. Yet Shakespeare exposes Viola to the broad farce of her duel with Sir Andrew, and Rosalind to the anticlimax of her fainting fit. When Greene's pathetic Dorothea—who changes her clothes but not her manners—is wounded in combat, the effect is disastrously incongruous; but the ironic situations in which Shakespeare's heroines are plunged by their lack of masculine courage are so contrived as to be purely entertaining. Complying with an *expected* note is also a source of ironic amusement. Slaying a lion was no more than was to be demanded of a romantic hero, and Orlando, as his name indicates, is the stage lover personified. His earnest pursuit of correct procedure even in the wilds of Arden, however, is mocked by the literary masquerades of Touchstone and Silvius. Soo, too, Olivia's decorous pose of mourning for her deceased brother is fortunately corrected by the prompt acceptance of a proffered bride on the part of Viola's living one. This development of character through disguise, or through the assumption of a conventional role, is an extension of the method of contrasted plot and subplot.

The two sides of Rosalind or of Viola have a different tone and yet each is allowed full play. If the fools are for the audience the chief purveyors of sympathetic irony, the heroines attract a teasing ironic sympathy.

An 'open' or undetermined nature in such a character is the element which makes for discovery. Each figure is no longer perfectly consistent and all of a piece, according to the received comic formula. It is complex enough to allow for a degree of bewilderment and self-deception, and for some ironic self-criticism and amusement.

> 'O time, thou must untangle this, not I:
> It is too hard a knot for me to untie.'   2.2.

The fluctuating depths in these parts also allows them to be played in a variety of ways. From the actor's and the audience's point of view the roles are flexible, though it is not of Viola but of the Duke Orsino that the clown observes: 'Thy mind is a very opal'. In *Love's Labour's Lost*, where the men have the deeper parts for once, the emphasis is strongly ironic. The formal role of scholar is stripped off in the discovery scene, where at first Berowne speaks in the accents of the pious moralist:

> 'Now step I forth to whip hypocrisy'

only to be uncased in his turn. But at the conclusion, the new and inexpert role of courtly lover is likewise stripped off by the ladies, and Berowne is commanded to jest a twelve-month in a hospital.

> 'Our wooing doth not end like an old play,
> Jack hath not Jill'

he observes in rueful echo of Puck:

> 'Jack shall have Jill,
> Naught shall go ill.'

Such a sharp conclusion beautifully balances the symmetry of structure of the artifice of speech: it is fittingly softened by the rustic conclusion, the ancient *estrif* of the Owl and Cuckoo.[15]

The School for Lovers which the ladies institute, and whose learning is extolled by Berowne in the great central tirade, continues in Shakespeare's later romantic comedies. Petruchio had tamed his shrew by fasting and watching—the approved method for reclaiming a hawk, and which he confides to the audience as his for a 'Kite' (the pun would then be much stronger), with a challenge to them to better it.

> 'He that knows better how to tame a shrew,
>   Now let him speak: 'tis charity to shew.'
>
> 4.1.194–5.

Courtiers are not so violent; Hero administers some sharp medicine to Beatrice, who is inclined to shrewishness, and Viola speaks some home truths to Olivia; but Orlando is most agreeably schooled in wooing by Ganymede, Orsino by Cesario, and Benedick by his brother officers. Only Malvolio, who is 'sick of self-love', proves incurable, and beyond the aid of the women or the fool.

These plays might indeed have been taken—if anyone wished to take them seriously—as Schools of Manners, Elizabethan refashioning of the Art of Love. The titles, however, scarcely suggest it: *Much Ado About Nothing*, *As You Like It* and *Twelfth Night* (the last and greatest of the twelve days of Christmas revelry) forbid such an intent. Moreover the preceptors in these Schools are in no position to dogmatize.

> 'Love is merely a madness; and I tell you, deserves as well a dark house and a whip as madmen do; and the reason why they are not so punish'd and cured is that the lunacy is so ordinary that the whippers are in love too.'
>
> 3.3.

The doctrine is the doctrine of Lyly: but the voice is the voice of Rosalind, not of the Sybil. Mockery of Orlando's sonneting does not save her in turn from the very skilfully aimed shafts of Celia's ridicule; her only protection is her readiness to turn the irony, lightly but unflinchingly, against herself. In each game of wit there is the shock of a new depth in an increasingly complex nature discovering itself—

> 'O coz, coz, coz, my pretty little coz, that thou didst know how many fathom deep I am in love! But it cannot be sounded: my affection hath an unknown bottom, like the Bay of Portugal.'
>
> 4.1.

as Rosalind cries after in the shelter of her disguise she had
gone so far as to rehearse the marriage service with Orlando.

In developing the heroine's parts Shakespeare was enabled
sympathetically to explore the subtle flow of unacknowledged
attraction between man and woman, or between two women.
His heroines are as different from the stiff goddesses who
stand to be wooed in duels of courtship as from the impossible pieces of devotion and long-suffering who follow their
lords, with Constantia in *Ram Alley*, not to the greenwood
but the stews.

While the wooing continues, other action is suspended:
'there's no clock in the forest', and everyone enjoys unlimited
rehearsals. In *Much Ado About Nothing*, physical disguise is
limited to the masks which are donned in the ballroom and
the final scene, for the discovery is more inward and subtle;
lovers are playing at being enemies and the taming of his
shrew costs Benedick less than it costs Petruchio because she
is already half-won.

Other assumptions of a role for protection may be a more
serious business, however, as in the case of Prince Hal,
where it costs him the sympathy of some modern critics,
though seldom of the modern audience. The role of prince
'frolicking' in disguise, as he did in many a comical history,
is here combined with the role of the prodigal, and also with
that less engaging role, the ruler on the prowl. Vincentio,
Duke of Vienna, a more cold-blooded prowler than Prince
Hal, and a more abrupt wooer than Richard III, has this in
common with both of them; that he knows how to play a part.
The ruler in disguise was a favourite figure in satiric comedy,
and some of his activities reached the superlative degree of
improbability.[16]

Measure for Measure is Shakespeare's most theoretic study
of disguise but it hardly comes within the scope of comedy.
The condemned prisoner and the bride have each their substitutes, and Lucio, the Vice of the play, is uncased in the
very act of uncasing the supposed friar. His 'open' characters culminated in Falstaff, about whose motives and character controversy still persists, and whose many roles, some
consciously assumed, range from that of Hal's royal father
to Mrs. Quickly's sponging client.

A role assumed for a given end, whether or not it involves disguising of apparel, is on the whole more characteristic of Shakespeare's tragedy, although Hamlet's antic disposition, Iago's assumption of the plain blunt man, and Edgar's transformation to Poor Tom have each their grimly comic aspect. More especially in Hamlet and Edgar the 'open' view of character invites a wide variety of interpretation, and as wide a variety of response. What emerges here is almost alternate secondary personality, as in some forms of real imbalance.[17] Hamlet himself takes over the part of the court jester; and when—accompanied by the rustic Clown as Gravedigger—he moralizes upon Yorick's skull, there is indeed a tragic metamorphosis.

With the final romances, the fixed characters of fairy-tale re-emerge and their disguises become transparent. In *Cymbeline*, the artifice is everywhere: Imogen in her page's disguise, her brothers and Belarius disguised as peasants, Cloten in Posthumus' garments, and Posthumus himself, as the poor soldier, change their habits merely; the characters are constant. So in *The Winter's Tale* the royalty of Perdita shows through her lowly habits, as even the 'muffled' Polixenes realizes: she is 'the queen of curds and cream'. Finally in Hermione's statue which comes to life, Shakespeare hints at the magic which is to pervade the last play of all. The varying of shapes in *The Tempest* belongs principally to Ariel, but no one is sure even of his own identity; Ferdinand thinks Miranda a goddess and she thinks him a spirit. The luminous haze which softens all outlines but one leaves the characters as formal yet as evanescent as the spirits of the masque which Prospero summons. He himself puts off not only his magic robe but his player's part to speak the epilogue, a humble appeal for applause and indulgence in spite of 'faults' such as a country stroller might use.[18]

> 'Now I want
> Spirits to enforce, art to enchant. . . .'

The enchanter's modest aim is but the traffique of the stage.

> 'Gentle breath of yours my sails
> Must fill or else my project fails,
> *Which was to please.*'

CHAPTER VII

CHARACTER AS PLOT
II: THE DEFINITION OF COMEDY: JONSONIAN FORM

1. The Poets' War

'By God, 'tis good, and if you like 't, you may.'

WITH this thrasonical brag, Ben Jonson concluded *Cynthia's Revels*, his second contribution to the Poets' War. Although the supposed opposition of Shakespeare and Jonson in this 'lamentable merry murdering of innocent poetry' rests on the word of the anonymous student who composed *The Return from Parnassus*,[1] their fundamental differences went deeper, yet were compatible with mutual admiration. Jonson was given his start with the Chamberlain's Men when Shakespeare was their chief writer and a shareholder whose word must have been decisive; whilst a quarter of a century later Jonson, writing in acknowledged eminence, could nobly yield the victory to his dead friend and 'what he hath left us'.

'Soul of the age!'

The epithet implies that Shakespeare, with a unifying and informing power, both harmonized and animated a society which he swayed by 'delight' and 'wonder', leaving no room for that critical detachment which Jonson in general required.

Yet in comedy at least, Jonson had quickly displaced Shakespeare, and throughout the seventeenth century led in critical esteem. Shakespeare, in so far as he held his own, was admired for his tragedies, histories, and such Jonsonian comedies as *The Merry Wives of Windsor*. His romantic plays quickly fell into neglect, and as he had eclipsed Lyly, so he was eclipsed in turn.[2] Falstaff still reigned, but no distinction was drawn between the Falstaffs of Windsor and Eastcheap.

The Poets' War was not purely a theatrical campaign. Between 1598 and 1601, when 'the Poet and Player went to cuffs in the question', the battle was also carried on in verse satire, epigrams and pamphlets. Donne's reaction against 'sweet' poetry had taken about four years to reach the stages. The 'sugar-tongued' and 'honey-flowing' Ovidian poems of 'sweet Mr. Shakespeare' were dropped by a select few [3] and fashion veered against his comedies with the reappearance upon the London scene of the boy players, in their new repertory, at the private houses within the City.

A two years' closure had wrought great changes in the public theatres between 1592 and 1594, but the Boys of St. Paul's, after their suppression in 1590, did not restart till 1599. They were followed by the Children of the Queen's Chapel; this double revival of the 'little eyases' was a startling dramatic innovation, and led directly to the War of the Theatres.

The children began at once to specialize in satire, as they had done in Lyly's day. Professor Harbage reckons that of fifty-five plays which can be assigned to them between 1599 and 1613, all but a dozen are satiric comedies, the rest being tragedies or tragi-comedies. Elizabethans enjoyed precocity in children, and the biting wit of Shakespeare's small Duke of York (in *Richard III*) is a model of what was expected of infants, court dwarfs and other apes of men.

Two-thirds of this repertory was written by half-a-dozen playwrights—Jonson, Marston and Middleton; Chapman, Beaumont and Fletcher. It was the work of professed poets, who made pretensions both to wit and learning. Conditions of acting in the halls of the City favoured something more like an operatic or concert technique than the style of the open stages; and though most of these playwrights also wrote for the men, yet for the boys they adapted their style. The vogue for satire gradually spread to the better of the men's companies; these in turn moved into the private theatres. Shakespeare's company, which produced Ben Jonson's mature comedies, took over the Blackfriars in 1608; and by 1642, when the Civil War stopped performances, all the main theatres were private ones.

The Poets' War began in the retirement of the University

of Cambridge. Joseph Hall, Fellow of Emmanuel College, and University Lector in Rhetoric, whose satires were so parochial and academic as to include a Cambridge pub-crawl, pasted an epigram into every copy that the local booksellers received of one of the satires of John Marston of the Inner Temple. Supported each by a faction, these two undertook with enthusiasm a 'whipping' of 'abuses' which was ostensibly modelled upon Persius and Juvenal, but really continued an ancient academic tradition of debate and invective. In so far as they are not purely personal, Elizabethan satiric sketches derive from the same tradition of social homily as Piers Plowman, or the moral play, or the Dance of the Seven Deadly Sins.[4] Perhaps in Marston's case, there was some fond hope that satire would prove a short cut to political power and influence: for Marston was Italian by his mother's side, and acknowledged as his original Pietro Aretino, with whom the writer of the Parnassus plays compared him. As the author of The Whipping of the Satire reminded him, however, in England the correction of vice belonged to the Queen's courts; and in 1599, his works were summarily ordered by the Archbishop of Canterbury to be burnt as scurrilous. Ten years later, Marston himself was ordained, by a considerable exercise of charity on the part of the ecclesiastical powers, while Hall eventually became a Bishop.

Ecclesiastical as well as academic bickering had always been full of violence;[5] the arrogantly corrective attitude of the Whippers recalls that of the Puritans who condemned plays. Controversy proceeded then as now, by the coining of rival definitions which the combatants hurled at each other, accompanied by much personal invective. Modern attempts to discuss the nature of peace or democracy would furnish the nearest parallel to this bandying of platitudes. The War of the Theatres resolved itself into an attempt to define the Poet and to establish his superiority to his employers, the Players, whose economic control of the situation supplied them with the most effective form of retort.

There is no true question to be followed through the various plays, but only the rival set of definitions, constituting a set of rival claims, and set forth by means of a common stock of images. In Histriomastix (1598), Marston opened the conflict with the portrait of Chrisogonus, an Artsman or academic, who starts as a teacher of mathematics.[6] The Players, a set of country strollers, are supplied with plays by one of their band—Antony Munday in very thin disguise. When the players will not give his price for a play, Chrisogonus laments for the presumptuous ignorance of Kyd, Shakespeare and Munday, in accents that recall Greene's old attack upon player-poets in general and Shakespeare in particular.

> 'O age, when every scrivener's boy shall dip
> Prophaning quills into Thessalies spring,
> When every artist prentice that hath read
> The Pleasant Pantry of Conceits shall dare
> To write as confident as Hercules.*
> When every Balladmonger boldly writes,
> And windy froth of bottle ale doth fill
> Their purest organ of invention . . .'

The play has a strong morality structure, in which the ruin of Respublica is the theme;[7] at the beginning, during the reign of Peace, the Seven Liberal Arts flourish, but as her sceptre passes successively to Plenty, Pride, Envy, War and Famine, the various members of the commonwealth, including the Poet and the Players, are involved in common disasters. Only the Poet escapes from the turmoils of war, and provides the happy solution, since he sits above the reach of fortune in stoic indifference to events.

> 'Affliction is the perfect way
> That leads to Jove's tribunal dignity:
> Ill hast thou governed thy prosperity
> That canst smile in mere adversity:
> Look upon me (the poorest slave in show
> That ever fortune buried in mishap),
> Yet is this nature's richest jewel house,
> And teacheth me to weep at all your wants.'

In conclusion, the Players are banished overseas as mere idlers and vagabonds, and on the advice of Chrisogonus, Law is re-established. The admiring warriors hail this brilliant suggestion:

> 'Thou son of knowledge, richer than a man,
> We censure thy advice as oracles.'

---

* Hercules bearing the world was the sign of the Globe Theatre.

Peace resumes her reign, and a *dea ex machina* descends in the form of Queen Elizabeth herself, arrayed as Astraea or Heavenly Justice, leading in her train once more the Seven Liberal Arts.

Such are the general themes of the War of the Theatres: the status of the Poet, with special reference to his rate of pay, the opposition of learning to the vulgar craftsmen and their vulgar poets, and the power of Envy. It is during the reign of Envy that the commonwealth falls into decay; and Invidia, originally one of the Seven Deadly Sins, is the devil specially appropriated to Satire.[8] Joseph Hall opened his first three books of Satires with a Defiance to Envy; the purgation of Envy by the sight of Queen Elizabeth was the original conclusion of *Every Man out of His Humour*; the demon reappears in the Prologue of *Poetaster* and both prologue and epilogue of *Mucedorus*. Ill-will or Detraction, the critic's prior determination to assert himself by damning the play, was to the Players the supreme danger; while the Poet feared that he would be attacked by 'the strong antipathy of bad to good', since, as Jonson explained, Envy is distinguished from Hatred by operating only against virtue.

The Player Whipt—the stage title of *Histriomastix*—was put on by Paul's boys; *Every Man out of his Humour* was the rejoinder of the Players at the Globe. Asper, the embodiment of Satire ('he is of an ingenious and free spirit, eager and constant in reproof'), presents the play. His accent and themes are identical with those of Chrisogonus.

> 'O how I hate the monstrousness of time,
> When every servile imitating spirit,
> Plagued with an itching leprosy of wit,
> In a mere halting fury, strives to fling
> His ulcerous body in the Thespian spring,
> And straight leaps forth a poet! '

He promises to 'scourge' the 'apes' of the time:

> 'My strict hand
> Was made to seize on vice, and with a gripe
> Squeeze out the humour of such spongy natures
> As lick up every idle vanity.'

This in fact is his function in the play, where he appears as

Macilente, a scholar who, unrewarded by the world, 'falls into an envious apoplexy'. Macilente is no stoic:

> 'I am no such pilled cynic to believe
> That beggary is the only happiness;
> Or with a number of these patient fools
> To sing, *My mind to me a kingdom is*
> When the lank hungry belly barks for food.'

Having thus satirized the satirist, Jonson allows Macilente, after he has purged all the other characters of their excessive humours, to receive his own transformation by the appearance, perhaps from the 'Heavens', of the embodiment of 'invaluable virtues', the Queen.

> 'In her graces,
> All my malicious powers have lost their stings
> Envy hath fled my soul at sight of her.'

In *Cynthia's Revels*, Elizabeth again appears to purge the characters of self-love, and to unmask all the vices. In both these plays Marston is satirically portrayed, and he replied with satiric portraits of Ben Jonson.[9] This quarrel between the two satirists was a personal affair; both were now writing for the boys' companies. In the culmination of the war, Marston sided with the Players: Jonson's *Poetaster* classed him with Dekker, and it was Dekker who replied for both, with *Satiromastix*. Both sides, protesting that they intended no reference to any living persons, moved their stories into the past: Augustus Cæsar supports Jonson-Horace, and William Rufus defends the native tradition. Envy appears at the opening of *Poetaster* in an attempt to ruin the play by reading personal meanings into it, but is defeated by finding that the scene is to be Rome, and is trampled down to Hell by the 'well-erected confidence' of a Prologue in full armour. Marston's academic coinages of strange terms and Dekker's ignorance are equally derided in the final judgement when a judicial pill is adminstered, and Horace's stoic enemy [10] spews up his hard words

> 'O . . . glibbery . . . lubrical . . , defunct . . . O !'

whilst Ignorance, convicted of Envy, is dressed in a fool's

coat and cap, but spared Cain's brand upon his brow at the intercession of the magnanimous victor.

More than one medicinal dose was adminstered by the Players. *The Untrussing of the Humourous Poet*—the stage name of *Satiromastix*—shows Horace and his friend Asinus Bubo first tossed in a blanket, then brought in for a wedding masque, bound and dressed as satyrs, in which plight they are crowned with stinging-nettles and forced to read a recantation exactly parallel to that administered to Dekker and Marston in *Poetaster*. In this combat, Jonson's position was anomalous, for though he was learned, and finally stood for the Poets against the Players, he was not a graduate and therefore not a gentleman. His plays were to be dedicated to the Inns of Court and 'to the special fountain of manners' the Court itself (subscribed 'Thy Servant but not Slave'); but as his opponents did not fail to remind him, he had been bred a bricklayer.

> 'Dost stamp, mad Tamburlaine, dost stamp? thou thinkst thou hast mortar under thy feet, dost?'

as his tormentors cry to Horace. Nor is he spared reference to his poverty, his taffeta sleeves and worn black suit, which melancholy garb he is forced to exchange for a player's cast-off satin doublet. His conviction for homicide and his branded thumb; his face 'punched full of holes like a warming pan': his Envious-looking countenance, 'a lean hollow-cheekt scrag', are retorted on him in return for his own insults. His Muse is arraigned of turning satirist through pride and scorn, and not through love of virtue. 'Tu Quoque' is the cry on both sides.

> 'Or should we minister strong pills to thee,
> What lumps of hard and indigested stuff,
> Of bitter satirism, of arrogance,
> Of self-love, of detraction, of a black
> And stinking insolence should we fetch up?'   5.2.

Satiromastix was put on by Pauls' Boys in defence of Marston, their Poet and by the Chamberlain's Men in defence of the Players, so that Jonson had succeeded in drawing fire from both sides; while to his astonishment and indignation, the general public read all kinds of personal allusions into his own play. His apologetical dialogue, denouncing all such intermeddling, was performed but once.

Meanwhile, the Players had refurbished the old romance of *Mucedorus*, a defiantly popular choice, with an Epilogue in which Envy, who has been at strife with Comedy from the beginning, threatens to raise

> 'a lean and hungry meagre cannibal,
> Whose jaws swell to his eyes with chawing malice,
> And him I'll make a Poet.'

This poet, stirred up by Envy to write topical scurrilities, will give the demon a chance to provoke the magistrates to a general 'inhibition'. But Comedy scorns such a plot:

> 'This is a trap for Boys, not Men, nor such
> Especially desertful in their doings,
> Whose staid discretion rules their purposes.
> I and my faction do eschew these vices.'

Each side ironically conceded the victory to the other. As Jonson had satirized satire, in the person of Macilente, and as Marston had declared that no one could think worse of his writings than he did himself, Shakespeare in *Hamlet* allowed that the 'little eyases' had demolished the Globe, and carried off its sign.

> 'Do the boys carry it away?
> Ay, that they do, my lord: Hercules and his load too.'

Jonson makes Captain Tucca of the opposite conviction, when he declares that Histrio and the other players have '*Fortune*, and the good year, of your side', the Fortune theatre being the home of Alleyn's troupe, the Admiral's Men.

The last word, and the popular verdict, was certainly with the Players; yet what finally emerged was not a definition, but an example, of a Poet. The War established Jonson's reputation amongst the judicious: henceforth he was 'dramaticorum sui saeculi facile princeps'. The pre-eminence which he claimed for himself had never been seriously challenged by the opposition: they objected rather to his arrogance and self-assertion in claiming it. Among the articles he was made to subscribe in *Satiromastix* was:

> 'You must forswear to venture on the Stage, when your play is ended, and to exchange courtesies and compliments with the gallants

in the Lords' rooms, to make all the House rise up in arms, and to cry, That's *Horace*, that's he, that's he, that pens and purges humours and diseases.'   5.2.

The sniping tactics of his opponents had produced a series of attacks which were thrust into plays of quite a different cast—*Histriomastix* is a moral play, Marston's other two plays are medleys, and *Satiromastix* a comical history. Jonson planned his plays as critical manifestoes; and though they are not confined in subject to the War of the Theatre, they belong entirely to the kind of the Comical Satire, as they are described upon their title-pages. There is virtually no action, but a series of satiric figures is displayed: in *Every Man Out of his Humour*, where the nature of this new comedy is carefully defined by the Presenters, society at large, but especially the wits of the city are satirized: in *Cynthia's Revels*, it is the court, and in *Poetaster* the literary world. Not only Crispinus and Demetrius, Jonson's opponents, but Ovid is banished from Rome. Ovid is all that Marston ought to be: a true love poet, a student of law at odds with his father over work, but given only to gentlemanly revelling. The stern temper of Rome has no mercy on his masquerading in the habit of the gods, and even his opening poem in defiance of Envy does not save him, though it marks him as of the right faction.

The Players of the City, whose clumsy suspicions procure his banishment, are deceived by the hope of popular success into employing Crispinus.

'There are some of you players, honest gentlemen-like scoundrels, and suspected to have some wit, as well as your poets; both at drinking and breaking of jests; and are companions for gallants. A man may skelder ye, now and then, of half-a-dozen shillings, or so. . . . If he pen for thee once, thou shalt not need to travel with thy pumps full of gravel,[11] any more, after a blind jade and a hamper: and stalk upon boards, and barrel heads, to an old cracked trumpet.'

The War ends where it had begun, in Cambridge. *The Return from Parnassus*, acted at the end of 1601 in St. John's College, is a Comical Satire on a distinctly local topic, its main theme being the urgent question of graduate employment. The two students who are driven by poverty to an audition with Burbage and Kempe are ironically encouraged by the news of 'our fellow Shakespeare's' triumph over the learned poets, and by the advantages of 'the quality'.

> 'Be merry, my lads, you have happened upon the most excellent vocation in the world: for money, they come North and South to bring it to our playhouse, and for honour, who of more report than Dick Burbage and Will Kempe?'

while Ben Jonson is snubbed as 'the wittiest fellow of a bricklayer in England'. Many of the characters in *The Return from Parnassus* could be paralleled from Hall's Academical Satires of three years earlier, but his dreary and conscientious moralizings have been replaced by a vivid and nervous style; and both in structure and characterization, the influence of Jonson is everywhere discernible.[12] This purely academic and ironic tribute to his success ends with the complete failure of all the students to find a place in society: two become shepherds, one fortunately returns to Cambridge, and the fourth decides to become a professional satirist, for which purpose he retires to the Isle of Dogs. This refuge for debtors, cutpurses and the scene of a scandalous play by Nashe, has more than its cynical title would at first imply to recommend it to the student fresh from another kind of college, and a privileged life of the Gown.

ii. The Definition of Comedy

Jonson's critical strength lay in his formulated restrictions upon the licence of popular art.

> 'If we fail,
> We must impute it to the only chance,
> Art hath an enemy called Ignorance.'

He made unceasing wars upon common taste, from the attack upon romance and 'York and Lancaster's long jars', prefixed to *Every Man in his Humour*, a Globe play, to his very last comedy, where he is still complaining of stuffed legendary adventures.

> 'If a child could be born in a play and grow up to a man in the first scene, before he went off the stage: and then after to come forth

a squire and be made a knight: and that knight to travel between the acts and do wonders in the Holy Land or elsewhere: kill paynims, wild boars, dun cows and other monsters: beget him a reputation, and marry him an Emperor's daughter for his mistress: convert her father's country: and at last come home lame and all to be laden with miracles.'

With the common trash he condemned *Pericles*, 'Tales, Tempests and such drolleries'. His aim was not to please but to assert a standard, of which the Poet, and neither the Players nor the Audience, was custodian.

> 'Thy bold and knowing Muse
> Condemns all praise but such as thou wouldst choose'

as Beaumont observed. At his most unbending he denied the spectators all right of judgement and confined them to the passive role of believing only what they were told:

> 'Our parts, that are the spectators, or should hear a comedy, are to await the process and events of things, as the poet presents them, not as we would corruptly fashion them. We come here to behold plays and censure them as they are made and fitted for us: not to beslaver our own thoughts with censorious spittle tempering the poet's clay, as we were to mould every scene anew.'

At his most genial, welcoming the spectators with Martial's simile of the Poet as Cook, he could not forbear an ironic fling at part of the auditory.

> 'In this age, a set of writers are
> That only for particular likeings care,
> And will taste nothing that is popular.
>
> With such, we mingle neither brains nor breasts,
> Our wishes, like to those make public feasts,
> Are not to please the cook's taste, but the guests.
>
> Yet if those cunning palates hither come
> They shall find guests' entreaties and good room. . . .
>
> Cates fit for ladies: some for lords, knights, squires,
> Some for your waiting wench and country wives:
> Some for your men and daughters of Whitefriars.'

Yet in spite of his learning, Jonson was fortunately not academic in habit nor pedantic in style. Art in his work had freed itself from the restraints of scholastic theory; the Induction to *Every Man out of his Humour*, his first manifesto, contains a definition of his new type of comedy, and a justification of his departure from classical models. He transported Art from the Schools to the boards; he had no single solution to propound, no fixed model to offer, but instead a series of experiments and a continuous stream of discussion upon them, with alternative definitions. At the same time he sought constantly to defend his Art, so that the inductions, epilogues and incidental comments in his plays furnish the most complete theory of the drama which the age produced, based not upon scholastic arguments but upon practical experience. His parody of old-fashioned parts, such as the amorous, the martial and the tyrant's, in the scene of *Poetaster* where the boys rehearse before the players, depends upon a practical knowledge of the way to build a traditional play, and is comparable with the mechanicals' parody in *A Midsummer Night's Dream*, or Hamlet's condescending catalogue of the King, the adventurous knight, the lover, the humorous man, the clown and the lady. He has all the old playtags at his tongue's end.

Jonsonian comedy more than qualified for the ironic definition of Horace, in the Satire which Jonson so often relied upon: for much of it was in prose.

> 'Some people have questioned whether comedy can be called poetry: for neither in language nor plot has it the fire or the force of inspiration, and save for the regular beat of the rhythm, it might as well be prose.'
>
> *Satires*, I.IV.

'Deeds and language such as men do use' were Jonson's materials. He agreed with few of the professed critics, who all, from Sidney to Bacon, conceived that the poet's function was to build a brave new world, a second Creation in which the limits of the first were transcended. 'Our erected wit maketh us to know what perfection is, and yet our infected will keepeth us from reaching unto it', Sidney observed; and to Bacon 'the use of this feigned history hath been to give some shadow of satisfaction to the mind of man in those points wherein the nature of things doth deny it, the world being inferior to the soul.' These are justifications at once Platonic and Christian; poetry restores man to his original self, brings back the Golden Age and rediscovers his true kingdom.

Though Jonson, like Marston and Chapman, was prepared to accept unpopularity and poverty as the poet's lot, he did not believe with them that poetry must be mystic and difficult, or 'shroud' himself in the 'darkness' of a complex style. The dark raptures and Hermetic secrecy of Chapman's divine inspiration by the Goddess Melancholy were foreign to Jonson, who allowed the senses full play, and even admitted that the dinners which the actors provided were an improvement on the beans and buttermilk which was all he could afford for himself.[13]

His admirers recognized his special position in evolving

'the Art which thou alone
Hast taught our tongue . . . far more
Than any English stage hath known before'.

Indeed, in his old age an admiring undergraduate asserted

'With thee all Art began, with thee it ends.'

Neither would have recognized that there was any truth in the defence which Jonson himself mockingly puts into the mouth of Antony Munday (Antonio Balladino):

'Why, look you, sir, I write so plain and keep that old decorum, that you must of necessity like it: marry, you shall have some now (as for example in plays) that will have every day new tricks and write ye nothing but humours: indeed, this pleases the gentlemen, but the common sort they care not for it.'

Still less would they have acknowledged the stranger decorum with which the players' poet imagined an exquisite Italian prince commending a ballad.

'Mark it, Cesario, it is old and plain:
The spinsters and the knitters in the sun
And the free maids that weave their thread with bones
Do use to chant it. It is silly sooth
And dallies with the innocence of love,
Like the old age.'   2.4.

Shakespeare's only direct contribution to the War was a question addressed not to the rival Poet but to the rival Players—those unlucky little boys, some kidnapped and pressed into service, whose wages must frequently have been the most literal kind of whipping. He merely asked what would happen when they grew up to be Players themselves, and this in the course of refurbishing a vulgar and popular old tragedy of revenge, into which, however, he imported some of the ironic bitterness, the scholarly meditation and the scorn of the world that were proving so fashionable.

> 'For who would bear the whips and scorns of time,
> The oppressor's wrong, the proud man's contumely . . .
> The insolence of office and the spurns
> That patient merit of the unworthy takes,
> When he himself might his quietus make
> With a bare bodkin? . . .'
>
> 3.1.

In an old-fashioned writer the success of the new comedy was met by a return to tragedy. For the belligerent Jonson, the even more surprising sequel was—silence. His next play, which came after a four-year interval, was a tragedy too.

Jonson's reforms were directed, like Shakespeare's, to the intrigue and the characters, both of which were seen as aspects of the plot or fable. When Francis Meres had called Antony Munday 'our best plotter' or Leonard Digges described Shakespeare's plots as 'pure his own', they were referring not to the story, but to the whole architectural design of the plays, their plot in the builder's sense. The final passage of *Discoveries* makes this plain.

Instead of the multiple fable, with contrasted groups, Jonson returned to a single complex intrigue. In this he was certainly providing a more useful general model. What Shakespeare had achieved in *A Midsummer Night's Dream* and *The Merchant of Venice* could not be attempted by lesser men; the plays of Dekker and Heywood show what incongruities could be joined together in 'the old decorum'. In his three Comical Satires, indeed, Jonson had almost dispensed with the intrigue; like the modern discussion play, they relied upon character and rhetoric alone. Through these explorations and experiments, Jonson evolved the characters which, with variations, were to serve for his maturer plays. The induction, which the older writer had used to set forth the theme or moral, was used by Jonson for the same purpose as the Shavian preface. His achievement in reshaping drama has many similarities with Shaw's. Both enjoyed battle, both were endowed with a double passion—the passion for language itself, for collecting words and epigrams, and the passion for social theory. Neither was a dramatist in the supreme sense in which Shakespeare and Molière were dramatists, for neither was able to lose himself in the world of his own creation. Both created a public image of themselves—half comic, half heroic—which they manipulated with great skill. With Jonson's comedy, intellectual drama was born upon the English stage; and the writer, no longer concealing his identity, began with a vaunting proclamation of his own worth and an attack on his rivals. His trumpetings, like the trumpets which sounded from the Fortune and the Globe, were intended as advertisement; the image of the stormy poet was not the least successful of his dramatic creations, culminating in the supreme arrogance of the *Ode to Himself*.

iii. Mirror and Image

Though Jonson's definition of comedy was complex and not to be reduced to any single formula, he quotes in the Induction to *Every Man out of his Humour* the dictum attributed to Cicero: Comedy is an imitation of life, a mirror of manners and an image of truth. This could readily be combined with the Horatian view that comedy satirized contemporary behaviour, and the general theory that comedy reprehended vice, since for an Elizabethan to imitate was to interpret and not to reproduce: a mirror would either flatter or warn, but would not simply reflect: and truth involved the revelation of eternal forms behind the distorting veil of events. In modern terms, comedy was an interpretation of life, a criticism of society and an embodiment of values. In the courtly plays of Lyly and in his *Euphues*, the mirror held up was a flattering one, and the image was one to be copied. So, to Ophelia, Hamlet had been 'the glass of fashion and the

mould of form'; so, when Jonson objected to Donne's idealization of Elizabeth Drury in *An Anatomy of the World*,
Donne justified himself by saying that 'he writ of the Idea
of a Woman'.[14] The Tragic Mirror, whether the popular
Mirror for Magistrates or *A Warning for Fair Women*, was a
memento mori. Players were but shadows—the metaphor
was common—reflecting the life of the audience: it was the
response to mirrored truth by the spectators which conferred
life upon the scene.

> 'For speculation turns not to itself,
>   Till it hath travelled and is mirrored there
>   Where it may see itself.'

When Hamlet holds up to his mother 'a glass where you
may see the inmost part of you' he was repeating the lesson
of the play scene to Claudius. The mirror was a magic one,
particularly the mirror of the stage. Each character had at
least three functions—a role to play, whether King, Queen or
Hamlet Prince of Denmark: a truth to shadow, and a reflection to project of the spectators' own life—a mirror held
up to nature, showing virtue her own feature and scorn her
own image, but also and simultaneously showing the age and
body of the time, that is, reflecting the present moment and
company—as Hamlet instructs the players. In Elizabethan
painting there was a curiosity known as the 'perspective picture' which seen from a particular angle would display objects which, if the picture were directly faced, would be too
distorted to be recognized.[15] Something of this double or
triple point of view was demanded at a play.

In the older moral drama of the learned tradition, a single
figure might combine two roles; in Bale's *King Johan*,
Sedition undergoes a metamorphosis into Stephen Langton,
and Usurped Power becomes the Pope: in *Respublica* Queen
Mary is Nemesis. The transition is made openly. In *Hicks-
corner* the allegorical characters find themselves in Newgate.
These early plays provide no measure for judging Jonson:
it would be as reasonable to judge the art of Henry James by
that of Walter Scott. Forty years of rapid development lay
between.

It is rather in the popular drama which Jonson scorned

that the continuity with allegory is to be found. *A Knack to Know a Knave* contains amongst its characters St. Dunstan, King Edward, Ethelwald, together with Honesty, the Devil, Piers Plowman, the Three Mad Men of Gotham, a coney-catcher, a Puritan and a profiteering farmer.

Jonson's art lay in his manipulation of popular devices and classical traditions, to his own purposes. He knew and valued the old moral plays—so clearly, that it has been suggested that when he proposed to model himself upon *Vetus Comedia*, he meant the moralities rather than Aristophanes.[16] The probability is that he meant both. The remark is made in the opening scene of *Every Man out of His Humour*, which is modelled upon the old medieval Induction, and as such would seem familiar to a popular audience. But in the published text the speeches of Mitis, Cordatus and Asper are labelled GREX, and just as clearly they represent a development from the classical chorus. The unmasking of all the Vices, at the end of *Cynthia's Revels*, repeats the familiar conclusion of all moral plays; but these Vices are led by Cupid, and unmasked by order of Cynthia, while the mock litany in which they confess their sins provides a catalogue of fashionable affectations, current in the year 1600. It is addressed to the God of lies and learning, but headed, in the medieval fashion, *Palinode*.

> 'From Spanish shrugs, French faces, smirks, irpes, and all affected humours
> > *Chorus:* Good Mercury, defend us. . . .
> From stabbing of arms, flapdragons, healths, wiffs and all such swaggering humours
> > *Chorus:* Good Mercury, defend us. . . .
> From squiring to tiltyards, playhouses, pageants, and all such public places,
> > *Chorus:* Good Mercury, defend us. . . .'

The manifold interpretations of such figures—as Vices, as traditional dramatic characters, deriving from familiar formula,[17] and as representations of Jonson's literary enemies—are equally applicable and equally distinguished. In almost every one of his subsequent plays, Ben Jonson denies that

he is satirizing individuals. In the apologetical dialogue to
Poetaster he declares:

> 'I used no names. My books have still been taught
> To spare the persons and to speak the vices.'

while in the Prologue, Envy had risen

> 'with a covetous hope
> To blast your pleasures and destroy your sports
> With wrestings, comments, applications,
> Spy-like suggestions, privy whisperings . . .'

only to be defeated by the notice of the scene.

> 'Rome? Rome? O my vext soul,
> How might I force this to the present state?
> Are there no players here? no poet-apes,
> That come with basilisks eyes, whose forked tongues
> Are steeped in venom, as their hearts in gall?'

Since Jonson had rushed his play out at top speed in order to
get ahead of Dekker and his *Satiromastix*, this might sound
disingenuous, especially coupled with the later admission
that he had been provoked for three weeks before venturing
on a reply:

> 'To shew that Virgil, Horace and the rest
> Of those great master-spirits did not want
> Detractors then, or practisers against them:
> And by this line (although no parallel)
> I hop'd at last they would sit down and blush.'

Yet, though Crispinus speaks in the vocabulary of Marston,
and Tucca is apparently drawn from Captain Hannam,
Jonson kept throughout the play the decorum of a general
literary discussion; and he was at pains to make his Rome as
authentic as possible, even to translating from the original
Ovid and Vergil. *Poetaster* is more than a mere lampoon:
if the prologue, epilogue and all traces of the Poets' War were
unknown it would not be meaningless. The protests may
not be the whole truth, but they are something better than
chicanery. The three-tiered structure of the play is complete
and self-consistent at each level separately. The armed

Prologue who treads Envy down into Hell represents the author's 'well-erected confidence' that he can protect himself against base detractors, illiterate apes and the common spawn of ignorance. Though it created a sensation, the Prologue was in fact insufficient protection for the author. For the rest of his life, the imputation of personal implications dogged his writing. He was imprisoned for writing 'popery and blasphemy' in *Sejanus*: in the Prologue to *Epicoene* he begs the audience not to wrest his meaning to any 'him or her'.

'They make a libel which he made a play.'

In the prologue to *The Alchemist* he 'doth not fear who can apply' the story, but in the induction to *Bartholomew Fair* he again draws up articles of agreement with the spectators, forbidding them to put personal interpretations or 'politic picklocks' into the scene; and in *The Staple of News* and *The Magnetic Lady* interpretations are still being offered by foolish figures, such as the old gossips and Damplay—a later incarnation of Envy.

The very real risk for the dramatist lay in the government's determination to stamp out all covert political and religious propaganda. Whatever Jonson was supposed to have implied in *Sejanus*, his imprisonment a year earlier for his share in writing *Eastward Ho!* depended on the prompt identification of the anonymous 'gentleman' in that play who spoke broad Scots:

'I ken the man weel, he's ane of my thirty pound knights.'

Twice, in fact, Jonson had brought James's royal predecessor upon the stage. The latest lingering of allegorical characters was at the two extremes of virtue and vice: the goddess or the devil, as the supreme embodiment of Truth or the father of Lies, might appear, particularly to point the moral, even in plays that were for the most part 'an image of the times'. Jonson declared that he had introduced Queen Elizabeth 'though boldly, yet respectively, to a Moral and Mysterious end'.[18] She so appeared in plays of Marston and Dekker as well as Jonson, and even—as the divine infant inspiring a Vergilian prophet—at the end of Shakespeare's *King Henry VIII*. Such use of a personage who was more symbolic than human—Elizabeth had taken over many of the attributes of a more exalted Virgin—united at one point only (the conclusion), the moral or embodied value, the dramatic, or interpretative art, and the life of the day. Every play in fact was concluded in a general prayer for the Queen.

The Devil, the most popular traditional figure after the fool, was the central figure of the old moral plays. Disguise had been the weapon of the original Serpent, and the Vices who disguised themselves as Virtues were regularly unmasked at the end of the play. A typical popular devil is the presenter of *Wily Beguiled* (1606), who begins by substituting his own plan for the *Speculum* announced on the placard. Within the play, this character plays the part of Robin Goodfellow, but eventually reassumes the devil's shape to terrify the hero: he is dismissed with a beating, and the couplet

> 'Sure he's no man, but an incarnate devil
> Whose ugly shape betrays his monstrous mind.'

Jonson's fiend Envy, however, is no longer simply a monster: he is an embodiment of a social as well as an ethical vice: his new guise clearly indicates the shift from a way of writing where the social and ethical are fused to one in which they are distinguished, for Envy essentially belongs to prologues and epilogues in Jonson. In his later skit *The Devil is an Ass*, the innocent young devil who takes a human form at the beginning finds himself everywhere outwitted by human beings. In this play Jonson parodies the old Forms, which were still being faithfully copied in such popular productions as Dekker and Massinger's *Virgin Martyr*, where the devil takes the form of his most efficient surrogate, Macchiavelli, and appears as a Secretary.

Jonson's pupil, Nat Field, who began life as one of the Children of the Chapel, follows his master in the same device. One of Field's plays, *A Woman in a Weathercock*, concludes with a double unmasking, the same character appearing first as a priest, then, throwing off his costume, as a devil, and finally as one of the ordinary characters in the play who assumed the devil's disguise to point the moral to the others.[19] The conscious control of different levels in the play is characteristic of Jonson, and allows him to vary the emphasis

from play to play. In *Volpone* the moral element predominates; the characters are strongly satirized, as their generic
names imply: all are variations upon birds or beasts of prey—
Corvino, Corbaccio, Voltore, Volpone. The presentation of
man as a beast was a favourite satiric device. In *Bartholomew
Fair* the image of the times predominates, and the characters
are much closer to the likeness of the audience. *The Alchemist*
is Jonson's most perfectly adjusted play. In his early works
he tended to be too static and to present merely a gallery of
oddities: in his last plays he tended to emphasize the moral
structure and even to reintroduce purely allegorical figures,
such as Clara Aurelia Pecunia, the Infanta of the Mines.

Jonson demanded at all times that the audience should

> 'think nothing true,
> Lest so you make the maker to judge you.
> For he knows, never poet gained
> By writing truths, but things like truths, well feigned.'

This was of course a critical commonplace, which could be
paralleled from Sidney ('the poet never affirmeth and so never
lieth') and from other critics; what Jonson is repudiating is a
mere literal reproduction of contemporary life and nothing
else. In one or two cases, popular writers actually staged contemporary events, even a famous trial for witchcraft which
was still *sub judice*,[20] on which Heywood wrote a play.

On the other hand, a fantastic glorification of the audience,
like Heywood's *Four Prentices of London*, is also subtitled
True and Strange. This Heywood justifies in the Prologue
on the grounds that

> 'If we should not believe things recorded in former ages, we were
> not worthy that succeeding times should believe things done in our
> ages.'

A sceptic observes:

> 'But what authority have you for your history? I am one of those
> that will believe nothing that is not in the chronicle.'

To which the bland answer comes back:

> 'Our authority is a manuscript . . . we seek to show rather such
> things as are not common with everyone, than such historical tales
> as everyone can tell by the fire in winter.'

In ballads and romances 'the chronicle will not lie' is usually the prelude to some particularly outrageous fiction, and so here, where one of the Nine Worthies, Godfrey of Bulloigne, appears with three brothers as 'prentices to London trades. When a popular drama is introduced by some ancient authority as Presenter—Gower in *Pericles*, Skelton in Munday's *Downfall and Death of Robert Earl of Huntingdon* and Higden in *The Mayor of Queenborough*—this indicates that history is being displayed as a series of examples for the present age. For this reason Heywood, hoping that his play will encourage the 'prentices of his day to resort to warlike exercise in the Artillery Yard, dedicates to them this legendary story.

Conversely, Shakespeare took the events of a very recent reign, remoulded them to the pattern of *The Mirror for Magistrates*, with three examples of the Fall of Greatness—Buckingham, from the original *Mirror*, Queen Katherine, and Wolsey—and entitled the result *All is True*. The final scene presents the christening of Queen Elizabeth and Cranmer's messianic prophecy. In another play on Queen Elizabeth, presided over by the figures of Time and Truth, Dekker admits that he has arranged the events of the Queen's reign to suit himself:

> 'I write as poet and not as historian, and these two do not live under one law.'

Against such plays as Dekker's and Heywood's, Jonson waged unceasing war in the name of Art; yet the Ignorance which he attacked had its own strength: the strength of unselfconscious habits. Jonson has the strength of planned analytic organization. He depended very largely on reaction from the older habits: witness his constant and creative use of parody. His pupil Beaumont's best play is a parody of Heywood's *Four Prentices of London*. In that older drama the imitation of life was an idealization of it: the mirror of manners uttered flattering words or warning prophecies, as it reflected back upon the audience an image of Virtue or of Vice.

In Jonson's critical world the spectators were shown a play that did not pretend to be other than a play: the actors might come on and discuss their parts, the critics might put opposing points of view. The play is judged as it is acted. The mirror of manners has vanished and the spectators find themselves, from the Induction to *Every Man out of his Humour* to that of *The Magnetic Lady*, no longer reflected as men, but projected as selfconscious critics of a work of art. They are through the Looking Glass, and Comedy is defined in the action, and by the action. This definition in itself constitutes an analysis, for the author was one who, in Marston's phrase for him, enjoyed

'Art above Nature, Judgement above Art.'

PART III
THE TRIUMPH OF ART

CHAPTER VIII

PASTIME AND GOOD COMPANY: DEKKER AND HEYWOOD

1. Red and Black

DEKKER once spoke of the card-play of love as the subject of comedy, and the playing-card, a medieval invention, had both intricacy and individuality of design, as well as some of the magic powers which still cling faintly to it. The characters of comedy, formally marshalled under humours sanguine or melancholy, red or black, were destined either to provoke mirth or to stimulate a sense of sin. As they led off in the final dance which was the accepted method of clearing the stage, the wedded couples hand in hand, or as they stood to receive the final distribution of rewards and punishments of bitter comedy,[1] these characters must have assumed the heraldic symmetry of pasteboard kings and queens.

By the end of the sixteenth century, the general form of comedy was settled. The moment of differentiation had arrived. The Shakespearean unity dissolved. This change of mood and temper has been delicately outlined in half a dozen pages by F. P. Wilson.[2] In the mid-fifteen-nineties, the formal comedy of Lyly was assimilated to the romantic comedy of Peele by the genius of Shakespeare; but the most popular form of all was the chronicle history. From about 1597 onwards, domestic comedy became popular at the public theatres. In 1599, the private theatres reopened: and the satiric comedy of Ben Jonson introduced what was to become the fashionable comic style of the early seventeenth century.

For the first time, there is a division between two kinds of English comedy which amounts almost to a class distinction. On the one hand, the popular domestic themes handled in sanguine and traditional ways: on the other, themes equally traditional, but handled in ways which were melancholic and satiric. Thereafter, popular comedy, though it continued sturdily enough, became attached to a special and limited audience. Much of it was written by Henslowe's band of journeymen-poets.

The entries in Henslowe's Diary indicate how much has been lost, and show that collaboration was as frequent in building a play as in building a tenement. Some writers are now little more than names: their work tempted no printer, as they succeeded each other and were as rapidly discarded. Chettle, Daborne, Haughton, Porter, Cooke have left a single play or perhaps two apiece—some, like Porter's *Two Angry Women of Abingdon* and Cooke's *Greene's Tu Quoque*, excellent of their kind. Anthony Munday the ballad-maker, who was satirized by Jonson as Antonio Balladino, wrote for Henslowe his immensely popular Robin Hood plays, which may not have been without influence on the choice of setting for the rival company's *As You Like It*. Many anonymous plays might be grouped with this popular drama, such as *The Trial of Chivalry* and *The Thracian Wonder: Fair Em*, *Mucedorus* and *The Merry Devil of Edmonton* from the Shakespeare Apocrypha, belonged to his company; of these, the last two are, again, excellent in their own kind.

Two writers, Dekker and Heywood, have left a considerable body of work, from which a general view of the popular drama can be obtained. Dekker is the more archaic, with a basis of the old moral play.[3] Heywood, the better artist, works within the more mundane boundaries of adventure story and domestic drama. He runs to Moorish kings, but not to devils: visits Jerusalem, but not Heaven and Hell. Dekker leaves the impression of a spendthrift talent, whose possibilities were never realized: Heywood was a natural dramatist with a practical interest in the stage. Both were capable of neglecting or destroying the effect of their own best work by incongruous additions; yet their achievement depends also on this very simplicity. Lightness and delicacy of fancy, unstudied pathos, a natural purity of diction and movement and a ready variety of prose and verse style spring from that incessant practice of their skill to which necessity drove them.

11. Thomas Dekker

Dekker, the most traditional of Elizabethan writers, was by nature little of a dramatist and practised intermittently. His plays have moments of tenderness, gleams of pathos, but the general effect is too often amorphous and blurred. His work is mingled with that of others and often survives in a poor state. The titles of forty-two of his plays are recorded; seventeen remain of which five are entirely his own—*Old Fortunatus, The Shoemakers' Holiday, The Whore of Babylon, If it be not a good play, the devil is in it* and *Match Me in London.* In plays where he collaborated, the other partner seems generally to have influenced the plot. Dekker tried all the popular forms, and he wrote for the men and the boys' companies over a period of more than thirty years. His drama falls roughly into three divisions: the early popular comedies, including *Old Fortunatus, Patient Grissel* and *The Shoemakers' Holiday*; the citizen comedies written with Middleton and Webster; and after an interval, the final tragic lyric mode of *The Witch of Edmonton*, inconsequently joined with some poor fustian.

Old Fortunatus and *If it be not a good play* are probably compressions of two double plays; the first includes both the life of Fortunatus and those of his sons, and the second gives an account of the adventures of Friar Rush, who had formerly been shown in a double play. Magic hats and purses, devils with magic shows, a golden head which drops coins, and a scene in hell with the torturing of Ravaillac, Guy Fawkes, a Usurer and a Prodigal, provided bait for the groundlings. Mingled with these are adventures for the king, set speeches for the clown: in *Old Fortunatus* there are long declamations, and Fortune, Vice and Virtue appear in the Induction: in *If it be not a good play*, three devils are despatched to earth in the shapes of a courtier, a friar and a usurer, and the play ends with their return to hell, bearing their human spoils to an infernal conclave which is broken up by a boatload of Puritans from Charon's ferry. There is no coherence in the episodes: all is haphazard, and the folk-tales of fabulous good luck allow any kind of augmentation. There is a faint and far-off echo of situations in Marlowe's *Faustus*, but nothing of Marlowe's power to realize an inward state of being [4] or even of Peele's brevity and delicate mockery.

A dramatic poem, which was perhaps not meant for staging, achieved success at the noisy Red Bull. This was *The Whore of Babylon*, full of dumb shows and written in Marlovian blank verse. It tells of the troubles of Queen Elizabeth under the name of Titania the Faerie Queen. She is opposed by the Empress of Rome and wards off the attacks of three kings and of three assassins, Campeius, Paridel (Parry) and Lupus (Lopez). The play concludes with a grand seafight; but Dekker in a preface of unusual spleen reproaches the actors [5] for their noisy additions.

Another history play was hastily adapted by Dekker to provide *Satiromastix*, his contribution to the Poets' War, directed chiefly against Jonson. These two writers, born within a year or two of each other and dying in the same decade, are in opposition throughout their lives. All Jonson's virtues of concentration, order and critical control were lacking in Dekker, while Dekker's virtues of sympathy, tolerance and spontaneity were equally lacking in Jonson. Jonson's work can be judged only as a whole: Dekker's demands to be judged by his happiest efforts. They were at one only in their devotion to London, its history and customs; both delineated the very streets and alleys, and named it over ward by ward. In *The Wonder of a Kingdom*, Dekker wrote a play in celebration of the founding of Dulwich College by his old friend Alleyn. The festival of Simon and Jude, when the Liveries' pageants turned out, is especially dear to Dekker. His foreigners are real denizens of London—the Italian writing master, the Dutch artisan; the cockney 'prentices and their sweethearts are his heroes. Dekker only once satirizes the Puritans, he never shows cheating tradesmen or professional thieves. His rebuke to Jonson, ''Tis the easiest and the basest art to rail', was fairly spoken, for he was free of acerbity himself. Vigour, fidelity and directness in the Dutch manner which his name suggests, were his to command, as well as lively caricature and a journalist's passion for detail. He is like an earlier Dickens who never got past the stage of *The Pickwick Papers*. *The Shoemakers' Holiday*, based on a popular

work by the ballad-writer Deloney, remains his one successful
play and the natural antithesis to *Bartholomew Fair*. Both delight in a popular festival of the city; both catch the flavour of
a proverb, the smell of a shop. Yet while Jonson's judicial
eye noted merely the follies and affectations of his characters,
Dekker shows only the happy, the faithful and the generous.
Here is the King who frolics among his subjects, the noble
who loves a girl of low degree but resigns her to another; the
somewhat anæmic pathos of Jane, which pales beside the
boisterous excitement of Simon Eyre and the humours of the
three 'prentices,[6] softens the revelry and introduces a new
note. Although the language is varied, this remains the most
consistent of Dekker's works. All his other plays have some
incongruity or other. His readiness to reflect the fashions of
the hour, coupled with his great facility, was his undoing.
His plague-pamphlets and book of prayers show a depth of
feeling which in his drama emerges only in short passages.
His early clowns echo Lyly, his heroes Marlowe, his magicians Greene, and his masque Nashe. In his last works,
Match Me in London and *The Wonder of a Kingdom*, he tries
the tragi-comedy of Fletcher and Massinger. He has certain
stock ingredients, such as a comic Dutchman and a comic
Welshman;[7] among his lost plays are treatments of such well-
known legends as Constance of Rome, Guy of Warwick and
The Faery Knight. Jonson describes him contemptuously:

'O sir, his doublet's a little decayed: he is otherwise a very simple
honest fellow, one Demetrius, a dresser of plays'

and at the end of *Poetaster* arrays him in a fool's coat, and
cap.
   Dekker's happiest characters are traditional: frolicking
men or patient women. Simon Eyre and Orlando Friscobaldo are merry, humorous old jesters of boundless high
spirits—Hazlitt and Lamb overworked the pathos of
Orlando, who is serious only in flashes.[8] The boisterous
gaiety of Simon Eyre as he rattles away to his sovereign is
typical of Dekker's comic rhetoric.

'Mark this old wench, my king: I danced the shaking of the
sheets with her six and thirty years ago, and yet I hope to get two or

three young Lord Mayors ere I die. I am lusty still, Sim Eyre still. Care and cold lodging bring white hairs. My sweet Majesty, let care vanish, cast it upon thy nobles, it will make thee always look young, like Apollo, and cry Humph!'   5.2

This headlong style is speeded up yet more in the speech of Matheo, the prodigal of *The Honest Whore*, who, as he strips his wife's gown off her back and orders her off to her old trade, proclaims himself one of the roarers:

'Must have money, must have some, must have a cloak and rapier and things. Will you go set your limetwigs and get me some birds, some money? . . . You will not, then? Must have cash and pictures, do you hear, frailty? Shall I walk in a Plymouth cloak, that's to say, like a rogue in my hose and doublet, and a crab-tree cudgel in my hand, and you swim in your satins? Must have money, come!'

The blunt style of his father-in-law, old Orlando, matches this torrent, with only an occasional note of pathos, as when he speaks of his dead wife:

'She's an old dweller in these high countries, yet she's not from me: she's here'.

Disguised as a servant, Orlando watches and adds to his daughter's trials with the same improbable detachment as Gualter shows to Grissel. Patience in adversity is Dekker's endowment of all his heroines. Patient Grissel, Lady Jane Grey in *Sir Thomas Wiat*, the other Jane of *The Shoemakers' Holiday*, Infelice and Bellafront in *The Honest Whore* and Susan in *The Witch of Edmonton* are all dedicated to it. The accent of constancy is the same in these and other heroines: [9] it is simple and penetrating as that of a ballad.

'Yet good sir, because I will not grieve you,
With hopes to taste fruit which will never fall,
In simple truth, this is the sum of all:
My husband lives, at least I hope he lives:
Pressed was he to these bitter wars in France.
Bitter they are to me by wanting him.
I have but one heart and that heart's his due.'

Dekker's good women emerge from their trials too often, like some perfect machine, guaranteed mechanically perfect under all conditions. To yoke their pathos with the noisy

fun and violent brutalities of a rake's progress is fatally incongruous. Grissel, almost completely medieval in concep-
tion, is set off by a termagant Welsh widow and her hen-
pecked second husband, and by the Lady Julia, who prefers
the freedom of virginity. If either were less natural, it might
pass; only because he cannot devise perspectives of artifice
Dekker, in his easy pity and boundless tolerance, appears
something of a moral sloven, and Jonson's rasping judgements
more than railing.[10] Dekker writes at his best when he col-
laborates with someone who will stiffen the plot and provide
him with clear outlines of character upon which he can impress his own lyric tenderness or gaiety. In his most considerable work, *The Honest Whore*, he worked with the satirist Middleton. The repentant whore, her father and her wild
husband are joined with an Italianate revenge story, and with
'the humours of the patient man' Candido, a linen-draper
from Cheapside. Scenes in Bedlam and Bridewell, ruffling
humours and the fights of 'prentices are interspersed with
tremendous moral tirades. Bellafront, careless and gay and
sluttish, is more engaging in her unregenerate state: she has
not the brilliant horror of Marston's Franceschina, who appeared in the following season in a Blackfriars play, but her
conversion leads to a deal of dreary sermonizing, and she
ends, with all the other characters, in 'Bethlem Monastery',
which has transported itself from London to Milan with remarkably little change of character. In a scene of savage
farce, between three of the real madmen, Dekker seems to
be recalling *Hamlet* as he does elsewhere in this play: the
sweeper of Bethlem moralizes on his charges in the very
accents of the grave-digger.

> *Duke:* And how long is't till you recover any of these?
> *Sweeper:* . . . An alderman's son will be mad a great while, a very
> great while, especially if his friends left him well: a whore will
> hardly come to her wits again: a puritan, there's no hope of
> him. . . .   5.2

A broken merchant and two men who have run mad for love
are displayed to the visitors by their doctor with the observation:

> 'They must be used like children, pleased with toys,
> And anon whipped for their unruliness.'

This is the formula by which all the characters in the play are brought to felicity. Bellafront is deprived of Hippolito, and married by the Duke to the man who first seduced her; the Duke himself is cheated of his revenge by the doctor-friar who helps the two young lovers to steal a marriage. The final exposition of a cure is given with the sudden transformation of Candido, the linen-draper. He has displayed his humour of patience in a series of appalling situations which his wife has devised in the longing to put him out of humour, and ends also in Bethlem, where she has committed him, after he has accepted and even improved on all her stratagems. When, thoroughly remorseful, she comes to procure his release, he coolly throws up his role, telling her that the only lunatic is herself, and that he had swallowed all the indignities she heaped on him simply to cure her perverse longing. This novel and strikingly up-to-date method of taming a shrew is much more convincing than the moral objurgations with which Hippolito converts Bellafront; but it requires that Candido should be played in a manner far from guileless. No doubt to the City, the Draper who attended the Guild Hall in a tablecloth with a hole cut for his head because his wife had locked up his livery was simply a farcical innocent; while the naive pieties of his final sermon on patience endeared him to the admirers of Patient Grissel. Candido is an 'open' character in the Shakespearean mode: he could be played in several ways and is complex enough to be inconsistent, like the play in which he appears. He was revived for Part II and given a second wife, whom he tames by the much simpler expedient of a threatened taste of the stick. The sequel is in general a poor copy of Part I: but a procession of Bridewell whores which concludes Part II achieves true dramatic objectivity, and is in the sharpest contrast with the conventional speeches of the reformed Bellafront. The women are displayed in a procession, beating hemp, pounding chalk, and going to a whipping at the cart's tail.

Enter Doll Target, brave.

Infelice: Dost thou not weep now thou art here?

Doll: Say ye? weep? yes, forsooth, as you did when you lost your maiden-head: do you not hear how I weep? (sings).

Lodowick: Farewell, Doll.

Doll: Farewell, dog. . . .
Enter Penelope Whorehound.
Penelope: I never was in this pickle before: yet if I go among citizens' wives, they jeer at me: if I go among the loose bodied gowns, they cry a pox on me, because I go civilly attired, and swear their trade was a good trade till such as I am took it out of their hands. Good Lieutenant Bots, speak to these captains to bail me.

Seen against the fate of Penelope (dressed like a citizen's wife), the cheating game of easy virtue played in Dekker's city comedies, *Westward Ho!* and its very inferior sequel, *Northward Ho!*, becomes more savage than farcical. Jaunts to the Three Pigeons at Brentford, to Staines, Ware and Hoxton are the occasions for gallants to press their suits, and for punks and thieves to ply their trades. The city husbands themselves frequent bawdy houses, and have their garden retreats in Moorfields; but at the end, adultery is avoided, the citizens' wives remain honest, and a general Act of Oblivion covers all faults. The sardonic judgement which the plays evoke is never delivered, for these are not true satires, but only 'domestic' comedy. Well-known scenes and occasions must have given them almost the air of an impromptu and could easily have suggested individual portraits.[11] In two of his more successful collaborations, *The Roaring Girl* and *The Witch of Edmonton*, Dekker depicted living persons as the heroines, and it is likely that Moll Frith, the Roaring Girl, made a personal appearance on the stage. In each case the story is built round the figure of a woman who is cut off from her kind. The paradoxical character of Moll or the desperate wretchedness of old Mother Sawyer could not perhaps have been achieved by Dekker alone, but the sympathy and warmth of tone are his.

Both the revelling plays and the moral *Honest Whore* depend upon popular traditions, but modify them to the taste of the day. The Prodigal Son, the hero of many mid-century moral plays, came back to general favour in the early seventeenth century. The novelty of Dekker's treatment lies in the fact that the roles of tempting harlot and faithful wife, opposed in such plays as *How a Man May Choose a Good Wife* and *The Fair Maid of Bristowe*, are combined by Dekker. Bellafront is the centre of interest rather than her prodigal husband.[12] In all the plays of the prodigal which appear between 1602 and 1607 (except *Eastward Ho!* which burlesques the whole tradition) the sinner is let off very lightly. When he sinks to crime, it is often laid at his father's door. The shift from moral examination of the prodigal to his portrayal as a sympathetic social figure is part of the general movement from a drama based on ethics to one based on the study of man in society; but an additional cause may have been an appeal to the sympathy of the young gallants in the audience. They would not wish to see their own kind too harshly treated. After the prodigal and the clown, the curst wife was probably the most familiar figure in the old comedy. Candido's first and second wives come of distinguished company;[13] but no full-scale treatment of married affliction by Dekker survives, though a lost play entitled *Medicine for a Cursed Wife* indicates that he did not neglect it. In *Westward Ho!* and *Northward Ho!*, as in *The Merry Wives of Windsor*, the cheating tricks which knaves put upon gulls are turned back by the virtuous city wives upon would-be seducers, and thus bitter comedy on the Jonsonian model is converted to somewhat wry-faced revelry.

If the violent moral condemnation of the traitors in *The Whore of Babylon* be excepted, Dekker reserves his denunciation for those who prey upon others: for usurers, brokers and bawds. A boundless charity and willingness to comply with all comers characterize such different figures as Candido and Jacomo Gentilli, the linen-draper and the lord. Ancient hospitality is praised, and though the subplot of *The Wonder of a Kingdom* might almost be called *A Contention between Liberality and Prodigality*, it is the meanness of the prodigal in refusing alms which condemns him, and not his riots.

On the other hand, Dekker never omits the traditional moral element; witness his masque, *The Sun's Darling*, which survives only in a late form refashioned by Ford, but is probably based on the lost *Phaethon* of 1598. This masque has something in common with Nashe's *Summer's Last Will and Testament*: its real subject is the enchantment of spring and the riches of autumn: the exquisite songs distil the best of the scenes into a few stanzas. Nevertheless its fable purports to show the progress of a celestial Prodigal Son through the realms of the four seasons. Raybright, child of the sun, is accompanied through his progress by the whore Humour and the clown Folly, and attended by such figures as Delight and Health at the same time as he is waited upon by a French tailor, an Italian dancing master and a Spanish pastry-cook. The play, though it includes some social satire, celebrates the rites of Nature rather than the judgement of Man. This is Dekker's most complete gallimaufrey, saved by its lyrical naïvety and the freshness of the songs.

It is significant that Dekker's finest work is either in lyric form or in prose. His generous and unforced humanity and his deep vein of piety show up best in his pamphlets, which are incomparably superior to anything he wrote for the stage. His style has always the merits of easiness and simplicity, but the blank verse lacks pulse and power. His range is so wide that no one consistent impression remains. The prose speech of his clowns is the most distinctive of all; this was generally true, of course, and is well marked in the early Shakespeare. From the antithetical wit of Shadow in *Old Fortunatus* (a style roughly equivalent to that of Speed in Shakespeare's *Two Gentlemen of Verona*) Dekker steadily progresses towards colloquial ease. Shadow defines hunger like a scholar:

> 'Hunger is made of gunpowder or gunpowder of hunger; for they both eat through stone walls: hunger is a grindstone, it sharpens wit: hunger is fuller of love than Cupid, for it makes a man eat himself: hunger was the first that ever opened a cookshop, cooks the first that ever made sauce: sauce being liquorish, licks up good meat; good meat preserves life: hunger therefore preserves life.'

This parody of school declamation might well end with a *Sic Probo*. But Cuddy Banks, the clown of one of the latest plays, *The Witch of Edmonton*, speaks in very different accents:

> 'Prithee look but in the lover's almanac: when he has been but three days absent, "O" says he, "I have not seen my love these seven years": there's a long cut! When he comes to her again and embraces her "O", says he "now methinks I am in Heaven" and that's a

pretty step. He that gets up to Heaven in ten days need not repent his journey: you may ride a hundred days in a carouche, and be further off than when you set forth.'   3.1.

As his early plays echo Marlowe and Greene, Dekker's middle verse reflects Shakespeare.[14] For formal passages he is addicted to couplets: his imagery is always unobtrusive. His is precisely that simple, lucid, unplanned style which was essential to establish a norm. He is interested in proverbs and in the contrast of foreign speech with English, but language is a tool that has grown into his hand: he does not seek, like Jonson, to polish it.

The delicate fancy and rough vitality of Dekker were quenched by six years' imprisonment in the King's Bench (1613–1619), after which he wrote but little. His pamphlets and pageants continued to appear, but his final comedies are sorry affairs. *The Witch of Edmonton*, a tender and barbarous story, has nothing of comedy in it but Cuddy Banks's jests.

Dekker could not achieve formal structure. The simple contrast of Maid, Wife and Widow in *Patient Grissel* is a traditional one. In *Westward Ho!* and *Northward Ho!* with the aid of Webster he had tried symmetrical grouping of characters, and had speeded up the love-intrigue. In his last plays, *The Wonder of a Kingdom* and *Match Me in London*, he allows three or four pairs of lovers to a play: the method is explained in the epilogue to *The Wonder of a Kingdom*:

> '. . . All these changes and these marriages
> Both how they shuffled, cut and dealt about,
> What cards are best, after the trumps were out,
> Who played false play, who true, who sought to save
> An ace i' the bottom and turned up a knave.
> For love is but a card play and all's lost
> Unless you cog: he that packs best, wins most.'

The card-play of love had already been summed up unfavourably by Ben Jonson:[15] it is curious that as Dekker in his old age overcrowded his intrigues and multiplied plots in an attempt to follow the style of Jonson and his 'sons', Jonson himself turned back to those old moralities which Dekker had drawn on in his youth. Jonson's failure infuriated him;

but his old rival, with characteristic gentleness, appealed to youth to bear with age's infirmity.

> 'I have been a priest in Apollo's temple many years, my voice is decaying with my age: yet yours being clear and above mine, shall much honour me, if you but listen to my old tunes. Are they set ill? pardon them: well? then receive them.' [16]

Long before this, the original Elizabethan audience which brought forth the best in the old writer had disintegrated. The later work commanded a much narrower public than that which he enjoyed in the old days when he wrote for Henslowe and Alleyn at the Fortune. The form of the drama too had set, and the inchoate comedies of the nineties were now left far behind. Yet Dekker still aspired to be one who could

> 'Call the banish'd auditor home, and tie
> His ear with golden chain to his melody. . . .
> Can draw with adamantine pen even creatures
> Forg'd out of the hammer, on tiptoe to reach up
> And from rare silence, clap their brawny hands
> T'applaud what their charm'd soul scarce understands.'

The power to magnetize the London artisan—an instinctive and unstudied sympathy with simple people in a comedy not merely spectacular—was the secret of Dekker's early success and of his slow alienation from the stage. Dekker was essentially an Elizabethan, and his free extemporizing style belonged to the age when comic form was still fluid. Like Drayton, his ancient collaborator, he lived on into bleaker times, when only the Lord Mayor's Show allowed him a chance to revive the 'old Elizabeth fashion' in all its glory. He died, as he had lived, in poverty, yet still keeping friendship with younger poets; his last poem is a commendatory verse for a play by a 'son' of Jonson—Dick Brome. His incorrigible cheerfulness and unteachable simplicity recall the merry old men of his own plays. Throughout his prolific, disorganized career, a clear piping note of the earlier music arises. In spite of his Dutch painting of Bedlam and Bridewell, a countrified innocence and sweetness cling to the Cockney poet.

What bird so sings, yet so does wail?
O, tis the ravish'd nightingale.
Jug, jug, jug, jug, tereu, she cries,
And still her woes at midnight rise.

.   .   .   .

Haymakers, rakers, reapers, and mowers,
    Wait on your summer queen:
Dress up with roses her eglantine bowers,
    Daffodils strew the green.

III. Thomas Heywood

By the turn of the century, popular comedy had evolved
its own traditions. New comic forms, if they proved a success, were rapidly copied. These forms were often adapta-
tions of the old kinds. For example, a very successful line of
comedies had dealt with the mad mistakes of a night, which
is the ancient pattern of *Gammer Gurton's Needle*. A group of
country-folk or tradesmen find their lives turned topsy-
turvy through muddles, disguises and midnight escapades.
In the new form, however, these nocturnals, as they were
called, nearly always involved the adventures of one or two
pairs of runaway lovers. *The Two Angry Women of Abingdon*
turns on a family quarrel, and midnight adventures in a
wood; so does the much applauded *Merry Devil of Edmonton*,
with the additional excitement of a magician in the party.
Englishmen for my Money is a city comedy in which three
foreigners are defeated by three English lovers.[17] Jonson's
Tale of a Tub and Shakespeare's *Midsummer Night's Dream*
belong to the same kind.

The great change between the popular comedy of the
earlier period and that of the late nineties depends on the
triumph of love over adventure. The trials of true-love include the opposition of parents and of rivals, as well as mistaken identity and groundless jealousy leading to lovers'
quarrels. One of the commonest incidents is the supposed
death of one of the lovers, who, after being mourned,
miraculously revives, like the hero of a mummers' play.
Often the hero leaps out of his coffin, and sometimes the
heroine miraculously revives after drinking poison which

turns out, like Juliet's drink, to be only a sleeping potion.[18] Sometimes the plot is untied by the substitution of another woman for the bride or, more infrequently, another man for the bridegroom.[19]

The revival of the prodigal play, which has already been noted, laid great emphasis upon its love interest. The prodigal is generally shown as having to choose between a faithful wife and a wanton mistress, choosing wrongly at first and later being brought to repentance. The prototype is *How a Man May Choose a Good Wife from a Bad*, generally attributed to Heywood.

Here Arthur is set between the wife he has scorned and the drab he has chosen, and after his wife has saved him from the worst consequence of his evil deeds, he comes forward between the two to point the moral. Addressing his 'saint' and his 'devil', as he calls them, he says:

> 'My first wife, stand you here: my second there.
> And in the midst myself: he that will choose
> A good wife from a bad, come learn of me,
> That hath tried both in wealth and misery.'

He then gives a short character sketch of each of his two wives and of himself, by way of conclusion. *The Fair Maid of Bristowe*, another of these plays, is very near to ballad-style in plot. In the opening scene the bridegroom turns to a whore on his wedding day and forces his wife to strip off her wedding dress and jewels to adorn her rival. In the final scene the heroine enters in disguise, to offer her life in place of her condemned husband's at the gallows' foot.

Surprising adventures, whether at home or abroad, were still however the requisites for popular comedy: the chief writer in this kind was Thomas Heywood, a more staid, more learned and more strictly dramatic writer than Dekker.[20] On his own admission, Heywood had a hand in two hundred and twenty plays, some of them amongst the best getpennies of the age. He was also an actor, and in his *Apology for Actors* he firmly placed them as good citizens, 'of substance, of government, of sober lives and temperate carriages, house-keepers and contributory to all duties enjoined them'. He

himself lived and died as a respectable householder of Clerkenwell without ever seeing the inside of a jail or the cabin of a
sea-going ship. He collaborated with Dekker in plays on
Queen Elizabeth [21] and both produced city pageants. But
Heywood, though he complied with the taste of London, was
not a Londoner in Dekker's sense, and in his plays he ranged
widely. His four 'prentices, the original inspirers of Ralph
the Grocer's boy in *The Knight of the Burning Pestle*, travel
to France, Italy and Jerusalem: Bess Bridges, the Fair Maid
of the West, travels to Fayal and Morocco in search of her
lover. In *Fortune by Land and Sea* and *Dick of Devonshire* the
exploits of pirates are set forth and the fighting quality of
Englishmen attested by examples taken from recent notorious
events.[22]

These heroic exploits, whether real or invented, involve
familiar types of characters: they are the equivalent of the
modern adventures in space-ships and time-machines, which
depend on contrast between the everyday hero and occasions
fantastic or remote. Heywood usually multiplies the heroes,
to give the effect of the modern child's Famous Five or Ter-
rible Twins. Three, four or more brothers or friends act in
concert, and are opposed by three or four villains. In *The
Four Prentices of London*, Heywood produced a magnificent
fantasy, a grand feast of heroics which can no more suffer
deflation from Beaumont's parody than *The Conquest of
Granada* can be injured by *The Rehearsal*. The four princely
'prentices (all nobles in disguise), apart and all unknown,
fight combats with each other, rescue distressed maidens,
and finally destroy whole armies to achieve the conquest of
Jerusalem. Perhaps the best scene is that in which their sister Bella-Francia, fleeing from a ravisher, is saved by two of
of her brothers, Charles the Outlaw Chief and Eustace, who
happen at the moment to be engaged in a duel. None of the
family recognize each other and the brothers fall to quarrel-
ling afresh over the damsel in distress.

In his epistle to the reader of 1615, Heywood apologized
for lack of 'accurateness both in plot and style that these more
censorious days require . . . as plays were then, fifteen or sixteen years ago, it was in the fashion'. There is, however,
no need to justify the naïve splendours of this old romance,

which had so dignified a pedigree and so many imitators in its day.[23]

In *The Wise Woman of Hogsdon*, Heywood gave unusually gay and farcical treatment to the Prodigal. Not only is there a patient wife, but two other would-be wives; young Chartley, who is described as Lusty Juventus, is not a serious character, and his repentance is boyish and unabashed. The *dénouement* is a most ingenious piece of unmasking; for Heywood had at times an exceptionally fine sense of construction. *The Four Prentices of London* has the gaudy symmetry of a painted roundabout, with the Mercer, Goldsmith, Haberdasher and Grocer circling the stage in their golden crowns at the end, conquerors of Jerusalem and bridegrooms to royalty. It is as superior to *Old Fortunatus* as *Tamburlaine* is to *The Battle of Alcazar*. But Heywood, like Dekker, was also willing to expand his story if there were a demand, even at the cost of incongruity. This is seen in *The Fair Maid of the West*. Bess Bridges, the barmaid of Plymouth and Fowey, who goes adventuring in search of her love, is a heroine out of ballad-lore, vigorously and attractively drawn. She leads a sea fight, and charms a Moorish king with equal zest while accumulating money in a practical fashion; she shows almost the spirit of Moll Cutpurse, in her challenge of a coward to fight a duel. In the exasperating Second Part, this bouncing lass becomes a romantic heroine of the Fletcherian sort, while her honest Spencer is turned into a copy of the jealous Amintor, and the naïvety of their adventures among the Moors into a complex double-intrigue.

The Fair Maid of the Exchange, a milder shopkeeping beauty, is wooed by three brothers, of whom the youngest is naturally successful. This sprightly story has affinities with *The Merry Wives of Windsor*, and some sharp humours in the part of the valiant cripple of Fenchurch.

One of Heywood's most delightful plays, *Fortune by Land and Sea*, has been already mentioned.[24] This is the story of a poor but worthy family and a rich and wicked one, in which all the deserving reap splendid rewards, while all the bad characters are most magnanimously forgiven, except two ferocious but patriotic Pirates, whom history requires to be hanged at Wapping.

Clinton: 'Now our last night's done,
   And we must sleep in darkness.
     Worthy mate.
Purser: We have a flash left of some half hour long,
   Then let us burn out bravely, not behind us
   Leave a black noisome snuff of cowardice
   I' the nostrils of our noble countrymen.
   But now our sun is all setting, night comes on,
   The watry wilderness o'er which we reigned
   Proves in our ruin peaceful: Merchants trade
   Fearless abroad as in the river's mouth,
   And free as in a harbour. Then fair Thames,
   Queen of fresh water, famous through the world,
   And not the least through us, whose doubled tides
   Must overflow our bodies, and being dead,
   May thy clear waves our scandals wash away,'   5.1.

They go off arm in arm to execution; while the two distressed
lovers who had been forced to work as servants in the house
of a hard-hearted parent are enriched by their gains, since the
hardened old man conveniently dies of an apoplectic fit upon
suspicion that his goods have been lost to the pirates.

The story is lucid and the plot relatively uncomplicated:
the accent of simplicity and good humour prevails throughout. Heywood draws simplified normal humanity, while
Dekker draws moral types. In Heywood the blood and fighting are conventional, but the pain and devotion are real: his is
not a comedy of revelry, but a tragi-comedy. His constant
women have more individuality than Dekker's, and more
emotional colour. They are faithful, but not, like Patient
Grissel, Fidelity itself.

        'I was every morning
Down on my knees and with the lark's sweet tunes
I did begin my prayers: and when sad sleep
Had charmed all eyes, and none save the bright stars
Were up and waking, I remembered thee:
But all, all to no purpose.'

In his depiction of women, Heywood was not only sympathetic but subtle.[25] In his greatest play, *A Woman Killed
with Kindness*, though the heroine is but faintly portrayed in
comparison with her wronged husband, he achieves a rare
picture of a woman who is frail but not condemned. The
domestic drama usually demanded the sternest punishment

for sin; Heywood retained the traditional form and characters, but varied the moral—a notable blend of the unexpected and the expected. His highest powers reveal themselves in a poignant reticence, and his treatment of infidelity in this play makes almost every other Elizabethan look garish by comparison. The decorously artificial story of chastity which supplies the underplot contrasts unobtrusively with the penetrating simplicity of the main story. The conventional pattern of domestic tragedy is reversed to produce a most unconventional study of marriage not as a state but as a relationship. It is a pure appeal to sympathy, without tragic aloofness or ironic undertone.[26]

Heywood, like Dekker, relied on the traditional taste of a popular audience in producing his best work. He was a natural dramatist who could conceive a number of simple but warmly sympathetic characters grouped in a conventional but none the less active and fruitful relationship. This rare and essential dramatic gift he shared with Shakespeare, and by it was enabled to triumph over his own weaknesses.

Webster classed both Dekker and Heywood with Shakespeare for their 'right happy and copious industry'. All three were artisans of the theatre, without the professed loftiness of Chapman or Jonson: this united them, however absurd the collocation may now appear. All three practised a popular art, which they modified without destroying. Dekker and Heywood had merely accepted their opportunity: Shakespeare transformed it. Yet something may also be attributed to the kinder fate which gave Shakespeare a share with the Lord Chamberlain's Players.

CHAPTER IX

THE ANATOMY OF KNAVERY: JONSON, MARSTON, MIDDLETON

1. The City Wits

THE 'prentice who, fired by Heywood, saw himself as Godfrey of Bulloigne, might well have envied the opportunities of acting princely parts which fell to the young gentlemen of the Inns of Court. When in the Christmas sports of 1594 at Gray's Inn, Mr. Henry Holmes, a Norfolk man, was elected

> 'Henry Prince of Purpoole, Archduke of Stapulia and Barnardia, Marquis of St. Giles and Tottenham, Count Palatine of Bloomsbury and Clerkenwell, Great Lord of the Cantons of Islington, Kentish Town, Paddington and Knightsbridge, Knight of the most Heroical Order of the Helmet'

his glories outshone those of the Lord Mayor's Show, the city's great festival. They were financed by 'benevolences' exacted from all Grayans. Henry sent an embassy which was graciously received by the Queen, as well as receiving ambassadors himself, and from six counsellors such good advice on the conduct of his affairs as he might have heard seriously from Dekker.[1] This spirit of masquerade is traceable in the sports of every class in London, and with every shade of self-approval or of denigration for others. 'Prentices were imprisoned in Bridewell for libelling the Lord Mayor in *The Hog hath Lost his Pearl*; on the other hand, the heroic Shirleys, heroes of *The Travails of Three English Brothers*, were in life rather shabby adventurers, and Moll Firth a transvested termagant, rather different from the Roaring Girl. Gresham's Exchange was put upon the stage, and *The Launching of the Mary* is pure advertising. Only the most magnificent of such achievements reached the scene, but even these, the glories of the city, invited parody from the young lawyers and courtiers, whose attitude to trade aped that of Gown to Town in Oxford or Cambridge. The university stooped to writing English comedies only that the insults of *Club Law* might be intelligible to the Mayor of Cambridge, who was specially asked to Clare Hall to witness the play: and ten years after the Gray's Inn revels, the Children of the Queen's Revels invited the combined talents of Jonson, Marston and Chapman to caricature the lawful ambitions of an Industrious Apprentice. The first day out of his articles he is elected Master Alderman's deputy for the ward.

> 'Worshipful son! I cannot contain myself. I must tell thee, I hope to see thee one of the Monuments of our City, and reckoned among her Worthies, to be remembered the same day with the Lady Ramsey and grave Gresham: when the famous fable of Whittingdon and his puss shall be forgotten, and thou and thy acts become posies for hospitals, when thy name shall be written upon conduits and thy deeds played in thy lifetime by the best companies of actors and called their getpenny. This I divine. This I prophesy.'

Such rejoicings from his master, Touchstone the Goldsmith—or Simon Eyre as seen by the sophisticated—represented virtue's triumph in a play whose prologue politely concluded 'We only dedicate it to the City', a play which, by reason of a slight jest at the expense of Majesty itself, landed the three authors in jail.

The hero of *Eastward Ho!*, the idle apprentice Quicksilver, is a great frequenter of plays of the vulgar and obsolete kind: through dicing he is 'seven score pounds out in the cash' when the play begins, but justifies this gentlemanly rioting boldly:

> 'Marry fough, goodman flatcap: sfoot, though I am a prentice I can give arms and my father's a justice of the peace by descent.'

His virtuous fellow, Goulding, recites trencher verses and pious mottoes directly to the audience:

> 'What ere some vainer youth may term disgrace,
> The gain of honest pains is never base:
> From trades, from arts, from valour honour springs,
> These three are founts of gentry, yea of kings' [2]

Quicksilver's Virginian voyage, after leaving his master, extends no further than the Isle of Dogs, where he is shipwrecked; the wreck being described in a tremendous 'perspective' speech by Slitgut, a butcher of Eastcheap, from the vantage of Cuckold's Haven. Quicksilver ends in the Counter, where he experiences conversion, and perpetrates a Puritanical ballad of repentance.

> 'Farewell, Cheapside, farewell sweet trade
> Of Goldsmiths all that never shall fade:
> Farewell, dear fellow prentices all,
> And be you warned by my fall.'

The jailer almost weeps as he describes the prisoner keeping all the neighbourhood awake, 'singing psalms all night, and edifying all the prison'. As his final request he is led home through the streets in his rags as an example to 'the children of Cheapside' and Touchstone moralizes, pointing out the various characters:

> 'Now London, look about,
> And in this moral see thy glass run out:
> Behold the careful father, thrifty son,
> The solemn deeds which each of us have done:
> The usurer punisht, and from fall so steep
> The prodigal child regained and the lost sheep.'

And then, with a sudden jerk, actors and audience are turned out of the theatre into the street, the artifice is broken: the galleries become windows and the yard a lane.[3]

> 'Stay, sir, I perceive the multitude are gathered together, to view our coming out, at the Counter. See if the streets and the fronts of the houses be not stuck with people, and the windows filled with ladies as on the solemn day of the Pageant
>
> > O may you find in this our Pageant here
> > The same contentment which you came to seek:
> > And as that Shew but draws you once a year,
> > May this attract you hither once a week.'

Both virtue and vice, whatever their absurdities, are jested with sympathetically; from time to time there is a malicious glint in the words of Golding, and more than a glint in those of his master: Quicksilver's charm is infectious.

This parody is in good-natured contrast to the acerbities of the Poets' War. Four years' interval, prolonged idleness in a plague-struck season and the death of the old Queen lay between those days and the new collaboration of old enemies. In Jacobean comedy, satire predominated; but it ranged from the mischievous badinage of *Eastward Ho!* to the dark power of *Volpone*.

The City comedy of the next decade is modelled upon Jonsonian lines, and he himself provided the best of it. Marston and Middleton imitated him, with personal variations, and even Dekker, in collaboration with Webster, followed the trend with *Westward Ho!* and *Northward Ho!* The obvious characteristics of these plays are first, the artificial plotting, with symmetrically grouped characters, based upon the old learned moral play as modified by Jonson's theory of social humours: second, the vigorous and direct recording of the London scene, its language, habits and sometimes its features: third, the constant rousing of the spectator's critical judgement by literary parody, comment and discussion; the inclusion of extra-dramatic moments at the beginning and end of the play when the actors step out of their roles, or assume other roles, to guide the spectators' appreciation of what is being done. At once a moral mirror, an image of the times, and a work of literary pretensions, the play is directed to the few rather than the many. Marston stresses the critical aspect, and Middleton the humours and observation of the London scene: the one gives the maximum of satiric intensity, the other of detachment.

ii. Ben Jonson

If Jonson had not succeeded in suppressing his own popular plays, he might appear an even greater, if less consistent writer. He once collaborated with Dekker to write a domestic tragedy *Page of Plymouth*, which appears from a surviving ballad to have resembled *Arden of Feversham*: he also wrote historical tragedies on Richard Crookback, Robert II, King of Scots and the Fall of Mortimer.

The suppression of these plays, however, was essential to Jonson's creation of his own public personality; one whom Drayton called 'Lord of the Theatre' and Lucius Cary 'Poet Paramount' could not afford lapses from learning. It is true that Taylor the Water Poet wrote some respectful verses to Jonson, and the irascible dictator apparently unbent to show kindness to the poor sculler. But he could be extremely rude about the Lord Mayor and his Show: clearly he saw the city's centre in the Inns of Court rather than the Guild Hall. London for Jonson was a centre of wit and a pageant of folly : it was already an Augustan city. In his *Ode from the Country*, Francis Beaumont virtually identifies Jonson with the sophistication of the town ; and this sophistication is called out by the city vices which it satirizes. In the country, ancient simplicity still prevails :

> 'for our best
> And gravest man will with his main-house jest
> Scarce please you: we want subtlety to do
> The city tricks, lie, hate and flatter too:
> Here are none that can bear a fained show,
> Strike when you wink, and then lament the blow'

and with it, ancient ignorance. Exiled from the Mermaid Tavern, Beaumont finds himself amongst alluring country pastimes:

> 'I see my days of ballating are nigh :
> I can already riddle, and can sing
> Catches, sell bargains, and I fear shall bring
> Myself to speak the hardest words 1 find
> Over. . . .'

The mock-simplicity of this jesting poem turned to earnest for Jonson's other son, Robert Herrick, exiled permanently in his Devonshire parsonage, and patiently building an artificial world out of aboriginal materials.

Jonson's 'humours and observation' were to his city audience so familiar as to be startling. He presented the unexpected and freshly collected habits of Cockney streets and taverns in a form that was dignified with all the requirements of art. The shock to his contemporaries must have been as great as the pleasure, much like to the shock of Donne's familiar style in love-poetry. The growth of London, and in particular the growth of its underworld, a class of professional sharkers, had been depicted in the earlier pamphlets of Greene and Nashe, largely by a refashioning of traditional material Jonson drew from the life. In the chorus to *Every Man out of his Humour,* the play in which he first found himself, Jonson invited the spectators to reflect on tragic moral themes:

> 'the earth cracked with the weight of sin,
> Hell gaping under us, and o'er our heads
> Black ravenous ruin, with her sail-stretched wings,
> Ready to sink us down and cover us.'

But in going on to define the particular sinners, he becomes satiric:

> 'Well, I will scourge those apes,
> And to these courteous eyes oppose a mirror
> As large as is the stage whereon we act:
> Where they shall see the time's deformity
> Anatomiz'd in every nerve and sinew.'

The basis of the play is in fact the analysis and dissection of identity. Action is secondary, and the number of roles is such that it cannot be developed. The stage is crowded with a parade of eccentrics, and the catastrophe is the destruction of all their pretensions. A fine court lady cannot distinguish a gentleman from a clown; and an elegant fop is left in the debtor's prison. Each character assumes a role which is stripped from him; and the role varies from the horseplay of Puntarvolo with his dog to the deadly earnestness of Sordido with his halter. Sordido, the only character of a traditional ethical sort, is a hoarding farmer who is ready to hang himself on the expectation of plenty; he suffers the one true conversion of the play when he is rescued by his poor tenants.

> 'My barns and garners shall stand open still
> To all the poor that come, and my best grain
> Be made almsbread to feed half-famished mouths.' 3.8.

But Sordido is a countryman, and most of the scenes are set in Paul's Walk and the Counter: here a lighter kind of folly brings a lighter penalty.

When Jonson revised his first comedy, *Every Man in His Humour,* for the definitive printed edition, he lightened the penalties of the fools, perhaps because the original punishments—Stephen to stand in a fool's coat of motley and

Matthew to have his poetry publicly burnt—were too close to the final judgement in *Poetaster*. In this revision he also made a very significant excision: Edward Knowell's eloquent defence of poetry is cut. This defence, though fine, is not characteristically Jonson's: indeed it sounds much more like Chapman; Poesy is 'blessed, eternal and most true divine', though she may look poor. She tastes philosophy, and

> 'hates to have her dignity prophan'd
> With any relish of an earthly thought . . .
> Then is she like herself, fit to be seen
> Of none but grave and consecrated eyes.' [4]   5.3.

This transcendental Muse never appears again in Jonson's plays; his first play bears in other respects the impression of Chapman. It is built on a rapid Plautine intrigue, and celebrates, like Chapman's successful play of the previous year, *An Humourous Day's Mirth*. This is largely engineered by Brainworm, who resembles the puppet-masters of Chapman's comedies as much as he does the Plautine *servus*, yet who in his Cockney wit and unscrupulousness belongs decidedly to the age itself. In the revised version he is selected as partner for the feast by the Justice of the play, who compliments him on his 'day of metamorphosis'. Cob the water-carrier plays the traditional clown, in the scene where he weeps over the hard fate of his princely coz, the Red Herring; his wife, as she sets to fisticuffs with him, recalls a distinguished line of frampole women stretching back to Mrs. Noah.

> 'I'll see an you may be allowed to make a bundle of hemp of your right and lawful wife thus at every cuckoldy knave's pleasure,'
>   4.3.

she cries as she is haled off to justice.

The two forms of this play are a clear index to Jonson's development.[5] It is not radically reshaped, yet in the later version, where the scene is transported to London, and the quibbling speech loaded with ore, the whole effect is quite different. The early Plautine comedies (*Every Man in his Humour* and *The Case is Altered*), followed by the static critical plays of the Poets' War,[6] were in the nature of experiments. He found his true form with *Volpone*, where in the dedication he finds doctrine to be the principal end of poetry: 'to inform men in the best reason of living'.

This savage and violent play, with its blend of ancient crimes and Elizabethan cupidity and daring, can hardly be described as satire: the moral flavour is there, but the magnificent claims of Volpone to a life of unbounded desires and royal splendour recall Faustus and Tamburlaine rather than Sir Giles Overreach or Old Hoard. The assumption of different identities by the pair of cheating villains is so enthusiastic that to each of their dupes and to each other they show a slightly different character: they live for action and in their soliloquies they contemplate with enjoyment their public art. Volpone's heroic vitality leaves the anæmic virtue of Celia and Bonario to the chilly recompense of a final judgement scene in which all the characters are reduced to puppets, the strings are folded up, and they are laid in the right box, labelled Felicity or Perdition. Jonson's plays contain no true lovers or friends, no true fathers and sons: there are characters which bear these titles, but each exists in a general relation to all the others, and not in particular relations with any one of them. The action in this sense is simple. Such characters are incapable of development: they may be converted or destroyed, not modified.[7]

The characters of *Volpone*, human beings transformed into beasts of prey, have a more than mortal energy: the violence of the opening, with its perverted religious imagery, mirrors an insatiable pursuit of self-destruction which is general.

> 'Good morrow to the day; and next, my gold!
> Open the shrine, that I may see my saint.
> Hail, the world's soul and mine!'

Having delivered himself of this bitterest comedy, Jonson reverted to lighter themes. In his next play he positively wooed the audience; *The Silent Woman* was, however, written for the private theatres, whereas *Volpone* and the subsequent comedies belonged to the King's men. It is not on the level of the other plays, since its plot does not depend on a controlling idea. It embodies no vision, and all its technical competence cannot compensate for lack of a theme.

In *The Alchemist* there is something like a return to the

pattern of *Volpone*, but the satiric intention is modified: sympathy is now permitted, the scene becomes familiar and the crimes diminish. False gold replaces true, Ananias's old iron the treasures of Venice, two cheats of the London under-world a Magnifico and his Machiavellian follower; in contrast, the dupes include the simple tobacconist Abel Drugger with his vision of the Fairy Queen, as well as the magnificent Epicure Mammon, in whose sensuous robustness Jonson transmuted his own gluttonous relish for words. The theme of this play is the power of illusion: like fairy gold, the treasure eludes all seekers, but the victims are enriched with potent gifts of imagination and hope: they are characters seen almost in the round.

Bartholomew Fair expands the vision of society still further; the fair, a great home of trickery and shams, was itself a mirror of society. The cutpurse is the most heroic figure: among the fantastics are madmen, and Justice herself is a little wanting in the wits. The Puritans are more absurd than those of *The Alchemist*, Cokes is more foolish than any earlier foolish young heir; the atmosphere is one of holiday and the traditional judgement scene at the end is a complete farce.

> 'Look upon me, O London! and see me, O Smithfield! the example of justice and Mirror of Magistrates, the true top of formality and scourge of enormity. Hearken unto my labours. . . .'

In the process of delivering judgement, the scourger is silenced by the discovery of his own wife in the gown of a prostitute. Jonson was becoming increasingly susceptible to rogues. Intellectual ability always captivated him, but he gradually warmed to the human qualities of roguery; here the delicate balance between admiration and contempt for the rogues, or delight and contempt in the fools, makes it impossible to regard them as improving moral studies. The rogues frequently get off scot free, and virtue's reward is chilly disregard. The genial mixture of farce and irony is here almost Chaucerian.

In *The Devil is an Ass*, Jonson approached the popular tradition.[8] Here he, who had scorned the fool and the devil, produces a devil of his own, and asks for the countenance lately bestowed upon 'your dear light, *The Devil of Edmonton*'. The Induction is a parody of an old moral play complete with a Vice, Iniquity.

> 'Who is he calls upon me and would seem to lack a Vice?
> Ere his words be half spoken, I am with him a trice;
> Here, there and everywhere, as the cat is with the mice.
> True *Vetus Iniquitas*. Lacks thou cards, friend, or dice?
> I will teach thee to cheat, child, to cog, lie and swagger,
> And ever and anon to be drawing forth thy dagger:
> To swear by Gogswouns like a Lusty Juventus,
> In a cloak to thy heel and a hat like a penthouse.'   I.I.

The devil of this play is no true fiend, he is a literary and theatrical revival, made only to be gulled. Wittipol, the young gallant who rescues virtue in distress, is of the same family as the subtle young heroes of Jonson's earlier and Fletcher's later plays, the Wittipates and Valentines.[9] In this play Jonson has shown almost all the main dramatic types of his time to form a literary gallimaufrey corresponding to the social gallimaufrey of *Bartholomew Fair.* All the human characters combine to cheat the devil, who has finally to be rescued from Newgate jail by Satan and the Vice.

> 'Whom hast thou dealt with,
> Women or man this day, but have outgone thee
> Some way, and most have proved the better fiends?'

With this cheerful conclusion, the part-author of *Eastward Ho!* allows a ray of London pride to shine upon fools and knaves alike.

III. John Marston

Marston, Jonson's opponent in the Poets' War, had begun by offering a tribute which was unfortunately mistaken for an insult. Marston's aims were always being misunderstood, not least by himself. The obliquity of his work led him to write an erotic poem which he justified as a satire on erotic poetry, to dedicate his first play to his Maecenas, 'the most honourably renowned Nobody',[10] and to protest against publication with a frequent and self-defensive effusion that implies little tenderness for the reader.

'Only one thing afflicts me, to think that scenes invented merely to be spoken, should be inforcively published to be read, and that the least hurt I can receive, is to do myself the wrong. But since others otherwise would do me more, the least inconvenience is to be accepted.'

Preface to *The Malcontent.*

'Comedies are writ to be spoken not read: remember the life of these things consists in action. . . . If any shall wonder why I print a comedy, whose life rests much in the actors' voice, let such know it cannot avoid publishing.'

Preface to *The Fawne.*

It is perhaps worth noting that the motto for *The Malcontent*, which was originally *Me mea sequentur fata*, subsequently became *Sine aliqua dementia nullus Phoebus*. Marston's violence of language and high-pitched tirades surprised even his own headlong times; he is the original of Furor Poeticus in the Parnassus play. His best work was done in collaboration, and is exclusively satiric, even if the connexion between his poems and his plays is not so strong as has sometimes been implied. There is little doubt of *The Fawne*, as the address to the reader shows:

If any desire to understand the scope of my comedy, know it hath the same limits which Juvenal gives to his satires:

'Quicquid agunt homines, votum, timor, ira, voluptas,
Gaudia, discursus, nostri farrago libelli est.'

No quotation could be more inappropriate as a description of Marston's narrow intensity and what Eliot has called 'the significant lifelessness of his shadow show'. In so far as his work is not introspective, its affiliations are literary. *The Malcontent*, his most successful achievement, is a distillation of Jonson's comical satire—the play is dedicated to him, and he receives another compliment in the epilogue. It also, however, adopts the well-marked structure of Italianate revenge tragedy, already used by Marston in *Antonio's Revenge*, and the flattery which Shakespeare receives is of the sincerest sort, large discounts upon *Hamlet*.

The complexity and intensity of this tragi-comedy depend upon the constant springing of a new betrayal in the action, the ironic reversal of every situation, the engineer hoist with his own petard every time. All this develops from the unmasking of layer below layer in the motives of the principal character, from whose initiative all action flows. The scene opens with an Induction between the actors in Jonsonian style, wherein Burbage, who is to play the hero, appears in his own person: he then acts Malevole, the discontented and embittered railer at court, used by the duke as a spy.[11] Malevole, however, is really the rightful duke himself: he has been banished by treachery and contracted melancholy through grief, but he uses his own disease as a disguise, to spy upon his own account. The usurper's wife and his favourite have become lovers, and they employ Malevole to kill the usurper, intending afterwards to dispose of their hired assassin. Malevole saves the usurper and puts him forward in disguise as confederate: he is then suborned to kill Malevole, but a counterplot is sprung, with Malevole and his party disguised as Revellers: they unmask to effect a *coup d'état*.

The inspiring power of melancholy, that subtle disease of fine wits, was well known, but it hardly covers the ingenuity of Malevole. Melancholy was also known to be a breeder of seditious plots: the term *malcontent* applied to a disaffected subject. Here the successful overthrow of a régime is justified by the plotter happening to be the rightful ruler in banishment: but Marston, in the customary protest against the application of his play to particular individuals, finds it necessary to stress that it is written to discourage insurrection and show the disgrace of 'those, whose unquiet studies labour innovation'. The point indeed is not self-evident. All certainly concludes happily: the villains are all converted except one, and even he is pardoned. The spectator is asked to applaud the magnanimity of the restored ruler, who had earlier aimed at something more painful than mere assassination.

> 'The heart's disquiet is revenge most deep.
> He that gets blood, the life of flesh but spills,
> But he that breaks heart's peace the dear soul kills.'[12]
> 1.3.

One of Malevole's tasks in his Malcontent role is to tempt his own wife to infidelity; he is justified in acting as his enemy's agent in order to protect her from the solicitations of a real pander. The satire upon lust and the treachery of women centres in the horrible character of Maquerelle, the old bawd, but as theme it is hardly secondary to that of political treachery.

The two combine when Mendoza, the arch traitor, is given a speech in praise of women—with obvious indebtedness to Hamlet's encomium, 'What a piece of work is man'—to be delivered as he prepares to betray his benefactor:

> 'Sweet women, most sweet ladies, nay Angels . . . in body how delicate, in soul how witty, in discourse how pregnant, in life how wary, in favours how judicious, in day how sociable, in night how . . . O pleasure unutterable, indeed it is most certain, one man cannot deserve only to enjoy a beauteous woman: but a Duchess?'
>
> 1.5.

In the following scene, betrayed as he thinks, though the plan to make him think so is itself a trap, Mendoza recants.

> 'Women, nay furies, nay worse, for they torment only the bad, but women good and bad . . . rash in asking, desperate in working, impatient in suffering, extreme in desiring, slaves unto appetite . . . their words are feigned, their eyes forged, their sights dissembled, their looks counterfeit, their hair false, their given hopes deceitful, their very breath artificial. . .'
>
> 1.6.

Such artificially opposed tirades betray Marston's weakness as a dramatist. The minor characters fail to live: the panders and betrayers who surround Malevole give him material for his comments, but have little more than their generic Italian names to supply them with a core of identity. Malevole himself is a 'humorous' character: his assumed role of railer and flatterer has more importance than his stoic inner self, and each of his roles is highly stylized, almost a professional pose. It allows Marston to vary his power of satiric epigram; the phrasing is often brilliant: [13]

> 'Did your signiorship ne'er see a pigeon house that was smooth, round and white without, and full of holes and stink within, ha' ye not, old Courtier?'

but it is too 'dramatic' for drama; that is to say, there is no light nor shade, and no variety of tone; no rising or falling. Marston's is not a truly dramatic world; it is the world of the homilist, the academic satirist. His brilliant stabbing similes are technical exercises in the low style, as his groups of buffoons are variations upon characters of 'the old decorum'. For example, Wilson in his *Art of Rhetoric* had characterized the nations of Europe according to their proclivities:

> 'the Englishman for feeding and change of apparel, the Dutchman for drinking, the French for pride and inconstance, the Spaniard for nimbleness and much disdain: the Italian for great wit and policy: the Scot for boldness and the Boeme for stubbornness.' [14]

Such a distinction is burlesqued, yet followed in the burlesquing, when Malevole and Maquerelle enter from opposite sides of the stage singing a duet:

> 'The Dutchman for a drunkard,
> The Dane for golden locks,
> The Irishman for usquebath,
> The Frenchman for the pox.'

Such songs must have sounded exceedingly rancid upon the lips of boys.

The fine writing and the static characters do not coalesce with the rapid intrigue: Marston succeeds only with his central figure, the secretive autocrat, pulling all the strings in his base disguise of railer and assassin; but even here there is no such positive power as resides in the tragic counterpart of Malevole, Tourneur's Vindice. Marston (like Swift) has no positive values whereon to take a stand: his pessimism is beyond the tragic, which has its own exaltation. The stoic attitude of scorn for the world, *contemptu mundi*, is offered only to be rejected: it is the consolation of the noble Malcontent who urges Piero Jacomo to despise a dukedom while taking energetic steps to regain it for himself.

> 'Come, be not confounded, th'art but in danger to lose a dukedom, think this: this earth is the only grave and Golgotha wherein all things that live must rot: tis but the draught wherein the heavenly bodies discharge their corruption, the very muckhill on which the sublunarie orbs cast their excrement: man is the slime of this dungpit and Princes are the governors of these men.' [15]   4.5.

In *The Fawne*, Marston produced the mirror image of *The Malcontent*: Duke Hercules disguises himself as a flatterer and surrounds himself with fools whom he pampers openly and lashes secretly, to conclude with a judgement scene and an unmasking, in which the áncient Ship of Fools, setting sail from the court of Urbino, bears off all those who have been sentenced in a Parliament of Cupid. This includes most of the leading characters, save Tiberio, the duke's son, a cold youth who has been persuaded to steal a wife by being set to court her for his father—the assumption of the Fawne correctly being that stolen fruit is sweetest.

Many of Marston's plays, including his contributions to the Poets' War, are shapeless medleys, but there remains his one masterpiece in dramatic portraiture, *The Dutch Courtesan*. This play, perhaps a counterblast to Dekker's *Honest Whore*, illuminates the contrast of the old drama and the new. Dekker's basis is ethical: his whore is judged explicitly, both in her original and her reformed state: her passionate pleas have the eloquence of persuasion. Marston's whore is drawn with Dutch fidelity; she is displayed without exposition as a savage, murderous, treacherous beauty, whose sweetness of appearance, and whose dancing and songs are shown making their full effect upon a man who despises her but cannot free himself from her enchantment. She is the Dark Lady of the Comedies. This study of Franceschina, the 'fair devil', is a social and an ethical one: she is the kind of figure that might appear in a novel. Her brutality is shown in action.

> *Franceschina:* O *Divela*, life a min art, Ick sall be revengde, doe ten tousand Hell damme me, Ick sall have de rogue trote cut, and his love and his friend, and all his affinitie sall smart, sall dye, sal hang, now legion of devil seize him, de grand pest, St. Antony's fire and de hot Neopolitan poc rotte him!
> *Freevile:* Franceschina.
> *Franceschina:* O min seet, deerst, kindest, mine loveing, O mine tousand, ten tousand, delicated, petty seet art (*cantat Gallice*) mine alderleevst affection. 2.1.

The Argument, as prefixed to the play, is 'the difference between the love of a Curtezan, and a wife . . . which intermixed with the deceits of a witty City jester, fills up the comedy.'

Beatrice, the faithful wife, though slightly drawn, is the least unattractive of Marston's heroines, approached only by Katherine of *Jack Drum's Entertainment*. Her younger sister, Crispinella, who is perhaps meant to resemble in sprightliness the Beatrice of Shakespeare, is more typical and serves to show the distance between the player's notion of good manners and that of the future cleric.

> 'O i' faith tis a fair thing to be married and a necessary to hear this word *must* : if our husband be proud, we must bear his contempt, if noisome we must bear with the goat under his armholes, if a fool, we must bear his bable, and which is worse, if a loose liver, we must live upon unwholesome reversions. . . .'

The underplot includes such well-known *lazzi* or jests as robbery in pretending to shave the victim, and pretending that he is the robber instead of the robbed.[16] As all the characters in this underplot are equally vicious, the fact that no harm comes of it adds to the general tone of moral indifference that pervades the play. The principal victim, a vintner, is led out to be hanged, and, his ruling passion strong, he pleads:

> 'I pray you do not lead me to execution through Cheapside, I owe Mr. Burnish the goldsmith money and I fear he'll set a sergeant on my back for it.'

while his wife laments in the very accents of Mrs. Peachum:

> 'O husband I little thought you should have come to think on God thus soon: nay, and you had been hanged deservedly, it would never have grieved me, I have known of many honest innocent men have been hanged deservedly, but to be cast away for nothing!'

A last-minute reprieve parodies the reprieve of Malheureux, accused of murder through the wiles of the courtesan. The two scenes are related as masque and antimasque and as the hero, by retaining his disguise, has brought his friend to the gallows' foot on a charge of murdering him, and his betrothed to the point of dying of grief, these characters cannot be taken as more than pivots of the intrigue. Franceschina remains the one strong and individual figure in Marston's comedy; a full-length, overpowering study, suggesting a portrait from the life.[17]

Marston's power as a writer, which is an unpleasant and highly personal power, does not lend itself to dramatic variety; but the very oddity, violence and rankness of his style freed comedy from traditional limitations. He was very generally mocked; but his influence, even on those who opposed him, and perhaps especially upon them, cannot be ignored.

iv. Thomas Middleton

If the typical figures of Marston's plays are the painted harlot, fair and adorned to hide disease, and the spy, secretly controlling and manœuvring all, the typical figures of Middleton's city comedies are the rich widow and the young spendthrift. For Middleton, the hunting of a widow and the setting up of a broken gallant are the favourite bases of intrigue: in his plays the prodigal is treated even more sympathetically than by Heywood and is almost invariably furnished with handsome means to continue his career.

Middleton evinces neither the moral nor the combative tendencies of Marston and Jonson—who called him 'a base fellow'. He was equally at home with the lawyers, displaying an exact and extensive legal knowledge in plays directed to the ridicule of the City tradesmen, or in writing pageants of the old style for the Lord Mayor's Show. He served both the public and the private theatres, collaborated with Dekker and Rowley, wrote the most famous and audacious of all political allegories of the period in *A Game At Chess* and a moral masque in *The World Tost at Tennis*, which ends with a dance in 'the sphere of harmony', where Law confounds Deceit and the Church the Devil. He was a Jack of all trades, but a true 'Chameleon poet'.

The range of Middleton's work through satiric and romantic comedy, tragedy, and tragi-comedy rivals that of the false players of *The Mayor of Queenborough*, who, coming to play in the local town-hall, boast themselves

'Comedians, tragedians, tragi-comedians, comi-tragedians, pastorists, clownists, satirists: we have them, sir, from the hug to the smile, from the smile to the laugh, from the laugh to the handkerchief.'

5.1.

His greatest play, *The Changeling*, encompasses the full range of his art, combining the supernatural with the mundane, fantasy with close analysis of motive and behaviour, rough horseplay with a study of degeneration. The unity of its plot and subplot which is immediately seen in the acting, depends on the theme—the irrational swamping the rational, overbearing 'the pales and forts of reason'. This complex unity recalls the Shakespearean tragic mode, especially that of *King Lear*: [18] and Middleton, much rather than Heywood, deserves to be called a prose Shakespeare.

His style is on occasion highly poetic, but it is without the rich elaboration of Shakespeare, as his low style is without the stabbing similes or highly flavoured rhetoric of Jonson. It relies on implication.

'Love woven slightly
Such as thy false heart makes, wears out as lightly;
But love being truly bred i' the soul like mine,
Bleeds even to death at the least wound it takes.'

The Roaring Girl, 1.1.

In these lines, the adage that the body is the garment of the soul underlies the implied contrast between love bred in the one and in the other; but the paradox, which follows logically, that the soul bleeds (and the body merely frays) gives an echoing depth to the passage which Marston's feverish brilliance and Jonson's loaded deliberations never attain. It is more truly dramatic, in being more condensed.

Irony is Middleton's characteristic device of style, and it depends closely upon the dramatic situation, rather than on language, though the inflation of Sir Bounteous Progress, recommending his grandson to the service of a Lord:

'Shall I be bold with your lordship to prefer the aforesaid young Ganymede to hold a plate under your Lordship's cup?'

is well matched by the discreet reply from the Lord, who is

no other than the same grandson in disguise for the purpose
of cozening his elder:

> 'Sir, I have heard much good of that young gentleman. . . .
> Well, sir, for your sake and for his own deserving, I'll reserve a place
> for him nearest to my secrets.'
>
> *A Mad World, My Masters*, 2.1.

So the impassioned oaths of the supposed widow in *A Trick
to Catch the old One*, renouncing Witgood:

> 'on my knees, I vow
> He ne'er shall marry me'

are answered by Witgood, poking his head out of hiding with
the brief observation

> 'Heaven knows he never meant it.'
>
> 3.1.

These two conspirators, the reformed courtesan and the repentant rake, who finally drop into short moral epilogues,
have been shown throughout as the lively leaders of a well-
planned racket. The marriage of a sharker and a whore, the
cheating of a rich uncle or grandfather, the gulling of young
spendthrifts are common to both these plays: and it seems of
little significance that Witgood's mistress marries his foe,
while Sir Bounteous's courtesan is wedded to his grandson.

Middleton's world is one in which money rules so
thoroughly that there is no possibility of love or hatred, and
scarcely of lust: cupidity is the sole power. In *A Trick to Catch
the Old One*, the mutual hatred of the two old men, Hoard
and Lucre, which is the most passionate feature of the play,
depends on their common devotion to wealth. Lucre decides
to advance his prodigal nephew some money: this on the
prospects of his marrying the rich widow.

> 'The chief cause that invites me to do him most good is the sud-
> den astonishing of old Hoard, my adversary: how pale his malice will
> look at my nephew's advancement! with what a dejected spirit he
> will behold his fortunes, whom but last day he proclaimed rioter,
> penurious makeshift, despised brothel master! Ha! ha! twill do me
> more secret joy than my last purchase, more precious comfort than
> all these widow's revenues.'
>
> 2.1.

When old Hoard steals the widow, nearly loses her through a claim of precontract, pays handsomely to retain her and eventually discovers her identity, she justifies herself at considerable length; whereas the marriage of Witgood with Old Hoard's niece is never even mentioned in the conclusion. Joyce Hoard, the most perfunctorily drawn of virtuous heiresses, has a slighter role than the corresponding Molls and Janes of other plays: but the romantic interest in Middleton is entirely a matter of schematic convenience. The four poetic lines of Mary Fitzallard, quoted from *The Roaring Girl*, serve to fix her character, which is indistinguishable from that of her near namesake Jane Fitzallen of *A Fair Quarrel*, or Moll of *A Chaste Maid in Cheapside*. The pattern of these plays is constant: light relief is provided by the technicalities of lawyers and the legal practices of sharking— there is a soliloquizing drunken lawyer in *A Trick to Catch the Old One*, who replaces the clown. Gangs of thieves add variety of legerdemain: a rich widow brings shoals of suitors.[19] There are few sheer fools in Middleton: all at least aspire to some degree of knavery. It is the kind of world which might have been described or inhabited by Chaucer's Pardoner. Jonson's firm moral basis, and Marston's agonized, twisted preoccupations with sin and foulness have completely disappeared from the clear transparent honesty with which in Middleton knavery is displayed.

In rehandling the story of *A Trick to Catch the Old One*, as *A New Way to Pay old Debts*, Massinger softened and moralized the hard ironic terseness of Middleton to a complacent loquacity. There is but one miser, and the hint given in Middleton's title is expanded so that Overreach in the last scene becomes delirious and literally possessed by devils. On the other hand, the prodigal and the youthful suitor become two separate characters, the courtesan a really rich and benevolent widow who lends herself to the scheme, and who ends with a noble match. A comparison of these two plays shows how far Middleton retained the formal and stylized qualities of Jonsonian satire, although the accent of judgement is heard in Jonson's plays from beginning to end, whereas in Middleton the silent judgement is provided by weight of irony—by all that is left unsaid.

Both Middleton and Jonson rely at times upon Plautine narratives—*The Case is Altered* and *No Wit, no Help like a Woman's* are both based on *The Captives*. A son who spends the money given to ransom his mother and sister from captivity upon fine living is ready shaped for Middleton's use; courtesans who are tossed between fathers and sons, like the heroine of *Mercator*, and witty servants who help their master in gulling, belong also to the Plautine world, a slave society, where sheer indifference to human claims is taken for granted. Middleton's appeal to his audience is likewise intellectual and not sympathetic. He presents the Police Court News for the delectation of the Inns of Court, and knows better than to try barristers' rhetoric upon such very hard judges; at the same time, he remains himself indifferent to the censure of audience and critics which so troubled Marston and Jonson, and keeps his distance from both.

Middleton's material is similar to that which Dekker used in his pamphlets, but their points of view differ completely. Dekker's mirror of the world could never be mistaken for the likeness of the world itself: Middleton, in spite of the fact that he portrays only knavery, establishes a familiar and everyday feeling, through his easy style, which gives to his shallow society a deceptive solidity. Because they are devoid of any passion, except for money, and of any ethical utterance, because hero and villain are distinguished only by superior craft, and events point to nothing beyond themselves, Middleton's six early satiric comedies [20] achieve the impersonality of pure observation and wit. The audience may remain untroubled by any qualms about a Jonsonian 'weight of sin' or any recollection of the Four Last Things. The endorsement of popular morality has ceased. The death's head does not appear in Middleton's comedy, and there is comparatively little brawling or bloodshed, though a moral dumb show precedes *Your Five Gallants*, and in *Michaelmas Term* the numerous disguises undertaken by the woollen draper's two apprentices, Falselight and Shortyard, who are called his 'spirits', give a momentary reflection of the supernatural. In *A Mad World, My Masters* Penitent Brothel is visited by a succubus in the likeness of his mistress. The singing, dancing and rhymed patter of this she-devil are not at all alarming, nor does it justify being repelled, as it is, with scraps from *Hamlet*.

> 'Celestial soldiers guard me! . . .
> Shield me, you ministers of faith and grace!'

Tradesmen, though labelled as woollen drapers, vintners and brokers, bear no special stamp of their occupation: the Five Gallants alone are suited to their various cheating styles —broker, bawd, gamester, pickpocket and cully. The five, in the final masque, present themselves to the heiress for her choice of a husband, but are unmasked in the Jonsonian manner by the hero, and as the alternative to lawful punishment they are married off to five courtesans. These women, like others of their kind in Middleton's comedy, are not shown as particularly sensual creatures; they have none of the savagery of Franceschina, and except for the Country Wench of *Michaelmas Term* all are simply women of a trade. Diamond-cut-diamond continues to be the theme, as when the five gallants and the courtesans rob each other in turn of the jewels they are wearing, or a highwayman finds his booty, taken from another man, consists of the purse and chain he had given his whore.[21]

> 'Does my boy pick and I steal to enrich myself, to keep her, to maintain him? why, this is right the sequence of the world. A lord maintains her, she maintains a knight, he maintains a whore, she maintains a captain. So in like manner, the pocket keeps my boy, he keeps me, I keep her, she keeps him: it runs like quicksilver from one to another'.

> *Your Five Gallants*, 3.2.

The unfortunate and the unlucky, the happy clown and pleading lover have no place in Middleton's city plays: court and country seldom appear. The atmosphere is that of the tavern, the brothel and the thieves' kitchen, with no hint of the jail, the bedlam or the bridewell which Dekker so emphasized. Middleton too was born a Londoner, but unlike Dekker and Jonson, he does not apply local colour. We hear of the 'two colleges of Wood Street and Poultry' (the two Counters or debtors' prisons) but never see them. The plays are not closely localized, and some of them are theoretically set in foreign parts. *The Phoenix*, which belongs to the same kind as *The Fawne* and Sharpham's *The Fleire*, is set in Ferrara, and the earliest of these satiric plays, *Blurt, Master Constable*, in Venice, though its merriment is provided by a fantastic named, significantly, Lazarillo de Tormes.[22] Many characters have type names—the heroes are labelled for their intellectual agility as Follywit, Witgood, Touchwood: others are Easy, Fidelio, Lucre, Hoard, Gulf, Frippery, Primero, Sir Bounteous Progress, Frank Gullman.

Such type-names link Middleton's characters, through Jonson, with the tradition of the moral play; and both writers use disguise in the manner of the moralities. Here the medieval tradition that the Devil originated all disguise when he took on himself the form of the snake was unmodified by any inclusion of the counter-balancing idea—the disguise of the Incarnation, Christ taking on Himself the form of the Suffering Servant. So the moralities concluded with a general stripping of disguise from all the Vices; this was transferred to the political sphere in such plays as Skelton's *Magnifycence*, where the wicked counsellors are revealed in their true light and given their true names at the end of the play. The essence of this disguise, which is the opposite of the Shakespearean kind, is not fusion but dissection, not synthesis but analysis of the separate roles. Character is not discovered: by disguise, it is betrayed.

This popular social tradition modified in time to a contrast between honest countrymen and false courtly splendour, gorgeous without and worthless in fact; the contrast between Cloth Breeches and Velvet Breeches was always in favour of the first.[23] With Jonson and the satiric writers a closer and more exact application to the image of the time appeared:

> 'I'll strip the ragged follies of the time
> Naked, as at their birth.'
> *Every Man out of his Humour*, Chorus.

The end of this play and of *Cynthia's Revels* both exemplify such an uncasing: it coincides with a Judgement. The disguisers at the end of *The Malcontent* unmask to meet treachery with counterplot: in spite of Malevole's transformation back to the 'merciful' Altofront, he can hardly be said to execute a Divine Judgement, as the satirists were accused of doing by their opponents.[24] The judgement scene at the end of *The Fawne* is frankly farcical, but its connexions with *Cynthia's Revels* are plain enough, and throughout the play Duke Hercules has certainly indulged his power to lash folly behind the scenes, while outwardly pampering it.

With Middleton, as with the later Jonson, the wicked disguised characters become attractive through their very wickedness and ingenuity: the devil really has succeeded in transforming himself to an angel of light. Lovers cheat their mistresses into surrender, whores pose as heiresses, kings as jesters. Increasingly dexterous and malicious use of disguise, as by Volpone, Subtle and Face, and the majority of Middleton's cheating plotters, leads to its association with the witty hero or heroine. Such disguise must be bold, startling and assumed with some clear objective in view: to gain a throne or a fortune, a woman's chamber or a man's promise, to test a wife's fidelity or a child's obedience. His audacity transforms the feigning character into a new role, or very often seems to promise his total disappearance, for one of the most popular devices is to feign death and to appear in the guise of a corpse. Here the resurrection provides a happy ending.[25]

Such is the conclusion of *A Chaste Maid in Cheapside*, a play which follows upon the earlier comedies of Middleton at some five years' interval, in 1613, and which was designed for the robust audience of the public theatres. It is built to the older model, but of the new materials. The theme is Chastity and Wantonness; with the emphasis upon Wantonness. Sir Walter Whorehound marries off his cast mistress to the rich goldsmith's son by producing her as a Welsh heiress, lady of 'some nineteen mountains'. He himself is cheated in the end by Allwit, who has allowed him to keep Mistress Allwit, and rejoiced in the birth of seven bastards to be brought up at Sir Walter's cost, but who sees him hauled off to prison and ruin with the bland lie:

> 'I must tell you, sir,
> You have been somewhat bolder in my house
> Than I could well like of: I suffer'd you
> Till it stuck here at my heart: I tell you truly
> I thought you had been familiar with my wife once.'

The weight of irony can be measured only if this is set against the exultation of his opening soliloquy on the joys of being a wealthy man's cuckold.

Sir Walter has been disinherited through the activities of Touchwood Senior, an unfortunate reduced gentleman with too great an ability in the begetting of children. To conserve his estate he has separated from his lawful wife, but he restores his own fortunes and destroys Sir Walter's by acting as proxy for the impotent Oliver Kix, and providing him with a son and heir whose doubtful origins are a fitting punishment for the getter of Allwit's children.

The younger brother of Touchwood is the lover of the Chaste Maid, whom her parents wish to marry to Sir Walter, and he and she finally achieve their end by the trick of the pretended deaths and resurrection of both. Their parts, however, are of little importance, except in the conclusion: they are crowded off the stage by the knaves, and the fool, Moll's brother, the Cambridge graduate who rejoices in his learning but ends by marrying the Welsh widow.

The scene at the christening of Allwit's latest bastard, 'a fine black eyed slut', is amongst the rankest in all Elizabethan drama, with the Puritan gossips and complacent mother exchanging compliments and filching sweetmeats. This is the latest of Middleton's many hits at the Puritans; all the characters in this play can be paralleled from his earlier comedies, but the total effect is quite different. The underlying morality structure is self-evident; the London scene is here more detailed, and the effect is far closer to an image of the times; the usurous goldsmith, father of Moll and Tim, might be Cupidity by name, but he is in fact placed firmly in Cheapside, neighbour to Touchstone of *Eastward Ho!*

In *The Roaring Girl*, Middleton and Dekker brought upon the stage an actual personage, Moll Firth, commonly called Moll Cutpurse, who in 1612 did penance at Paul's Cross for an unknown offence, with apparent contrition; it was discovered, however, that 'she had tippled off three quarts of sack before she came to her penance'. In this play she is allowed to characterize herself at the opening in a noble passage that does *not* suggest a portrait from life.

'Sir, I am so poor to requite you, you must look for nothing but thanks of me: I have no humour to marry: I love to lie a both sides a' the bed myself: and again, a' the other side, a wife, you know, ought to be obedient, but I fear me I am too headstrong to obey: therefore I'll ne'er go about it. I love you so well, sir, for your good will, I'd be loth you should repent your bargain after: and therefore we'll ne'er come together at first. I have the head now of myself, and am man enough, for a woman: marriage is but a chopping and a changing.' 2.2.

The dignified self-knowledge which her rejection of a rich suitor implies is counter-balanced in the last sentence by a quibbling play upon her masculine appearance, which may have provided the spectators with that kind of entertainment which is now furnished in reports by the popular press of sexual freaks and abnormalities. In her masculine attire—which the real Moll wore—she is addressed as Jack: she fights a duel, rescues a spendthrift from the catchpoles who would arrest him, and talks mysterious canting language with thieves, from whom she has the power to extract stolen goods for her friends. The final justification which she gives—that a knowledge of evil is necessary at times—

'You'd proclaim
Your knowledge in those villainies, to save
Your friend from their quick danger'
5.1.

is spoken to a Lord, implying that a knowledge of Venetian courtesans would be useful to him in his travels; and it is identical with the argument of Old Hoard's courtesan to excuse her previous way of living. When therefore Moll ends the play with an old-fashioned riddling prophecy that she will marry when various impossibilities take place,[26] the accent is no longer quite so noble, or her character quite so unequivocal as it was. She has appeared as a kind of feminine Robin Hood, aiding the weak against the strong, and in her final disguise as 'bride' to Wengrave she is deputizing for Mary Fitzallard, whose pathetic self-characterization has been instanced already as amongst Middleton's most poignant lines. The two, Moll and Mary, appear together in male dress in the most significant scene of the play: Mary is disguised as a page, in a suit made by Moll's tailor, but as she takes up this Shakespearean role, that of a Jessica or a Rosalind, her lover abruptly destroys the old decorum with an innocently ironic remark that reduces her to Epicoene

'I'd kiss such men to choose, Moll:
Methinks a woman's lip tastes well in a doublet. . . .
Every kiss she gives me now
In this strange form is worth a pair of two.'

4.1.

The identities and roles of Moll and Mary are so intertwined that the rest of the story is of very minor significance: it consists indeed largely of merriments or jests which serve to show off Moll's virtuosity, from her skill in singing bawdy songs to the viol de gambois to her ability in talking canting jargon. She provides entertainment for her betters, seemingly a harmless jester: but the edge of Middleton's writing was seldom keener than here.

He had strayed far from the satiric order of his early plays; yet in his later plays he strayed still farther. *The Witch*, *The Fair Quarrel* and *The Spanish Gipsy* are Fletcherian in mode, though in one at least he was collaborating with Rowley. Middleton's power to work with other men and produce a play of apparently seamless unity is one of the most astonishing features of the Jacobean drama. The collaboration of Shakespeare and Fletcher, or Fletcher and Massinger also produced plays of extraordinary vitality; and the named partnership of Beaumont and Fletcher was only an open acknowledgement of a very general practice. In these later stages of the drama it is possible that the old collaboration between actors and audience, which had formerly been so fruitful, was replaced by the more delicate, though more limited one between two writers. *Eastward Ho!*, *The Honest Whore*, *The Puritan* (sometimes ascribed to Middleton and clearly influenced by him), *The Changeling*, *The Roaring Girl* almost rival those more mysterious examples of Shakespearean cross-breeding, *Pericles* and *The Two Noble Kinsmen*.

CHAPTER X

A SET OF WIT WELL PLAYED: DAY, CHAPMAN, FLETCHER

1. From Symmetry to Sophistry

THE courtly game, 'a mark marvellous well shot', a set of wit, a game at chess or bowls, which Lyly had so elegantly developed, did not disappear with the discarding of the Euphuistic style. Comedy of wit, flavoured with satire, but also with fantasy, devoid of the moral weightiness of Jonson or the complex irony of Middleton, continued in the private theatres; and in the second decade of the seventeenth century, when the men's companies shifted over to these theatres by degrees, it enjoyed a notable revival in the work of Fletcher. The problems were literary, the answers were cooked, the disguises were frivolous and the audience and author met as equals. Neither flattery nor instruction coloured the address. Airy trifles, depending largely on the grace with which they were presented, these plays grew up side by side with the more stately court masque, to which they are in some respects akin.

The men who wrote them were also capable of writing very differently; for with growing ease and flexibility in the use of the low style, even the high style could no longer retain its old formality, and the stiff pattern of Lyly's plays has softened in the work of Day. These authors restricted real familiarity with the audience to the prologues and epilogues, where the note of careless ease is clearest. It is recognized that all the audience cannot be gratified.

> 'Since all our labours are as you can like,
> We all submit to you: nor dare presume
> To think there's any real worth in them:
> Sometimes feasts please the cooks and not the guests;
> Sometimes the guests, and curious cooks condemn them.'
>
> Epilogue to *All Fools*.

In their time the skill and control required to produce

comedies of wit were greater than it is easy to appreciate now. The besetting sin of the Elizabethan writer was the production of indigestible mixtures. Miss Doran has noted the tendency of romance to creep into satiric plays, and suggests that the classical models upon which the comedy of wit relied had in some ways been read with an emphasis different from the modern one.[1] Even in Lyly's day, Sir Philip Sidney had exemplified the courtly grace of *sprezzatura*, which in terms of style reveals itself as irony: in Fulke Greville's *Life* this is noted as his distinguishing quality. But Sidney was ahead of his time in lightness of touch; and it was Shakespeare who translated this grace into dramatic form. Upon Shakespeare's foundations, both the popular comedy and the comedy of wit were re-established; while the alternative form of satiric comedy developed by reaction. The language of satire—familiar, violent and gusty—when practised on such a scale as in the first decade of the seventeenth century, could not but impress by mere contiguity; the barriers of the various kinds were no longer so rigid: and the comedy of later Jacobean times is altogether more conscious of the graces of negligence than of the need for consistency. Fletcher almost made a virtue of inconsistency; his readiness to collaborate and the speed at which he worked are virtues achieved at the cost of some shallowness and softness; his top notes were shrill, and his unexamined grossness is as different from the laughing frankness of the older writers as from the polished sophistication of the Restoration wits. His tragedies are offensive, for he was incapable of work at that level; his pastoral, though the language is lovely, reveals that true innocence was something beyond his power of portrayal; his tragi-comedy, which may have been something of a technical feat in its day, is now rather uninteresting: but his light comedy of wit remains as a genuine contribution both to literature and the theatre.

II. John Day

John Day, although a minor writer, may be taken as typifying the transition from the work of Lyly to that of the boys' theatres in the early years of James. He has been improbably credited with the authorship of *The Maid's Metamorphosis*, a play almost completely in Lyly's style (it is included in the standard edition of his works) and with the writing of the Parnassus plays.[2] His college was Caius, and his connexion with Cambridge is tenuous: indeed, very little is known of him at all. But his three plays for the children's companies—*The Isle of Gulls, Humour out of Breath, Law Tricks*—prove him capable of delicate and witty fancy, although sadly deficient in dramatic art. He was also a voluminous writer for the popular theatres—Jonson called him a rogue and a base fellow. He collaborated with Dekker, Chettle and other of Henslowe's hacks in twenty-three plays within the space of the four years 1598–1603, ranging from the legend of Guy of Warwick to Moll Cutpurse, or the depicting of familiar scenes, like *The Boss of Billingsgate*. Only two popular works have survived: *The Blind Beggar of Bednal Green*—a second and third part both being lost—and *The Travails of Three English Brothers*. These are mere fountains of rant, and the second was justly satirized by Beaumont in *The Knight of the Burning Pestle*. Nevertheless, the fact that Day achieved some popular applause, yet is now remembered for his poetry alone, suggests that his various potentialities were never successfully embodied in any one work. The most delightful of his writings is *The Parliament of Bees*, a series of allegorical dialogues: they have a long literary ancestry, stretching beyond Chaucer's *Parliament of Fowls*, yet the judgements of the parliament to which the bees are summoned recall the final judgement scenes of satiric comedy. This, however, constitutes the sole event of the work, which could not have been intended for the stage. The mixture of moral fancy and personal 'shadowing' concludes with the appearance of Oberon to receive gifts from his subjects, pronounce blessings and exact penalties. All is highly traditional, but the freshness and delicacy of phrasing which is Day's individual gift is here employed upon themes which brought out the countryman in him.[3] Vintager and Flora are blessed in language of limpid simplicity:

'May thy grapes thrive
In autumn and the roots survive

In churlish winter: may thy fence
Be proof 'gainst wild boars' violence:
As thou in service true shalt be
To us and our high royalty.

'Honey dews refresh thy meads,
Cowslips spring with golden heads,
Gilliflowers and carnations wear
Leaves double streaked with maidenhair.
May thy lilies taller grow,
Thy violets fuller sweetness owe:
And last of all, may Phoebus love
To kiss thee and frequent thy grove,
As thou in service true shalt be
Unto our crown and royalty.'

Drones, wasps and bumble bees are characterized with sins of monopoly, engrossing and chicanery, treachery, riot and loose living: they are punished, a viceroy is appointed, a bride bestowed upon him, and finally the Golden Age restored.

'Prorex shall again renew
His potent reign: the massy world,
Which in glittering orbs is hurled
About the poles, be lord of: we
Only reserve our royalty . . .
Apollo and the Muses dance,
Art hath banished Ignorance.'

This gentle Virgilian conclusion reveals the underlying strength of a yet simple unity of morality and letters: [4] by contrast, Fletcher's *Faithful Shepherdess* betrays the disintegration of standards, although technically it is the more accomplished drama.

On the other hand, *The Isle of Gulls* is relatively sophisticated, but lacking in co-ordination. It is a literary *jeu d'esprit*, based on Sidney's *Arcadia*; and if it be compared with the popular *Mucedorus*, also based on *Arcadia*, the sophistication becomes evident: yet *Mucedorus* has more life in it, as time demonstrated.[5] The most interesting feature of *The Isle of Gulls* is its Induction, a gay variant upon the satiric Jonsonian model, in which three nameless spectators, representing three literary types—the satirist, the amorist and the bombastic ranter—make incompatible demands upon the players and poet.

> *First Gentleman:* Look to't, if there be not gall in it, it shall not pass.
> *Second Gentleman:* If it be not baudy, 'tis impossible to pass.
> *Third Gentleman:* If it be both critical and baudy, if it be not high written, both your poet and the house too lose a friend of me.

In the Prologue the professionals hit back:

> 'Neither quick mirth, invective, nor high state
> Can content all: such is the boundless hate
> Of a confused audience.'

The Player boldly declares for himself that if 'our merits nothing, yet our hopes are great' and from the Poet he brings a message:

> 'His play shall pass, let Envy swell and break,
> Detraction he scorns, honours the best.
> *Tanti* for hate: thus low to all the rest.'

The concluding bow was evidently preceded by some physical gesture of defiance; which received indeed an unequivocal answer, for next month 'sundry were committed to Bridewell', as Sir Edward Hoby reports, presumably because the two rival nations depicted in the play were thought to bear political implications.[6]

Such interest is needed, for though the rhetorical set pieces —a definition of a maidenhead, a parody of a Puritan's sermon or of a lover's sonnet—are often amusing from the literary point of view, the characters are so faint and the narrative so weak that the only possible articulation would be to 'figure' some 'certain state or private government'. This the Prologue-speaker strenuously but perhaps not very convincingly denies.

The writing is in the highly artificial style of *Love's Labour s Lost* or *Romeo and Juliet*: in the definition of a dream, in *Humour out of Breath* there would seem to be an echo of Mercutio on Queen Mab.

> 'Why, your whole world doth nothing but dream: your Machievel he dreams of deposing Kings, grounding new monarchies: the lover he dreams of kisses, amorous embraces: the new married wife

dreams that rid of her young husband she hugs her old lover and likes
her dream well enough too: the country gentlewoman dreams that
when her first husband's dead, she marries a knight, and the name
of lady sticks so in her mind, she is never at heart's ease till she gets
her husband dubbed: the captain he dreams of oppressing the
soldiers, devising stratagems to keep his dream. . . .'

I.2

The whole play is an elaborate game; one of the central
scenes is actually a tennis-court, where the repartee flies to
and fro like the tennis-balls. So also, in *Humour out of Breath*,
a pair of lovers steal away from the jailer by engaging him in
a game of Blind Man's Buff. In this play the action, in contrast to that of *The Isle of Gulls*, is likewise rapid, even be-
wilderingly so; the characters are grouped with the symmetry of Lyly. But whereas Lyly was evolving a form, Day
was repeating a formula. More than a dozen crucial years
had intervened, and the old tricks had become outworn. The
noble lovers, disguised in rustic weeds, encounter in a volley
of words as though time had stood still:

> *Hippolito:* Fair maids if so you be, you are well met.
> *Hermia:* Shepherds, or be what else you are, well met.
> *Francisco:* Tis well, if that well met we be unto you.
> *Lucida:* If not to us, you are unto yourselves.
> *Hippolito:* We did not meet, you saw us come together.
> *Hermia:* Whate'er we saw, you met ere we came hither.
> *Francisco:* We did, we met in kindred, we are brothers.
> *Lucida:* So, shepherd, we did meet, for we are sisters.

The formula is at least more coherent than that of *The Isle of
Gulls*: it is no parody of Arcadia, but the place itself. *Law
Tricks*, the least successful of Day's comedies, attempts to
include the pathetic. As in the others, disguises, improbabili-
ties, intrigues and fantastic reversals of situation abound:
at the same time, a ferocious test of patience is imposed upon
the Countess, the Griselda of this play. The theme of *The
Isle of Gulls* and *Humour out of Breath* is a prize at fence in the
game of love, that of *Law Tricks* is cozenage; but it is the
moments of lyric pathos, totally irrelevant to the play in itself, which redeem it

> *Countess:* Here's a fault, little one, what work make you?
> *First maid:* True-stitch, forsooth.

170

Countess: Then see you work it true.
Third maid: Pray, madam, teach me how to take out this knot
        Of heart's ease.
Countess: Heart's ease, I have almost forgot.
        I could have wrought it well when I was young,
        But in good sadness I have had none long.
        What's that?
Second maid: A branch of rue.
Countess: A common weed.
        Of all herbs else, I work that well indeed. . . .
        You are like April, or rose buds in May,
        You never wither till the wedding day,
        Even so did I: so, pretty souls, will you.
        Youth wears mild heart's ease, marriage bitter rue.

                                 3.1.

Here the poet of *The Parliament of Bees* reappears; perhaps also the copyist, fresh from Ophelia's scene of rosemary and pansies.[7]

III. George Chapman

The comedies of George Chapman, like those of Day, may be divided into the popular, the academic and the tragi-comic. His early plays were written for Henslowe, and *The Blind Beggar of Alexandria* (1595) achieved great success on the stage, besides setting the fashion for a whole series based on the feats of a quick-change artist.[8] In *An Humourous Day's Mirth* (1599), also written for Henslowe, Chapman initiated the Jonsonian comedy of humours. His chief contribution to the drama seems to have lain in the provision of models for better men. Although he practised almost every literary form of the day, Chapman never succeeded in devising a satisfactory mode for himself. His preference for the difficult and involved situation, his cult of Hermetic and mystical philosophy, and his sense of separation from the world at large might have been expected altogether to unfit him for the writing of comedy; on one occasion he openly proclaimed his dislike of the stage.[9] His comedies are exercises in art rather than animate theatre; the success of the early plays must have depended upon the helter-skelter actions which were Chapman's own invention. Irus, the Blind Beggar, is subtlety personified: like Malevole, he controls all the action and dominates all the other characters. A ruler disguised in various roles, he runs through murders lightly, seduces both his own wives, and amasses a vast fortune, eventually reaching a crown to which he was not born. In *An Humourous Day's Mirth* there is a comparable character, Lemot, who directs all the intrigue, which is here, however, subordinate to display of humours in Blanuel, Labesha, Labervele and the rest. These lords of the ascendant, who are devoid of moral purpose or satiric intensity, reappear in the later comedies which Chapman wrote for the children's companies. Rinaldo, Ludovico, Vincentio, Vaumont and Tharsalio are variants upon the type, which is summed up by Rinaldo in *All Fools*:

> 'Fortune, the great commandress of the world,
> Hath divers ways to advance her followers.
> To some she gives honours without deserving.
> To other some, deserving without honours . . .
> My fortune is to win renown by gulling.'   4.1.

Cheerful and reckless gulling is the basis of *May Day*, translated from the Italian of Alessandro Piccolomini, and of *All Fools*, based upon two plays of Terence. Chapman was proud of his learning—it sometimes got in his way—and was no doubt anxious to transplant learned comedy to the boards. These are both revelling plays, crammed with minor characters, who in *May Day* put on a bewildering variety of disguises. A man disguised as a girl and a girl disguised as a man fall in love with each other and discover that they are already long-lost lovers: a wanton dresses in man's clothes and an old lecher assumes the mummery of a chimney-sweep's costume. *All Fools* is filled with elaborate hoaxes inflicted by children on their parents, and adorned with long set orations on Love, Women, the Fop, the Cuckold and the Horn. Ludovico in *May Day* is the kind of hare-brained young mischief-maker that Fletcher was later to delight in: he is good-humoured, gay and without ambitions. The setting of the plays is indifferently Florence, France or Alexandria; in any case, a mere label. Grand tirades, practical jokes and humorous character-sketches are the raw material; they are drawn from literature, not from observation. Perhaps the figure of the poor scholar, Dowsecar or Clarence,[10] who leaps into success, fame and love, may be taken as a wishful dream on the part of his creator; if so, the dream is very dim. The successful tricksters have not the dramatic strength which makes Middleton's rogues so formidable: on the other hand, the fools are not satirized, but merely enjoyed as freaks, and even petted a little, as a great man might indulge his jester or a lady her dwarf or monkey.

In two of his comedies, Chapman includes a higher strain of his own transcendental idealism; they can hardly be called tragi-comedies, for the different moods, though technically well linked, do not cohere. Unlike Shakespeare's blended or contrasted plots and subplots, the alternating levels of *The Gentleman Usher* and *Monsieur d'Olive* merely serve to show the division in Chapman's mind between doctrine and the life of the scene.[11] The two gulls who give their names to these plays are somewhat alike: both are deluded by hopes of false glory, to which they are led by their own good conceit of themselves. The gentlemen usher is fooled by a prince into thinking himself a favourite when he is really being used as a go-between for the prince and his lady. Monsieur d'Olive, who is intoxicated by being appointed ambassador for his duke, acquires a huge train of fools to escort him, only to find his embassage cancelled. While claiming that he has no ambitions and wishes to live in retirement

> 'his mind is his kingdom . . .
> His chamber is a court of all good wits,'

he appears a compound of Armado and Malvolio. He is not without wit, though deplorably lacking in sense, and his magnificence in playing the part which is offered him is its own reward. He sees himself as the equal of a king, and the glory of his dream is worth the price of disillusionment.

> 'The siege of Bulloigne shall be no more a landmark for times: Agincourt battle, St. James his field, the loss of Calais, and the winning of Cales, shall grow out of use; men shall reckon their years, women their marriages from the day of our embassage, as "I was born, or married, two, or three or four years before the great embassage". Farmers shall count their leases from this day, gentlemen

their mortgages from this day: St. Denis shall be razed out of the calendar, and the day of our instalment entered in red letters: and as St. Valentine's day is fortunate to choose lovers, St. Luke's to choose husbands, so shall this day be to the choosing of lords.' 4.2.

After his cozening is over, Monsieur d'Olive is kindly welcomed to the court and his role of fool is by no means unsympathetic. The minor figures include the usual witty pages, but the hero of the serious action, Vandome, is the principal wit. He returns from travel to find his virtuous mistress, because of her husband's jealousy, has vowed never to see the light and rises only at night time; while his sister having died, his brother-in-law keeps her embalmed body above ground to feed his grief. Here is an allegory of Chapman's doctrine of contemplative melancholy, in which mystic illumination is associated with the shadow of night; but Vandome's method of cure is a summary one; he sends his brother-in-law on a wooing embassy, in which of course he succumbs to the charms of the lady; and entices his own mistress out of doors with a tale of her husband's infidelity.

The heroic story in *The Gentleman Usher* contains even more clearly a measure of doctrine. Strozza, who is wounded by an arrow whilst hunting, despairs of his life, but is counselled to patience by his wife Cynanche, and as a result of submitting to 'patience in torment' and waiting on 'Nature's secret aid' he is not only cured but gifted with miraculous prophecy by his 'free submission to the hand of Heaven'. His mind 'spreads her powers' till he can say

'Humility hath raised me to the stars.'

The Platonic marriage of Margaret and Vincentio, celebrated by the sort of rite which Chapman loved to devise, is the other heroic theme. When Vincentio is reported killed, Margaret destroys her own beauty with a disfiguring ointment, but both are eventually reunited and cured.[12] Strozza's happy state is owing to his wife, who persuaded him to submit in the first place; and his description of her might equally typify the union of Vincentio.

'Oh, what a treasure is a virtuous wife,
Discreet and loving. Not one gift on earth
Makes a man's life so highly bound to heaven;

She gives him double forces to endure
And to enjoy by being one with him,
Feeling his joys and griefs with equal sense;
And like the twins Hippocrates reports,
If he fetch sighs, she draws her breath as short,
If he lament, she melts herself in tears;
If he be glad she triumphs: if he stir,
She moves his way: in all things, his sweet ape,
And is in alteration passing strange,
Himself divinely varied without change.'   4.3.

The sentiments of Strozza and the stratagems of Vendome
are inverted, when from this empyrean height virtue crashes
to the ground in Chapman's most powerful comedy, *The
Widow's Tears.* This coherent and ironic play has a violent
simplicity of action. In tone and temper, although not in
dramatic achievement, it anticipated Middleton's *Chaste
Maid in Cheapside.*

The theme of *The Widow's Tears* is that all the acts, intentions and outward evidence of virtue presented by the two
widows, Eudora and Cynthia, are direct evidence for a contrary state of mind. The more they protest, the more certain
they are to belie themselves; the play consists of their two
stories, which are not intertwined but succeed each other. In
the first, Tharsalio, committing himself to the three blind
deities, Fortune, Love and Confidence, rushes into the presence of his late master's widow, and by sheer impudent proclamation of his intents, aided by the testimony of a bawd
upon his extraordinary virility, he overcomes the scorn of
the lady, baffles her suitors and wins her. In the second
action, his brother, feigning death to test his wife's fidelity,
finds that after a show of inconsolable grief she allows him
in the guise of a common soldier to seduce her within her
husband's tomb. The collapse of both women's resolution
is sudden as the fall of a mined building, and entirely unpre-
pared by any precedent action. In the final judgement scene,
instead of the dignified pronouncement which such a story
demands, the image of a fool in office proclaims a general
saturnalia: [13]

'Shifters shall cheat and starve and no man shall do good but
where there is no need. Braggarts shall live at the head, and the

tumult that haunt taverns. Asses shall bear good qualities, and wise
men shall use them. I will whip lechery out o' the city: there shall
be no more cuckolds. They that heretofore were arrant cornutos,
shall now be honest shopkeepers, and justice shall take place. . . It
shall be the only note of love to the husband to love the wife: and
none shall be more kindly welcome to him than he that cuckolds
him.'   5.3.

Neither the rage of the deceived husband nor the joy of
his brother at proving the inconstancy of Cynthia are permitted to give rise to satiric reflection. The goddess of
chastity—Chapman has used the name which in his earliest
poem typified all virtue—sinks so low that when her disguised
husband, in a final attempt to shame her, proclaims himself
the murderer of the corpse she was mourning, she does not
shrink from him. She has undergone some horrible metamorphosis of an inward kind, in which her previous self has
been destroyed. The situation would justify even the accents
of Hamlet:

> 'A little month or e'er those shoes were old
> With which she followed my poor father's body
> Like Niobe, all tears: why she, even she—
> O God, a beast that wants discourse of reason,
> Would have mourned longer . . .'
>   1.2.

but nothing of the kind is heard. The strange incomplete-
ness and echoing silence of this play are its strength. The early
scene, in which Tharsalio rushes into Eudora's presence,
confidently proclaiming her real desires in face of her blank
denials, gives the key. The effect is almost that of a modern
problem play, and the end is a large question mark. In
Bussy's words:

> 'Fortune, not Reason, rules the state of things,
> Reward goes backward, honour on his head.'

Here fantasy touches the borders of horror. That Cynthia
saves herself in the end by the old trick of pretending that
she had penetrated her husband's disguise is only in keeping
with the irony of the whole structure. The protestations of
widows were a common target for the comic writers, and the
theme could be treated with gaiety, and reduced to farce: [14]

in Chapman's play it is not common hypocrisy which is portrayed, but a stranger and more bewildering dualism of nature.

iv. John Fletcher

Fletcher was a Son of Jonson, but he also collaborated with Shakespeare. To Dryden he appeared almost their literary equal, certainly comparable, and their superior in depicting the manners of gentlemen. Shakespeare purchased his status; Fletcher, the son of a bishop, was born to it. It was for gentlemen that he wrote; a special code of manners—that of the Cavaliers—and a special range of topics—those concerning love and friendship between individuals—combine to limit the appeal of his plays to the class from which he sprung. Its literary ideals were no longer intellectual, like those of Lyly's audience, or moral, like Jonson's; they were ideals of behaviour, of manners and deportment, which the playwright presented in a heightened but uncritical form. Banter, artifice and a taste for the sensational, together with a sense of the absurd, provided the bond between author and audience. The disentanglement of authorship within the group of plays ascribed to Beaumont and Fletcher would demand close analysis; the general attitude is consistent enough for the group to be treated as a whole.[15] While the tragedies and tragi-comedies are stunningly and unashamedly factitious, the pure comedy is a genuine variant upon earlier kinds. Such plays as *The Wild Goose Chace, The Scornful Lady, Rule a Wife and Have a Wife* and *The Tamer Tamed* present a sharpened conflict in the merry war of lovers: it is the amatory equivalent of Middleton's comedy of city cheats. The struggle for domination between man and woman, viewed with airy, fantastic mockery, does not preclude shrewd observation and occasional flickers of sympathy. In all these plays, pursuit not only of love but also of the right matrimonial status is eventually gratified.

In *The Wild Goose.Chace*, Mirabell, who like Don Juan carries with him his catalogue of seductions, is reclaimed by Oriana after a series of stratagems that include a mock wooing by her own brother, a scene in which she feigns to be mad for love, and finally the disguise of a rich heiress, which, after she has entrapped him, Mirabell confesses he had penetrated. In *The Scornful Lady*, a haughty beauty is tamed by a similar series of tricks, the last of which is the hero's forthcoming marriage to another woman. This 'woman', a second suitor in disguise, is thus enabled to conquer the lady's younger sister in a manner exactly parallel to Don Juan's conquest of Doudou in the seraglio. The plays at their best are in the spirit of Don Juan; the lively, apparently callous but not totally unfeeling farce, the unprincipled bravado and the tone of easy lordly insolence are very similar. There is no possibility of real catastrophe in this world, but its ridicule is not altogether thoughtless. The Scornful Lady sums up her own predicament and that of several other heroines.

> 'Is it not strange that every woman's will
> Should track out new ways to disturb herself?
> If I should call my reason to account
> It cannot answer why I keep myself
> From mine own wish and stop the man I love
> From his, and every hour repent again,
> Yet still go on. . . .
> I'd rather die, sometimes, than not disgrace
> In public, him whom people think I love,
> And do't with oaths and am in earnest then.
> O what are we? Men, you must answer this,
> That dare obey such things as we command.'
> 5.1.

This is far from the world of Dekker in which Viola torments Candido, the patient man; the natural perversity of woman is treated far more seriously. In Fletcher's plays older situations are often reversed: *The Woman's Prize* is a sequel to *The Taming of the Shrew*, in which Petruchio, married to a second wife, is tamed by her with the methods of Lysistrata. This feminist, who leads a troop of other wives, recalls Petruchio's original metaphor of taming the hawk: [16]

> 'Hang these tame hearted eyasses, that no sooner
> See the lure out, and hear their husband's hollo,
> But cry like kites upon them: the free haggard
> (Which is that woman that hath wing and knows it,
> Spirit and plume) will make a hundred checks,
> To show her freedom, sail in every air,

> And look out every pleasure, not regarding
> Lure nor quarry, till her pitch command
> What she desires.'
>
> I.2.

In the end, having overcome her husband, she suddenly capitulates:

> 'I've done my worst and have my end: forgive me.
> From this hour make me what you please: I've tamed you
> And now am vowed your servant.'

Natural perversity rules these ladies: the heiress of *Rule a Wife and Have a Wife* marries a servant whom she thinks will prove a complaisant screen for her amours, only to find herself in the grip of the tamer. The steady determination and cool mastery of Leon are based upon his control of his wife's vast wealth, but equally upon his knowledge of her flightiness. Until he won her he played the harmless fool: then, in a manner almost recalling the sudden revelation of Middleton's de Flores, he displays his true character.

> 'I stand upon the ground of my own honour,
> And will maintain it. You shall know me now
> To be an understanding, feeling man,
> And sensible of what a woman aims at,
> A young proud woman that has will to sail with;
> An itching woman that her blood provokes too.
> I cast my cloud and now appear myself,
> The master of this little piece of mischief!'

So grave a note is seldom struck: usually the high spirits of the men-tamers, one of whom appears in the subplot of this very play, are matched by the reckless jests and masquerades of the young gallants. In nearly all these plays, lovers feign madness, sickness, death, or disguise themselves to bring their cause to victory.

Fletcher makes free use of disguise, but it is the use of Jonson, Middleton and Chapman, not of Shakespeare; the trickery which is the chief weapon of wit finds expression in the masquerade of witty heroes and heroines, and the helter-skelter intrigues of the dramatist gather speed from it; but it is not a means of deepening the implications and widening the scope of the comedy's intent.[17] It is true that sometimes symbolic disguises are used: in *The Nice Valour*, the mistress of the Passionate Lord appears throughout in the disguise of Cupid, in which role she follows her distracted lover about the court; this is part of an elaborate stratagem to cure him and make an honest woman of her, for on a promise of marriage he had got her with child. Such a story, with its queer mixture of allegory and vulgarity, evidently pleased the age, for the epilogue makes a particular boast of it.

> 'But for the love scenes which he ever meant
> Cupid in's petticoats should represent,
> He'll stand no shock of censure. The play's good,
> He says he knows it (if well understood).'

Nevertheless, such masquing, like that in Chapman's *The Gentleman Usher*, fails singularly to control or illuminate the main theme in the manner of older masque scenes: it is not poetically harmonious, but a stage trick merely.[18]

Disguise in Fletcher is generally of another sort: in Middleton's *The Widow* and *Wit at Several Weapons*, women who rather arbitrarily disguise themselves as men are bound and robbed; in *The Widow* the disguised woman is wooed by another woman, but by a timely revelation of her sex is able to protect her protectress from a jealous husband. In *Monsieur Thomas* and *The Wild Goose Chace* a man disguised as a woman gains access to a girl's bedchamber; this trick may lead to one man 'marrying' another, or another hero pretends to be about to marry a man disguised as a woman in order to bring his mistress to capitulate. In *The Wild Goose Chace* and *The Mad Lover*, the wooers pretend to be sick or dead. Such tricks in frequency and improbability rival the metamorphoses of the earliest comedies of wit; but here they are combined with natural dialogue and a human story. The effect is one of gaiety, and the joy of the carnival or the masked ball. Such disguise is indeed the permanent basis of high comedy of manners. When Beaumarchais constantly substitutes Susanna for the Countess or Figaro for the Count, when the figure concealed in the closet always turns out to be somebody other than was expected, the spectator receives an exquisite satisfaction. The action implies that cause and effect may not really always work in an iron chain, that a sinner may be able to get away with his crime undetected, that a glutton may be able to eat his cake and have it. This release from the ordinary limitations which impose virtue on our daily existence is one form of the comic katharsis.

Fletcher's heroes have at all times a gay negligence; the young prodigals are no longer even faintly guilty, they are agreeable lunatics; while the widow hunt is pretty completely discredited. The pursuit of wealth in *Rule a Wife and Have a Wife* and *The Elder Brother* seems to occur as a dramatic device without any acknowledgement of its being a true motive, or any stress being laid on it except in farcical under-plots. Fletcher's spendthrifts are harebrained, their estates are not substantial enough for the squandering to be a serious matter. In *The Noble Gentleman*, the gull Marine is fooled by his wife into selling all his land, in spite of the pleas of his tenants: in *The Scornful Lady*, the prodigal younger brother sells up his elder's estate in spite of the pleas of his distressed steward. In Dekker or Jonson these distressed dependants would have had the author's full support: here they are ghostly characters, liable to be mocked and summarily dismissed. In *Wit Without Money*, the hero has not only spent his own fortune but also his younger brother's, and he insists that to live on the bounty of friends is preferable to the possession of estates. Unlike Timon of Athens, he finds his friends remarkably accommodating, and when he joins in their behalf in the pursuit of a wealthy widow, he not only succeeds in winning her, but his brother wins her sister. Both ladies secretly succour their lovers, and the verbal contests which continue throughout the play are palpable fencing. All the traditional butts—the Puritan hypocrite, the grasping citizen, the Jewish usurer, even the phrasemonger and the braggart soldier—have disappeared from these plays. Eccentricity is itself a desirable quality, the badge of wit. One of the most notable figures in Fletcher is the comic madman: these fantastic characters, looked at with close observation and amused indifference, are seen as the victims of love and therefore always curable. The melancholy of lovers, unlike that of malcontents, is sympathetic, and interest in it became more pronounced upon the late Jacobean and Carline stage, stimulated perhaps by the appearance of Burton's

Anatomy of Melancholy in 1621. Ford in particular uses Burton as his source-book for *The Lover's Melancholy*.

The madness of lovers is a heroic passion, and in Fletcher soldiers are specially prone to it; it is the defeat of wit by passion, and since wit is the standard of excellence, these madmen are legitimate comic butts.

The hero of *The Mad Lover* is a soldier who falls in love with a princess. When he sees her, he is struck dumb, and can only stammer out his love directly in broken words. A mocking phrase which she throws at him about sending her his heart is taken literally, and he seeks ways to win her by making this alarming gift. As nearly all the other characters in the play are in pursuit of the same beauty, while she is in love with the hero's younger brother, the solution is complex: the younger brother feigns death, which cures the Mad Lover, who returns to his trade of soldiering. Other madmen are Shatillon of *The Noble Gentleman*, who believes he is heir to the throne and has delusions of persecution: the Passionate Lord of *The Nice Valour*, who passes through a cycle of exhilaration and anger and is finally cured by a blow on the head; and Shamont, in the same play, a kind of Cyrano de Bergerac, who cannot endure the shadow of an affront, even from the Duke. He is contrasted with a clown who will endure any insult, and he has to be cured by violence. The play is a study upon the point of honour and of madness: every character, from the Duke, who dotes on Shamont, to the clown, is infected. The doctrine that virtue is the true nobility is put in characteristically Cavalier manner by Shamont, after he has been insulted by a flick on the shoulder from the Duke—a blow which he may not return.[19]

> 'If your drum call me, I am vowed to valour;
> But peace shall never know me yours again,
> Because I've lost mine own. I speak to die, sir:
> Would you were gracious that way to take off shame
> With the same swiftness as you pour it on!
> And since it is not in the power of monarchs
> To make a gentleman, which is a substance
> Only begot of merit, they should be careful
> Not to destroy the worth of one so rare,
> Which neither they can make, nor lost, repair.'   2.1.

The Passionate Lord, attended by his fantastic Cupid, is more absurd, but the absurdity has an undernote of horror: the masque and songs designed to cure him are full of obscene horseplay. Shatillon of *The Noble Gentleman* has on the other hand a touching nobility, which is contrasted with the folly of Marine, gulled into the belief that he is a Duke by his witty wanton of a wife. The two delusions of grandeur are set against each other in the scene in which Marine and Shatillon dispute; here the very subtle blend of fantasy and irony is worthy of Don Quixote.

> *Shatillon:* But had not the tenth Lewis a sole daughter?
> *Marine:* I cannot tell.
> *Shatillon:* But answer me directly:
> *Marine:* It is a most seditious question.
> *Shatillon:* Is this your justice?
> *Marine:* I stand for my King.
> *Shatillon:* Was ever heir apparent thus abused?
> I'll have your head for this.   3.1.

In the final scene, Marine, 'deprived' of his false titles, has them proclaimed in defiance by a champion, and Shatillon, rushing in to the defence of the King, though he regards it as another of the plots against his own life, is restored to sanity by the sight of his mistress.

These mad lovers are contrasted with the romantic figure of Charles, the hero of *The Elder Brother*, drawn by love from a melancholy absorption in scholarship to an active display of self-interest and even of swordsmanship. Gallant rivals such as Charles and his younger brother, Memnon and his younger brother in *The Mad Lover*, Valentine and his unknown son in *Monsieur Thomas*, allow of a final contest of nobility which was evidently much to the popular taste. In the last play, the noble theme is set off by the exploits of Tom, who is upbraided by his father for being too tame and by his mistress for being too saucy. After trying to satisfy both, he dresses in his sister's clothes, goes through a mock marriage with a courtier, thus regains the approval of his father and forces his mistress to disclose her real affection. Like some of the other heroes, Tom is only enabled to face his lady's scorn by an infusion of Dutch courage: in these plays, drunkenness, like madness, is always amusing.[20]

On the other hand, woman-haters can be savagely tormented. Goldarino, in the play of that name, is tied up and tortured by the caresses of a group of women: Jacomo in *The Captain* is pursued mercilessly. The peculiar passions of minor characters range from a craving for scholastic argument to a craving for rare dishes. The pursuit of the umbrane's head in *The Little French Lawyer* is the most boring of subplots.

Outside the region of courtship, trickery in love and fantastic madness, the comedies falter. Fletcher's field is the same as Lyly's, though his method is in complete antithesis. *Wit at Several Weapons*, in which a son gulls his father into giving him an allowance, is unsuccessful, because the city manners, copied from Jonson and Middleton, are not rooted in city life; tricks are multiplied in an effort to give sprightliness to a play which is dead at the core. In Fletcher's world, no serious issues should be allowed to intrude: his plays are in holiday mood, and the fantasy of the story is matched by the fragile, indirect motives of the characters. They may be allowed a generous impulse or a freakish whim: very rarely are they permitted to drop the mask or pause in the gay galliard. Madness itself evaporates into nonsense, and crime does not exist.

Yet the holiday mood cannot be achieved without some contact with ordinary life; this in Fletcher arises from his fluent colloquial style. His characters are not defined by personal qualities of speech like Shakespeare's or Jonson's: they speak an unaffected easy verse, which, except in the occasional tirades, is free of rhetorical devices.[21] The broad farce of *The Woman's Prize* may demand a heightened diction and the politer exchanges of *The Wild Goose Chace* a cooler one; but in his comedies, unlike his tragi-comedies, Fletcher is neither ranting nor raucous. His characters do not indulge in sets of wit in the old manner, but in more natural exchanges; except for his simple soldiers and his few fops, no one has any special marks of speech. Repetition and parenthesis, the easy movement of an oiled sentence, give to the comedies their air of lightness and insubstantial elegance: the older style is occasionally glanced at, with a few mocking quotations from *Hamlet* or *The Spanish Tragedy*.

The style of Fletcher's plays and the whole mode in which they were conceived look forward to that of Restoration comedy; they retained their great popularity till the end of the seventeenth century. Their difference from the plays of popular writers like Dekker and Heywood is hardly greater than their difference from the satirists' work of Jonson or Middleton. Here the appeal is both to the sympathy and the ironic disclaimers of a small group of gallants, wits or cavaliers: the standards are those of contemporary good manners. Yet these are not social comedies in the old sense, for there is no feeling of the structure of society in any of them. The comedy of individual relationships is presented within a single group, that of the gentry and their servants. The scene may be England, France or Spain; the City, Court and Country are no longer valid divisions. The individuals who constitute this world have no roots; they are allowed to play out their jests in the anterooms of great houses, with no particular suggestion of day or night, winter or summer, the real flavour of London, Paris or Madrid.

Fletcher's is an inward world; not the world of tragedy, but none the less of *pathos* rather than *ethos*, a world of motive and of sentiment. Protean changes of mood are the method of conducting the story forward; the intrigues are for the most part loosely woven, compared with Chapman's or Jonson's, yet they are skilfully calculated to keep the interest of the audience without absorbing it. The sentiments, tone and air of witty comedy count for more than the action, but the two are in general well balanced.

These are the comedies of a man whose one partially successful tragi-comedy depends on a sense of bewilderment and privation. In *Philaster* the most dramatic scene occurs in the wood where all the characters have lost their way.[22] They stumble about, if not 'in a deep pit of darkness', at least in a dim and pathless gloom. In the comedies gay recklessness and bravado conceal the fact that the path is lost; madness is made a jest, and death itself only a lover's trick to win a lady's hand. Beyond their own wilfulness and wit, Fletcher's heroes have nothing to rely upon. The world they inhabit offers them no support. It is one in which all the comforts and all the judgements reside in private affections and in-dividual standards. The bonds of society are loosed, and the territory of art is circumscribed. It is no longer as wide as England or as high as the stars, but a private chamber or the anteroom of a palace.

THE GHOST AT THE REVELS AND THE GOLDEN AGE RESTORED: JONSON'S MASQUES AND SHAKESPEARE'S LAST PLAYS

1. Jonson's Masques

BEN JONSON'S masques and Shakespeare's final plays, in very different ways, mark the end of the earlier comic tradition. Each exerted his art upon works at once delicate and complex, coloured with the afterglow of that 'old Elizabeth way' which their joint achievement had inevitably eclipsed.

Jonson's masques, elegant confections designed for one performance only and sometimes for royal actors, paradoxically reveal something of that popular writer whom Jonson the Poet Paramount rigorously suppressed. It was the invention of the antemasque, the comic or burlesque introduction to the main masque, which enabled Jonson to bring into his Christmas shows many figures of popular lore and a Shakespearean contrast of plot and subplot, reduced to the tiniest scale.

His earliest entertainments were filled with allegorical forms, in the strictest Italian taste. *The Masque of Blackness* is emblematic: *Hymenæi* celebrates the virtue of Union, Concord or Harmony in the marriage of two young nobles, with all the moral and symbolic weightiness of Chapman's marriage Sestiad in *Hero and Leander*.[1] It was in the following year, 1609, with *The Masque of Queens*, that Jonson discovered the possibilities of the antemasque. The hideous hags who precede the gorgeous vision of the Queen and her ladies may have been conceived through scholarly researches into demonology, as the notes imply: they certainly released Jonson's fancy from the bounds of classical decorum. The more startling the antemasque, the greater its success. The ancient tradition of Misrule was strong, and permitted all kinds of primitive grotesques within the courtly show. An early arrival was the figure of Nobody from the old interludes, dressed in a pair of breeches which came up to his neck, with his hands sticking out of the pockets and a great cap drowning his face. In other masques, the 'four ancient poets', Chaucer, Gower, Skelton and Lydgate, appear; or Skelton and Scogan come on to lead a troop of *sots*, traditional figures from ballads and old revels.[2] There are reminiscences of *England's Joy*, the mythical play on Queen Elizabeth, by then some twenty years old,[3] and themes from Jonson's own plays appear in miniature—alchemy in *Mercury Vindicated*, newsmongering in *News from a new World*. The masque belonged to the season of good will, to Christmas and Shrovetide in chief, or to such occasions of rejoicing as a great wedding, or the coming of an embassy. It celebrated social harmony, either through marriage seen as a social contract, or through the direct idealization of the monarchy as symbol of government and unity.

Jonson expended all his art upon the majesty of *Hymenæi*, the triumph of the marriage god, the Goddess Reason and her servant Order. But his greatest dramatic success was *The Gipsies Metamorphosed* (1621), which was enacted three times in all. The bold familiarities of the gipsies, their canting and impudent fortune-telling, evidently tickled the susceptibilites of James when he heard it on the lips of his favourite, Buckingham, who played one of the chief roles. Such badinage, intolerable in any other, would provide for Buckingham a great opportunity for self-display, and for the royal auditor a delightful mixture of flattery and raillery. It would have been inconceivable at the court of his predecessor.[4]

> 'With you, lucky bird, I begin: let me see
> I aim at the best, and I trow you are he.
> Here's some luck already, if I understand
> The grounds of mine art: here's a gentleman's hand.
> I'll kiss it, for luck's sake. You should, by this line
> Love a horse and a hound, but no part of a swine. . . .
> You are no great wencher, I see by your table,
> Although your *Mons Veneris* says you are able;

You live chaste and single, and have buried your wife,
And mean not to marry, by the line of your life.
Whence he that conjectures your quality, learns
You are an honest good man and have care of your bairns.'

The elegant compliments to the ladies which follow are in a
high style; the great officers of court are jested with freely,
and then a company of clowns come in to have their wenches
dance with the gipsies, and their pockets picked of such
treasures as 'a dainty race of ginger, and a jet ring I had to
draw Jack Straw hither on holydays', 'an enchanted nutmeg,
gilded all over, was enchanted at Oxford for me, to put in my
sweetheart's ale a' mornings'. These treasures being restored
but not to the rightful owners, the gipsies are themselves
transformed into the gorgeous masquers of the final revels.
Yet these, however splendid, seem little more than an epilogue to the gay scene in which all the chief members of the
audience had played their parts. This device of including the
spectators in the antemasque as the gipsies' customers and in
the main masque as their partners made the entire performance a joint one; and the family jokes, directed at
Buckingham's wife and mother, bind the two groups yet
more closely.

> 'Lady, either I am tipsy,
> Or you are to fall in love with a gipsy. . . .
> Your pardon, lady, here you stand,
> If some should judge you by your hand,
> The greatest felon in the land
> Detected. . . .⁵
> I cannot tell you by what arts,
> But you have stolen so many hearts. . .'

This masque was the culmination of more than ten years'
experiment, during which the antemasque steadily grew
in significance. *Love Restored* (1616) is the first in which
the comic induction overshadows the main performance.
The costliness of previous shows had excited protest, and
Jonson neatly counters by opening with the declaration
that there is to be no masque at all. Plutus, disguised as
Cupid, enters and in the accents of a Puritan forbids such
vain toys.

> 'I will have no more masquing: I will not buy a false and fleeting delight so dear: the merry madness of an hour shall not cost me the repentance of an age.'

He is interrupted by the country sprite Robin Goodfellow, who has crept into court by assuming a variety of shapes: first he tried the straight way, then climbed over the wall and took shape as an 'engineer', then as tirewoman, musician, and finally a Puritan feathermaker from Blackfriars:

> 'and in that shape I told them, surely I must come in, let it be opened unto me; but they all made as light of me as my feathers; and wondered how I could be a Puritan, being of so vain a vocation. I answered, We are all masquers sometimes: with that they knocked Hypocrisy o' the pate and made room for a bombard man. . . .'

The goblin finally gets in as a citizen's wife, only to find one of the Blackguard making too free with his placket. He unmasks the false Cupid, the Puritan God of money, and brings in the true god of love 'wrapped up in furs like a Muscovite', whose icy fetters are thawed by the beams of the royal presence. Robin protests:

> 'I am the honest plain country spirit, and harmless: Robin Goodfellow, he that sweeps the hearth and the house clean, riddles for the country maids, and does all their other drudgery, while they are at hot cockles . . .'

Yet this is not truly the Puck of *A Midsummer Night's Dream*, still less the Robin Goodfellow of *Wily Beguiled*: rather it is his ghost, animated enough, but torn from the company and setting in which he naturally lived. The contrast of courtliness and rustic jests is made in the service of the court; and like the country sports of his son, Robert Herrick, Ben Jonson's are too exuberant, too richly loaded with local colouring, to convince outside the realms of spangles and candlelight for which they were designed. Within those realms, however, the revelry is genuine.[6]

These popular sports proved so much to courtly taste that when at the Twelfth Night revels of 1618, *Pleasure Reconciled to Virtue* failed to live up to its name and please, Jonson introduced a new comic antemasque of Welshmen, modelled on the similar Irish Masque of 1613.[7] The humours are

closely studied and Jonson was at pains to learn a little Welsh
or go to those who could provide it. The opening words:

> 'Cossin, I know what belongs to this place symwhat petter than
> yow'

give promise of the full-scale quarrel which afterwards develops.

> 'By got I am out of my tempers terribly well, got forgive me, and
> pyt me in my selves again. . . . Believe it, I will rub and break your
> s'ins for this, I will not come so high as your head but I will take
> your nose in my way, very sufficiently . . . well, before his madestee
> I do yet forgive him now with all my heart and will be revenged
> another time.'

The appeal to James to visit Wales is more respectful but
delightfully bathetic.

> 'Go to, see him once upon a time your own selve, is more good
> mean yow, than is aware of: by got, is very hard, but s'all make yow
> a shestice of peace the first days yow come; and pershance (say
> nothing) knight of the s'ire too: is not Worcesters, nor Pembrokes,
> nor Montgymeries, s'all carry him from yow.'

A dance of Welsh goats, to the sound of Welsh harps,
which leads up to riddling compliments for the King and
Prince of Wales, is the induction to Griffith's grave concluding speech in praise of the Principality:

> '. . . unconquered and most loving liberty, yet was it never mutin-
> ous, and please your majesty, but stout, valiant, courteous, hospitable,
> temperate, ingenious . . . religious preservers of their gentry and
> genealogy as they are zealous and knowing in religion.'

The likeness of such characters to the valiant Fluellen of
Henry V needs no emphasis; they are there to pay tribute to
the King by the simplicity of their attempt to treat him as
one of themselves ('all the water in Wye cannot wash your
Majesty's Welsh plood out of your body', as Fluellen observes to Harry Monmouth), and at the same time to demonstrate their own loyalty and good-heartedness. They are depicted wholly without irony, though not without ridicule;
as in the comical history or the pastoral, the King was put on

a level with his subjects and brought into their company only to acknowledge by this temporary confounding of it the great distance that lay between. Fair Elisa, Queen of Shepherds, had been sung by Spenser in his stateliest verse, and in many an Elizabethan lyric the full contrast of shepherd and monarch had been brought home by apparently disguising the monarch in subject's array. Jonson's many variations on country sports, gypsy lore and the fraternity of the citizens were each a means of producing an atmosphere of revelry and unity, while at the same time subtly manifesting just those social distinctions which were ostensibly being overriden. The familiar antemasque served always as preparation for the magnificent ceremonial of the masque proper.

At the court of James, the royal family were more actively engaged in the masquing than ever Elizabeth had been. She would descend from the dais to join the concluding dance, but Anne of Denmark appeared on the scene leading the troop of masquers, and Prince Henry led the tilters at his Barriers. Nor were such sports confined only to Whitehall and the Christmas season; like Elizabeth, James went on progress, and at country entertainments for the King, Jonson introduced the rural sport of tilting at the Quintain, performed by followers of Robin Hood and concluded with a bride-ale; or a troop of mechanicals, including such figures as Maul the freemason, Dresser the Plumber and Beater the Morter-man to give a dance. In the masque at Kenilworth, there appeared upon his hobby horse the ghost of old Captain Cox, who had led the mummers there before Elizabeth in the local antemasque to *The Princely Pleasure of Kenilworth*, more than fifty years before. This *Masque of Owls* significantly recalls the old freemason, a famous actor and leader of the Coventry town players, whose collection of plays, ballads and romances and whose passion for swordplay and acting would seem to epitomize the popular dramatic sports of the 'old Elizabeth way'.[8] When Captain Cox had actually appeared at Kenilworth, Shakespeare was a boy of eleven, living in a near-by country town; it was in the world of Captain Cox's mumming that he grew up. Now, ten years after his death, Ben Jonson revived Captain Cox's ghost to lead the revels of 'six owls out of an ivy bush'—that is, six bankrupts in hiding. These are all characters whose day is past, and among them is a maker of Coventry blue thread, who laments that with the passing of the Coventry plays, his trade is out of fashion.

> '. . . undone
> By the thread he has spun:
> For since the wise town
> Has let the sports down
> Of may game and morris,
> For which he right sorry is;
> Where their maids and their makes
> At dancing and wakes,
> Had their napkins and posies
> And the wipers for their noses
> And their smocks all bewrought
> With his thread that they bought,
> It now lies on his hands . . .'

Captain Cox's ghost at the Kenilworth revels is a more poignant symbol than Robin Goodfellow, for he embodies a still living memory. Here is the lament of Hamlet: 'For O, for O, the hobby horse is forgot'.

In London, on the other hand, the characters presented were very much alive. *The Masque of Augurs*, a more dignified variant of the gipsies' fortune-telling, which followed next year, was preceded by the citizens' antemasque of Notch and Slug, who,

'hearing that the Christmas invention was dry at court, and that neither the King's poet nor his architect had wherewithal to entertain a baboon of quality, nor scarce the Welsh ambassador, if he should come there',

conveyed their masque from St. Katherine's Dock and landed in a lighter with the mistress of their local inn, the Three Dancing Bears, and with the whole masque of the bearward, John Urson and his performing animals, who 'dance to present the sign, and the bearward to stand for the signpost'.

The most lively of all these popular incursions, however, was *The Masque of Christmas* (1616), not a masque proper at all, but a parody of a mummer's play, where the revellers enter to the sound of drums, led by the figure of Christmas.

'Why, gentlemen, do you know what you do? ha! would you keep me out? Christmas, old Christmas, Christmas of London and Captain Christmas? Pray you, let me be brought before my Lord Chamberlain, I'll not be answered else: *Tis merry in hall when beards wag all*: I have seen the time you wished for me, for a merry Christmas: and now you have me, they would not let me in: *I must come another time!* a good jest, as if I could come more than once a year.'

Though he comes out of Pope's Head Alley, Christmas claims to be 'as good a Protestant as any in my parish', and after his ten children are led in, he forbids entrance to 'one o' Friday Street' and 'neither of the Fish Streets, admit not a man! they are not Christmas creatures: fish and fasting days, foh!' Venus, however, a deaf tirewoman from Pudding Lane, is allowed, although she admits she is 'a fishmonger's daughter',[9] and Cupid, her son, 'prentice in Love Lane to a bugle-maker, leads the masquers 'on a string' in his 'prentice's coat and flat cap; according to Venus, he is a promising actor.

'I could have had money enough for him, an I would have been tempted and have let him out by the week to the King's Players. Master Burbage has been about and about with me and so has old Master Hemings too. . . .'

Brought forward, and loudly encouraged by his mother—''Tis a good child, speak out: hold up thy head, Love' the little 'prentice, in spite of his previous good performance at 'the Warmoll Quest', forgets his part and has to be hustled off.

Here Jonson's own London pride and his allegorical tastes combine to produce a scene at once familiar and fanciful, and a very different Venus and Cupid from the stately creatures of his earlier masques.[10] Christmas's rout represented Good Cheer: Misrule bears with him a rope, cheese and a basket, New Year's Gift gingerbread and marchpane: with Wassail, Baby-cake and the rest, they are introduced by Christmas under their citizen's names. Misrule is Tom of Bosom's Inn, and New Year's Gift is Clem Waspe of Honey Lane.

These revels of London appeared in the same year as Jonson's play *The Devil is an Ass*, where the old moral play returned in a new guise. Increasingly in his later work Jonson drew upon such fancies, as the ancient fashions grew more and more remote and a bleaker world came in.[11] He could not reconcile himself to his own old age, and the growing sense that his work was itself outmoded. The embittering quarrel with Inigo Jones over these very masques colours his writing. In *The Fortunate Isles* he introduces for the antemasque the old poet Skelton, and Scogan the jester leading a crew of fantastics.[12]

> *Merefool* (a melancholic student): But wrote he like a gentleman?
> *Johphiel:* In rhyme, fine tinkling rhyme, and flowered verse,
>   With now and then some sense. And he was paid for't,
>   Regarded and rewarded: which few poets
>   Are nowadays.
> *Merefool:* And why?
> *Johphiel:* 'Cause every dabbler
>   In rhyme is thought the same.

In one of the very latest shows, *Neptune's Triumph*, the Poet appears in his own person to provide the comic antemasque, in a dialogue with the royal Master Cook. The classic comparison of these two trades, which Jonson had used gaily enough before, has here a touch of bitterness.[13] The Poet introduces himself as 'the most unprofitable of the King's servants, sir, the Poet. A kind of Christmas ingine: one that is used at least once a year, for a trifling instrument of wit or so' whereas the Cook, in a tremendous encomium of his own art, proves it identical with poetry: 'A good poet differs nothing at all from a Master Cook.' Both have to please those ticklish ladies, Expectation and Curiosity: variety is what is required, and it is the Cook who produces the characters for the antemasque, the Poet ironically objecting to this as 'mere bye works and at best outlandish nothings'.[14] The contents of his pot furnish the dancers; a fine laced mutton (a prostitute), a poulterer's wife who 'plays the coney with eggs in belly', and various court figures, at whom Jonson tilts almost in his older manner. The Poet accepts the antemasque in the terms used in the forty-year-old masques of Lyly:

> I conceive
> The way of your *gallimaufrey*

and in this wry-mouthed jest the Cook finally triumphs:

> The broth's the best on't,
> And that's the dance: the stage here is the charger.
> And brother poet, though the serious part
> Be yours, yet envy not the cook his art.

The sacred term of Art is now applied to brothmaking.

In his masques Jonson was given to introducing two figures who appeared to be identical and who claimed the same identity.[15] Truth and Opinion, who dispute at the Barriers following *Hymenaei*, were 'so like attired as they could by no note be distinguished' although of course they are natural opposites. The two Cupids who dispute in *A Challenge at Tilt*: Plutus disguised as Cupid and the true Cupid of *Love Restored* are also in appearance exact counterparts: the Eros and Anteros of *Love's Welcome at Bolsover* are distinguished only by wearing a garland of roses for the king, lilies for the queen. In these opposed yet inseparable pairs may be seen a symbol of the popular comedy itself and the popular comedy as Jonson uses it. His mirror-image or reflexion is here the antithesis of what it resembles: the costly, gorgeous setting into which these humble sports were now caught up preserved them only like bees in amber.

ii. Shakespeare's Last Plays

Almost before Ben Jonson was launched on his series of court masques. Shakespeare's dramatic career was over. His four last plays, *Pericles, Cymbeline, The Winter's Tale, The Tempest*, can be dated fairly exactly between 1607, the date of *Pericles*, and 1611, when *The Tempest* was performed at court. The unity of theme within these plays, and their beauty and power in depicting a realm on the other side of tragedy, 'beyond hope and despair', has been sufficiently emphasized within the last few years. The wide variety of interpretations, ranging from the anthropological to the mystical, have not prevented a general agreement that here is perhaps the most characteristic and inimitable manifestation of Shakespeare's dramatic art.[16]

Yet the contemporary history of these plays differs widely.

196

Only one of them enjoyed an overwhelming popular success, and that the one which modern critics would regard as the weakest. *Pericles* may not be entirely from Shakespeare's hand—it was not printed in the First Folio, and on the grounds of style much of it has been rejected. Ben Jonson singled it out for his special disapproval, and in the *Ode to Himself* he considers the greatest insult he can throw at the critics who condemned his own play is that they would be satisfied with this:

> 'No doubt some mouldy tale
> Like *Pericles*, and stale
> As the shrieve's crusts and nasty as his fish—
> Scraps out of every dish
> Thrown forth and raked into the common tub,
> May keep up the Play-club.'

It was performed again and again: Betterton revived it after the Restoration: it was the first play to provoke by its success the issue of a narrative version, 'the book of the film', so to speak: [17] and five editions of the quarto text appeared, the last being in 1635. None of the other three plays has left any records of particular success: though *Cymbeline* and *The Winter's Tale* were both performed before Charles I. *The Tempest* was rewritten by Dryden and Davenant after the Restoration, with characteristic embellishments; [18] in which form it met with the approval of Pepys. The last three plays may well have been composed for performance at the private theatre in Blackfriars, which Shakespeare's company took over as their second playhouse in 1608: the delicacy of the verse, complexity and sophistication of the plots, and the close connexion with the new fashionable tragi-comedy of Beaumont and Fletcher suggest that they were designed for a select audience and indoor staging. On the other hand, Shakespeare did not abandon the public theatre; for *Henry VIII* was clearly a popular play, and it was the discharge of cannon at a performance in 1613 which set fire to the Globe and burnt it down. So ended, not unfittingly, the scene of Shakespeare's first triumphs.

The popular qualities of *Pericles* are easy to distinguish. The story is one of the traditional sort; it is actually found in

Gower's *Confessio Amantis,* and by bringing on the figure of Chaucer's friend to act as Presenter, the play is given the status of an old wives' tale.[19] Shakespeares' maieutic method here, as in *Hamlet,* forced him back for experiments upon hackneyed old material.

> 'To sing a song that old was sung,
> From ashes ancient Gower is come. . . .'

In Gower the story is told to illustrate the difference between lawful and unlawful love; and this theme remains in the play. The contrast between the daughter of Antiochus, who opens the play, and the daughter of Pericles, who concludes it, the one guilty of incest, and dramatically consumed by fire from heaven, the other preserving her chastity in a brothel, is a contrast of the old-fashioned moral sort. In the opening scene, Pericles comes to woo the daughter of Antiochus, and is set to guess a riddle; the scene is decorated with the severed hands of those princes who had preceded him in this dangerous enterprise, and who forfeited their lives by failure. The emblematic quality of such a fairy-tale scene cannot but recall the tale of Portia and the three caskets, in Shakespeare's earliest tragi-comedy; and having evaded the dangers of this trap, Pericles meets other symbolic dangers in the hatred of Antiochus, the shipwreck, and the tourney where he appears like a wandering knight out of the old romances, with emblematic device upon his shield. Pericles' adventures, which constitute the unity of this rambling story, show a man who, without being hardened or developing any false stoicism, is enabled to withstand the worst blows of Fortune. He preserves his humanity, his capacity for suffering, at the same time as he preserves his control. Shakespeare may have renamed his hero—who in the original story is Apollonius—from Pericles of Athens, one of the examples of Christian patience.[20] On the stage, the play is intensely moving, and centres entirely on Pericles: Marina, his daughter, a figure of angelic rather than human interest, is significant chiefly in relation to him: and Thaisa his wife is more shadowy still. Shakespeare's Pericles, whose journey is a mixture of an Odyssey and a Pilgrim's Progress, appears fully only in two scenes: the scene of the second storm at sea, where Marina is born, and Thaisa is thought to die; and the scene in which he is reunited with his lost child. There are few more exciting moments in all the plays than the beginning of Act III, scene I, when after two acts of emblematic postures in old-fashioned jogtrot verse:

> 'Unto thy value I will mount myself
> Upon a courser whose delightful steps
> Shall make the gazer joy to see him tread.
> Only my friend, I yet am unprovided
> Of a pair of bases'   2.1.

the authentic and unmistakable voice of Shakespeare is heard.

> 'Thou god of this great vast, rebuke these surges,
> Which wash both heaven and hell: and thou that hast
> Upon the winds command, bind then in brass,
> Having called them from the deep! O still
> Thy deafening dreadful thunders: gently quench
> Thy nimble sulphurous flashes!'   3.1.

Pericles, however, is fully characterized; he is more than a mouthpiece for poetry. The stifled control of his farewell to the corpse of Thaisa, who to placate the superstition of the sailors must 'overboard straight':

> 'A terrible childbed hast thou had, my dear:
> No light, no fire . . .'

is part of a large acceptance. There is only one cry, when Lychorida brings 'all that is left living of your queen':

> 'O you gods,
> Why do you make us love your goodly gifts,
> And snatch them straight away?'

before he turns to the child:

> 'Even at the first, thy loss is more than can
> Thy portage quit with all thou canst find here.
> Now the good gods throw their best eyes upon 't.'

The treachery which attempts the destruction of Marina leaves him stunned: and their reunion at Mitylene shows him a prey to the melancholy of grief, speechless and dishevelled.

The sureness of touch with which the revelation is made depends upon the simplicity of the writing—so like yet unlike the flatness of the opening scenes:

> 'A condition of complete simplicity,
> Costing not less than everything.'

'You are like something that. . . . What countrywoman? Here, of these shores?' to which Marina answers:

> 'No, nor of any shores.'

The magic of the scene, issuing in the unheard music which Pericles alone detects at its ending, is very close to the magic of an old wives' tale; and the scene of union with Thaisa which follows might have come straight from an old romance, with its bandying of tokens and its final moral epilogue from ancient Gower, who commends the virtue of patience to the spectators with additional and cheering information that Marina's betrayers, like the daughter of Antiochus, have been consumed with fire. But the fairy-tale, without ceasing to be a fairy-tale, and the Globe's best getpenny, has by this time been transformed. In Bacon's phrase it 'gives some satisfaction to the mind of man in those points wherein the nature of things doth deny it'.

Cymbeline, another fairy-tale, centres not upon a prince but on a princess. The sophisticated artlessness of its construction [21] includes a wicked stepmother, an 'Italian fiend' and two stolen children: set in the far-off times, it contains a mixture of many ages. Shakespeare, who had an acute sense of history, must have been aware of what he was doing when he made a Machievel, 'bold Iachimo, Sienna's brother' lead the troops of Augustus Cæsar. Elsewhere the gods descend to a condemned cell, where the rough jailers have been trying their Cockney wit on the prisoner in a mixture of good will and insensibility. Poisons, disguises and coincidences lie so thick in this play that the final scene opens out like a series of chinese boxes, each discovery lying within the disclosures of its predecessor.

Yet within this enchanted kingdom genuine passions stir. The remorse of Posthumus, the anguish of Imogen, the delicate lust of Iachimo are more rarified because they suffer no intermixture with mundane and heavy commonplace. They are 'all air and fire'. Each character may for a moment step forward from his simple, traditional role, to speak with the voice of individual but as it were disembodied passion, before sinking back into quiescence. They may actually disappear for long stretches, as do Posthumus, Iachimo and in the last act Imogen herself. Shakespeare, like Jonson earlier, is taking the puppets out of the box, and letting the audience see him do it. Yet 'the art itself is nature'. It is essential to the play that Posthumus, writhing as Iachimo injects his poison, or Imogen, silent for the most part in her grief but with one very human flash of self-pity and rage,[22] or Iachimo gloating and yet restraining himself, as he looks at Imogen or goads Posthumus, should have the material vividness of dreams. The tragic agonies are felt by the audience, even as they are witnessed, to be but 'the baseless fabric of a vision', yet the visionary quality only deepens the momentary effect; and each character is complete in its inner consistency. The momentary revelation does not falsify what has gone before: this is the distinction between Shakespeare's virtuosity and Fletcher's casuistry.

The most difficult scene for a modern audience is one depending on disguise. When Imogen finds the headless body of Cloten, her would-be ravisher, dressed in her husband's garments, and thinks that he has been murdered and she betrayed, the effect is so shocking as to be grotesque. Posthumus himself, often maligned as credulous and ignoble in his vengeance, though a minor figure is quite convincing. He is first of all an exile: through Imogen's eyes he has been seen diminishing, as the ship carries him away. His concealed need for reassurance, rising from his own 'unworthiness', makes Iachimo's attempt the secret mission of his own fears, though not in any doubt of Imogen. It is stressed even in the opening scene that Imogen is his 'queen', owing him obedience as his wife but claiming his allegiance as the heiress of Britain. The delicate double relation is exquisitely solved in their scenes together. Nor are his secret fears without counterpart in her: she at once puts down his brutal order for her death to 'some jay of Italy'. His return to fight for his own country—and Imogen's country—in the disguise of a common soldier is proffered by him as some sort of retribution for his madness, and the final discovery that the mountaineers are princes, the condemned prisoner husband to a princess, and the little page Fidele the one who holds the key to all the riddles may result in an ending that is the despair of the modern playwright,[23] but which was the beginning of a new dramatic form, the Jacobean tragi-comedy. On internal probability, it seems to me likeliest that Shakespeare led the way for Beaumont and Fletcher, and that his play preceded theirs.[24]

The Winter's Tale, based on a novel by Greene, that one of Shakespeare's predecessors who had most derided his early success, proclaims by its title that it is linked with the old romances. It was 'a winter's tale' that Madge told to Frolic and Fantastic in Peele's dream-play; such marvellous stories were still popular on the stage, and even the ancient gods and goddesses were enjoying a notable popular success at the Red Bull with Heywood's play on The Golden Age, which was to be followed by the Silver, Brazen and Iron Ages. The theme of The Winter's Tale, like all Shakespeare's final plays, is a variant upon The Golden Age Restored. In this play, tragedy is more nearly approached, in the madness of Leontes' jealousy and the suffering of Hermione; the parallels with both Othello and King Lear have often been noted.

Leontes' jealousy—a form of the disease of melancholy, as the Elizabethans would have recognized[25]—makes its onset with great violence, at the moment when he *sees* his wife and Polixenes in affectionate and familiar converse. The images that rise in his mind belong to the world of the brothel in which Marina was incarcerated; he includes with-in himself the power of torment which circumstance im-posed in the earlier play. He assumes that his view is the general one.

> Leontes: How came't, Camillo,
> That he did stay?
> Camillo: At the good Queen's entreaty.
> Leontes: 'At the Queen's' be't. 'Good' should be pertinent,
> But so it is, it is not. Was this taken
> By any understanding pate but thine?

For thy conceit is soaking, will draw in
More than the common blocks. Not noted, is't,
But of the finer natures, by some severals
Of headpiece extraordinary?

1.2.

This is ironic, for he has already declared that everybody is
whispering and gesticulating about him: 'Sicilia is a so-
forth'. The utter inaccessibility of Leontes' mind is recognized by Hermione.

'Mine integrity
Being counted falsehood, shall, as I express it,
Be so received.'

3.2.

It is useless to plead 'Not guilty' in a court where he is both
prosecutor and judge in his own cause; and unlike Paulina's,
who expresses exactly what she feels about the treatment of
her mistress, Hermione's defence is submission.

'Sir,
You speak a language that I understand not;
My life stands in the level of your dreams,
Which I'll lay down.'

3.2.

Not the word of the oracle but the death of his child kills the
madness in Leontes, which departs as suddenly as it had
arrived. This brief study cuts deeper than *Othello*, where the
hero had to be roused by the unnaturally clever tempting of
Iago. The very motivelessness which the fairy tale allows
produces a new kind of inward verisimilitude, for the horror
of Leontes' imagination is that of the truly private world,
the 'small circle of pain within the skull'.

In the original story, Hermione died and was not resur-
rected: in Shakespeare's version, the statue scene 'fills her
grave up'. Paulina commands Leontes:

'It is required,
You do awake your faith.'

5.3.

And, though without a word, the statue descends, the dead
returns, and Leontes has but three words:

'O, she's warm.'

203

As Lear regains Cordelia, 'a soul in bliss', Leontes regains both his wife and daughter, his counsellor Camillo and friend Polixenes, and in Polixenes' son, his own dead child Mamilius. The fairy-tale happiness of this ending is separated from the earlier part not only by sixteen years and the Chorus of Time but by the Arcadian love-making of Florizel and Perdita, and the cheats of Autolycus, the kind of country tricks which the popular stage still enjoyed.[26]

The Winter's Tale is the most audacious of the final plays; Leontes outgoes the melancholy jealous young men of Beaumont and Fletcher: he had indeed features of the stage tyrant,[27] and in this play the possibility of a genuine tragicomedy is fully realized, through the deceptive innocence of the fairy-tale. Yet Perdita's daffodils take the winds of March with beauty, she dances like a wave of the sea in her rustic finery; the world of the senses and of the seasons is here with a country freshness that the sophisticated pastoral of Jonson and Fletcher never achieved. Act IV of *The Winter's Tale* may resemble a masque, but it is not a masque; it is Hermione's own blood that looks out in Perdita's cheeks, as the last part of the scene makes clear.

The Tempest comes even closer to the masque, and it has sometimes been thought to be a wedding celebration for the marriage of Elizabeth of Bohemia. It has also been recognized as an allegory of Shakespeare's own history, as closely following the pattern of Italian tragi-comedy, even to the setting and the characters; it reflects the story of Sir Thomas Gates' wreck in the *Sea Venture* upon the islands of Bermuda; it has close affinities with several tales of magician princes in Spanish and German, and with Italian history. In fact, the multiplicity of sources and origins for *The Tempest* is baffling; and no less baffling is the quality of the experience transmitted.

The central character, Prospero, dominates the play to such an extent that the other characters may be said to be his creations. Miranda is of his begetting, Ariel and Caliban of his taming: the others are all absolutely in his power. The nature of his power is a subject of some disagreement: to those who see him as 'That four-flusher Prospero', and to those who see him as Shakespeare, breaking his magic wand, might be opposed the humble Elizabethan playgoer, who might have seen him as the equivalent of the Merry devil of Edmonton, John a Kent and John a Cumber (if they liked benevolent magicians and winters' tales) or as one of the breed of Duke Altifront and Duke Hercules, in *The Fleire* and *The Fawne* (if they enjoyed a dream of despotism). Dowden saw Prospero as a man closely akin to Pericles; one who 'displays in his grave harmony of character, his self-mastery, his calm validity of will, his sensitiveness to wrong, his unfaltering justice . . . a certain abandonment, a remoteness from the common joys and sorrows of the world'. But where Pericles has only sufferance, Prospero has power and is himself the ruling God of the island kingdom. Certainly in the two plotters, Antonio and Sebastian, the common evil of the world is very precisely realized. The smart innuendoes with which they lead up to the proposal of murder of the sleeping king are much more 'Machievellian' than Macbeth ever was.

> *Antonio:* Noble Sebastian,
>   Thou let'st thy fortune sleep—die rather: wink'st
>   Whiles thou art waking.
> *Sebastian:* Thou dost snore distinctly:
>   There's meaning in thy snores.
>   2.1.

Yet it is the fairy world, the 'brave new world' which Miranda forsakes for the crown of Naples that took the audience of the day, and which was most freely imitated on the Caroline stage. Caliban is a prototype for the witch's son in many a tragi-comedy; and Ariel's songs led to the play later being refashioned as an opera. The 'sea sorrow' is transmuted in the delicate atmosphere of the island where invisible music plays in the air. The idyll is not spattered with blood, though swords are drawn; and the garments of the mariners who were shipwrecked seem 'fresher than before'. Prospero's magic turns out to be a form of disguise: 'lie there, my art', and his magic powers are divested: while he appears at the end with rapier and plumed hat 'as I was sometime Milan'.

The Tempest can be read in almost as many ways as *Hamlet*; and therefore it is adapted for all comers. It is almost

indefinitely variable; it can be staged like a pantomime, or enacted on a plain scene. This Protean power, in part the gift
of the age, was yet Shakespeare's special endowment; and the
mastery of it was for him the triumph of art. In this play, the
classical unities are for once strictly observed, and the full
resources of the theatre, in dancing, songs and spectacle, are
certainly utilized; but the solvent is Shakespeare's power of
language, the mingling of concentration and restraint which
can sum up the play in a song.

> 'Those are pearls that were his eyes:
> Nothing of him that doth fade,
> But doth suffer a sea-change
> Into something rich and strange.'

The final note is one of discovery (and this is perhaps where
the sea-voyagers become relevant in more than a topical
sense). Miranda discovers more than is obvious when she
sees a brave new world of goodly people in a group that includes Antonio and Sebastian: they at least discover one who
can master them and yet not betray; as Gonzalo's summary
proclaims

> 'in one voyage
> Did Claribel her husband find at Tunis:
> And Ferdinand her brother found a wife
> Where he himself was lost: Prospero his dukedom
> In a poor isle; *and all of us ourselves*
> *When no man was his own.*'

5.1.

CHAPTER XII

ELIZABETHAN COMEDY IN THE THEATRE' OF TODAY

1. The Open Stage

THE nature of theatre in England has undergone radical changes in the second half of the twentieth century, when new physical structures reflect not only new technologies, but, even more significantly, the effects of social transformation on the theatre as social institution and social framework. New custom has broken up the old models, and national tradition has been modified by international developments.

The Elizabethan open stages offered a model viable in some respects, so that the new buildings enable Elizabethan plays to be put on in a live theatre more akin to the original playhouses than anything that has appeared in the intervening three hundred years; yet the new theatre is more eclectic in its origins. Tanya Moiseiwitsch's theatre at Stratford, Ontario, and its various derivations in USA and England, the Mermaid and the new Stratford stage, with their deep aprons and the use of exits and entrances through the audience, have united performers and spectators in full joint participation; but the audience itself is unified, being entirely or almost entirely seated in a single half moon or a continuous and steeply raked amphitheatre, in the manner of the ancient world.[1] Not only is there interaction between the two sides of the house, but the audience are regarded as a single unity, not a hierarchy of groundlings and gentry. When it was proposed at the World Shakespeare Congress of 1971 that the Globe Theatre should be reconstructed on its original site, even the most dedicated scholars were quick to point out that this would have only an educational interest. A usable theatre would need to be modified, not only to conform to modern safety regulations but to give an acceptable seating and acting area. Walter Hodges suggests that it should carry a glass roof, a stage capable of being sunk or raised, and that it should remodel the second Globe.

Although the new theatres were built for classic repertory, revivals have been selective. Shakespeare has more than maintained his predominance, so that all his plays have been put into production, many of them now reappearing on the boards for the first time since the closing of his theatre; the full sequence of English histories has several times been staged, and productions have been taken far afield, to Moscow, Tokyo and the Antipodes.

Other Elizabethan dramatists have been revived only sporadically; whenever this has occurred, tragedy and tragic farce or 'black' comedy has proved the most popular form. The Royal Shakespeare Company has revived, very notably, Marlowe's *Jew of Malta* and *Faustus*, Tourneur's *The Revenger's Tragedy*, Middleton's and Ford's tragedies have been seen, the Mermaid has produced *The Witch of Edmonton*, and the National Theatre recently staged Heywood's *A Woman Killed with Kindness*. Against this list can be set notable performances of Jonson's *The Alchemist* and *Bartholomew Fair*; some of Marston's plays, including *The Dutch Courtesan* and their joint play *Eastward Ho!*, have been seen at the Mermaid; an occasional performance of Green's *Friar Bacon and Friar Bungay*, or Dekker's *The Shoemaker's Holiday* has revived Elizabethan romance. But considering the original predominance of comedy, it has enjoyed only a limited revival.

Within the Shakespearean repertory itself, the outstanding successes have been the problem plays, formerly thought undramatic, of which *Troilus and Cressida* has proved much the most pungent. The romances and romantic comedies have been 'darkened' for presentation, while new horrific aspects of the tragedies are sometimes stressed; on other occasions, they have been treated to stress the 'black comedy' inherent in *Hamlet* or *King Lear*. 'Black' comedy is considered more profound and more realistic than tragedy because the heroic glories of tragedy disappear. The setting has often been continuous, or located by a few properties, whose symbolic character recalls such Elizabethan stage emblems as the throne or the flowery bank. The Council table of the English history plays, as staged by the Royal Shakespeare Company in the fourth centenary year, was finally battered to pieces to symbolize the disintegration of the reign of King Richard III, while *King Henry V* was given a sardonic comment by wheeling onto the field of Agincourt objects bearing a strong resemblance to Mother Courage's waggon.

The technical powers of modern lighting and hydraulic stage machinery allow to a relatively bare scene an unlocalized, rapidly changing, dream-like quality; action remains continuous, and the audience is not subjected to breaks or intervals. Rapid shifts of tone, lighting and perspective give the feeling of transformation and of a dream journey, not unlike that which children may get from riding on a roundabout at a fair. This accords with the Shakespearean imagination, as described by Theseus— the poet's eye glancing from heaven to earth, bodying forth the forms of things unknown, giving to airy nothing a local habitation and a name. It is fitly embodied by the subtle and flexible effects of changing lights, of suggested and vaguely adumbrated places, which evoke the audience's own fancy, while stimulating half-forgotten associations. In all this, the effect of other media—cinema and television —becomes pervasive, whilst the subliminal techniques of sales promotion are not neglected.

The classical London repertory theatres make full use of current and traditional Elizabethan scholarship. Programme notes may cite the latest critical views upon any play, social historians and art historians will be consulted for expert advice, but no longer with the aim of a Macready, to reproduce the authentic settings of an earlier age. An informed eclecticism seeks to interpret the Elizabethan version, translating it into terms readily apprehended by a modern audience, but also providing new insights for those who may have seen several versions of the same play. Every production must differ from the last production; nothing remains of the habit-governing tradition which led Godfrey Tearle to 'block' the temptation scene in *Othello* with the words "My father stood *here* for this speech. What was good enough for my father is good enough for you!" The classical approach—as it used to be practised at its sternest by the *Comédie Française*—has virtually disappeared within the new theatre, where change and mobility are characteristic not only of each presentation but of the nature of dramatic illusion itself.

In some modern plays actors may be 'planted' in the audience; at Stratford and elsewhere, actors may toss flowers to the audience, or run through the auditorium, 'exploding' the play[2] and, on occasions, shaking hands as they pass up the gangway. In some of the plays of Genet, the audience have replaced the chorus; participation reaches its limits in 'happenings' and in the activities of the Roundhouse. Mobility constantly verges on demonstrations, which the Elizabethan theatre dreaded; yet a disturbance in the theatre might today act as a valuable means of publicity. The 'theatre crowd' have never been as dangerous as the 'football crowd'.

Elizabethan festivity, though sometimes it got out of control, contained at least an element of ceremony and dignity; the sheep-shearing scene in *The Winter's Tale* originally presented Perdita as a Summer Queen, in splendid dress; the pop festival that enlivened the Royal Shakespeare Company's production of 1969 presented essentially the groundlings' version of this delicate scene, translated into modern terms. This was *The Winter's Tale* as Ben Jonson might have seen it—naive, a drollery. Trevor Nunn's intention may have been to fall in with that most popular image of renovation, Jan Kott's study of *Shakespeare, Our Contemporary*—a book introduced by Nunn's colleague Peter Brook with the words

> Shakespeare is a contemporary of Kott, Kott is a contemporary of Shakespeare . . . It is Poland that in our time has come closest to the tumult, the danger, the intensity, the imaginativeness and the daily involvement with the social process that made life so horrible, subtle and ecstatic to an Elizabethan.
>
> Preface to *Shakespeare our Contemporary*, London, 1964, pp. x-xi

It is not difficult to imagine what Marxists make of Duke Vincentio.

II. The Sociology of Shape Changing

The lighting bridge and the cat walk were allowed as part of the scene in what is probably the most successful modern comedy staging of Shakespeare, Peter Brook's 1970 production of *A Midsummer Night's Dream*. This took place in a bare white space—it was described by one critic as being 'staged in a gymnasium'—and depended entirely on the verve, agility and team work of the actors. The performance was introduced by some words from Brook's book, *The Empty Space*:

> Once the theatre could begin as magic; magic at the sacred festival or magic as the footlights came up. Today it is the other way round . . . We must open our empty hands and shew that there is really nothing up our sleeves. Only then can we begin.

Not only was there nothing up their sleeves but sometimes nothing under their feet; Hermia delivered one of her angry speeches suspended from a trapeze, where she had been put by Lysander (or Demetrius?) much as Peer Gynt puts his mother Aase on the mill-house roof.

The stage was bare, the costumes vaguely reminiscent of the *commedia dell'arte*, the principle not unlike that of the Expressionist stagings of the early 1920s. There was no attempt at illusion, yet the spirit of gaiety and of carnival presided in all the slightly dangerous wildness that the Elizabethans associated with summer festivities, whether May Day or Midsummer. Oberon shooting down on a rope, the garlanded Bottom borne shoulder high by outsize fairies, embodied the spirit denounced by Stubbes in his attack on May Games:

> . . . then march this heathen company towards the church and churchyard, their pipers piping, their drummers thundering, their stumps dancing, their bells jangling, their handkerchiefs swinging about their heads like madmen, their hobbyhorses and other monsters skirmishing through the throng.

as they move towards their 'summer halls, their bowers, arbours and banquetting houses,' where they spend all day and as Stubbes adds, 'peradventure all night too.'[3]

Brook revived—in a totally different mode—the festivity

behind this play, in a more authentic manner than could have been achieved by a stage filled with plastic gnomes, or a Puck who, like the infant Ellen Terry, rose through a trap while seated on a mushroom.

A Midsummer Night's Dream combines courtly and popular sports, and the bringing in of May to bless the bridal. It is often thought to have been written for special performance at a noble wedding, though there is no agreement about the parties. The adapting of their repertory to meet a given occasion was a speciality of Elizabethan players; in one sense, the more familiar and conventional the material, the more witty would be its precise and apt 'application'. (This is precisely what is happening on a larger time scale today). The City pageant-mongers might bring out their old pasteboard figures of King David and Arion for the Lord Mayor's Show, if the Lord Mayor happened to be called Harper.[4] It does not seem likely that a professional troupe would get up a play for one performance only, but by adding a few lines or a dumb show, by suitable costumes and 'blocking' they could fit many occasions neatly.

However, the association of plays with particular festivities and localities was traditional; the popular town players of early Tudor times had performed their play at given seasons only; the Court itself expected a Masque on Twelfth Night, perhaps also at Shrovetide. One of the most influential books to have appeared of recent years, C. L. Barber's *Shakespeare's Festive Comedy* (Princeton, 1959) relates Shakespeare's romantic comedies and his *King Henry IV* to the traditions of court and country, and to such earlier half-emergent forms between 'game' and full drama as Nashe's *Summer's Last Will and Testament*. Barber's work clarified the Shakespearean form, which must not, of course, be confused with the matrix of playing from which it sprang. The pretty and ceremonious wooing games, seen especially in *Love's Labour's Lost* as language games, were bound up with love poetry of the time, and with the other arts.

In the public 'game place' or 'playing place',[5] at least during the sixteenth century, plays alternated with other festive activities, with fencing, bear baiting, juggling, singing contests. An actor might set up a small theatre in the garden of his house at Newington Butts, then in a pleasant country neighbourhood, but this could not have much more floor space than is given to a modern floor-show[6]. At Court, as the setting differed, so would the tone of the playing.

It has been suggested that the regulation of Elizabethan theatres was tightened up very decidedly in 1597 and that this date marks the beginning of a professional London theatre for a few selected troupes[7]. If so, most of Shakespeare's early comedy belongs to the era of flexibility and 'open' playing. The new phase almost coincides with the arrival of Ben Jonson as a playwright. From the beginnings, however, Shakespeare enjoyed a sense of perspective, an ability to include elements of parody and of irony in his romance, especially in his mockery of love games (from Portia's sketches of her wooers to Viola's teasing of Olivia). This may have made possible the very much enlarged degree of adaptation and collaboration, as well as the much freer 'applications' which his plays are found to tolerate from later generations.

The modern theatre, still more the modern drama centre, serves a multiplicity of interests, combining perhaps a lecture theatre, a playhouse, restaurant, drama school, bookshop and tourist club; such for example, is the Centre for Visual and Performing Arts at Ottawa, which lacks only resident players. On a smaller scale, many university drama departments, such as the Northcott Theatre at the University of Exeter and the various drama centres in the Midlands, witness not only to an attempt to integrate the arts, but also to new alliances with sociology and psychology, as well as drama's traditional rôle in education.

Shakespeare's comic rôles usually include a large element of disguise or metamorphosis; the interaction of character with character, discussed above in Chapter Six, is assisted by disguises. Different facets of the same character appear, affording an illusion of depth and nature to the play. When to this is added the alternative views of parody or irony, it will be seen that Shakespeare's romantic comedy becomes very flexible indeed, and permits a wide variety of valid interpretation. The present vogue for strengthening the bitter element in his sweet comedy is intended to be stimulating and provocative.

Such comedy is well suited to an age in which the ability to play a variety of rôles is almost a necessity for the well adjusted character in a mobile society. The theories of Reisman or Boorstin assume that in modern society every man must be something of a chameleon;[8] this idea has become thoroughly familiar, and the 'image' projected by a successful politician or the 'rôle' cast upon him by the exigencies of office tend to make any account of events into a 'drama' for the mass media. This very considerable growth in a particular kind of self-consciousness has had its repercussions upon the drama proper and on the habits of playgoers and dramatists.

First there has been a general move towards self-consciousness of the play as taking place within a larger play ('meta theatre'). In a well known study of *Shakespeare's Idea of the Play* (1962), Anne Righter Barton explored such leading areas as the rôle of 'the player king' and 'comic deceit', the power of disguise. In the modern theatre, rôle-taking may form the whole subject of a play (as in Tom Stoppard) or the text may be abandoned, for improvising. Artaud, whose 'theatre of cruelty' made him one of the most influential of modern critics, refused to see a play as literature, and saw it as consisting of a performance of blocking-and-timing. The sub-text (i.e., the action implied but not stated in the text) becomes more important than the text itself.

Paradoxically, these views have had their effect upon the most delicate and powerful Elizabethan writers and pre-eminently on the treatment of Shakespeare in the theatre. The *Titus Andronicus* of Brook and Olivier sparked off Jan Kott's interpretation of Shakespeare's theatre of cruelty. '*Titus Andronicus* is already Shakespearean theatre; but a truly Shakespearean text is yet to come,' observed Jan Kott.

Shakespeare's text is seen as presenting a basis, or possibly a challenge to new interpretation. It is no longer sacrosanct. Some plays have been rewritten or amended—as they have not been since the days of Dryden. John Barton's version of the English histories, Gielgud's 'translation' of *Much Ado*, represent direct alterations, but cutting out the repentance of Edmund in *King Lear*, or allowing Coriolanus's 'gracious silence' to spend a fair proportion of her time on-stage screaming are in overt contradiction to the originals. Doubling, in itself an Elizabethan habit, was used by Brook to emphasize the perspectives of *A Midsummer Night's Dream*.[9] However much weight is thrown upon the actors on an open stage, this is predominantly a Directors' theatre, and these modifications are made in accordance with a consistent plan, which aims not at soothing but stimulating the audience, by playing 'against the lines'. This of course demands great acting expertise. Dr Jonathan Miller shews Orsino as a bed-patient, raging with frustrated love, Orlando as a gawping country boy; the Royal Shakespeare Company gives Hotspur an ignominious death toppled backwards into a meal trough and hangs Vernon and Worcester on stage. The Mermaid's colonial version of *The Tempest*, with Ariel a negro in blue knee breeches, the National Theatre's all-male *As You Like It*, do not measure up to the extremes of adaptation that have been tried out on the tragedies, from the magnificent Zulu *Macbeth* (*Umabatha*) to Marowitz's 'alternative' versions of *Hamlet* and *Othello* (designed for the present racial conflicts of USA, with a black Iago). Shakespeare provides a stage mythology which can be adapted, as stories from the Bible are now also being adapted, to produce a shock of contrast and recognition between the original and the 'new' versions. The pioneer in this movement was Brecht, who adapted Kipling, Marlowe, Shakespeare and Gay for his own stage, specializing in sardonic but exhilarating parody. Musicals are frequent—the Hungarians recently turned *Love's Labour's Lost* into a musical—or Shakespeare may provide a 'play within a play' as in *Rosencrantz and Guildenstern are Dead*.

Sometimes the mode of performance seems to challenge, invert or 'insult' the lines, as if to see how much the indestructible original can take. In a Stratford *King Richard III*, Richard and Richmond addressed their troops simultaneously, rendering each other inaudible. If Shakespeare is still there, after all resources for decreation (a term of applause for the removal of conventional constructs) have been brought to bear, and glory has been taken out with iconoclastic fervour, the audience may even surreptitiously venture to enjoy a little of his old-fashioned sentiments which they would not feel at liberty openly to acknowledge— a little humility, generosity or worship.

In milder forms of interpretation, the plays will be staged in terms of a new time and place, through which the director's version can be projected. In such versions, costume may be of first importance, especially as it helps the actor's projection also. *Much Ado* given in nineteenth-century costumes catches reflections from the stage of that day (operas and Oscar Wilde); Olivier's nineteenth-century *Merchant of Venice* lent a coarse commercial flavour to the Venetian scenes. When the Romans are left as Romans but the Volsces appear as nearly naked Mexican Indians (Stratford, 1972), the effect of Coriolanus' change of allegiance is more violent. Shakespeare, who had an unusually delicate sense of place and of history, finely distinguishing the holiday air of Arden from that of Illyria, or the qualities of Rome and Egypt, proves supple and accommodating to a wide range of fantasy here: but unless some vestiges of his original intention assert themselves, the requisite paradox or 'ambivalence' will not be felt. A total loss of tradition would deprive innovation of its power. Image-breaking can continue only while the images remain relatively intact. The writer who developed so fully the metamorphosis of character has thus himself undergone a truly Protean series of shape changes without losing his identity. The text is now regarded not as a monument of unaging intellect but as raw material for a director's realization in modern terms, of *performance*, which will differ subtly from one day to the next.

The structuralist view of literature applies with particular force to the drama, most social of all the arts. If French scholars of the Elizabethan stage have led the way in the exploration of drama's sociological implications,[10] the French structuralist critics have produced a methodology that can be used to consider the developing interactions between Shakespeare's plays and the English stage, of which his history plays provide the clearest example.[11]

As these evolved from the tragedy of *King Richard III* towards the comedy of *King Henry V*, the chronicle history, very largely Shakespeare's invention, drew together the social expectancies of the audience, which in an age of such violent and rapid change and development had evolved certain images and emblems of stability. These were quite deliberately used under the Tudors, especially in the public triumphs and spectacles of the City of London.[12]

The history plays of Shakespeare were the means by which he established his reputation; to them the ordinary playgoer would bring memories not so much of Hall's or Holinshed's Chronicles as of London's great civic street theatre. Chronicle history probably did more than any other form to give shape and stability to popular drama. By the end of the century, various different kinds of play had evolved, with self-regulating and self-correcting habits of parody built in, to assist in the dynamic evolution. In his final history play of the York-Lancaster series, *King Henry V*, Shakespeare raises some disturbing questions; the protests of the common soldiers to the disguised king are not really answered. Love comedy, comical history and—latest arrival—comical satire had meanwhile evolved as distinct 'kinds' associated perhaps with certain playhouses or certain actors, for the professional stage was beginning to meet specific and particular demands from audiences who were also beginning to develop new habits. It had started to split into the different groups that characterized Jacobean times.

ii. The Jacobean Theatres.

If Glynne Wickham's theory is correct, and 1597 was a turning point in the evolution of the English stage, leading from relatively free playing to a strong regulative system that reduced the number of actors, made for greater professionalism, and closer connection between players and government, this might help to account for the decline of playing in the provinces, and the growing coolness of provincial centres towards visiting troupes.[13] The first dozen years of the seventeenth century saw metropolitan drama reach the peak of its evolution, where three distinct forms predominate—Jonsonian comedy, Revenge tragedy, and the Court Masque, in which Jonson also took the lead.

The younger playwrights assumed attitudes much more critical and prescriptive than Shakespeare's. The tiny indoor theatre of St Paul's choristers may have been really something like a play-club; the Chapel Royal boys at Blackfriars performed in the first modern commercial indoor theatre, a form of much greater social pretensions, which was eventually to oust the open stages of the arenas and inn-yards. Yet, while certain Jacobean tragic writers have regained the boards in the present age, Jacobean comedy, which appears to have a much greater affinity with the mood and temper of the contemporary stage than Elizabethan comedy, has not appealed. The recent fourth centenary of Jonson produced no such theatrical revival as might have been expected.

Yet Jonson has enjoyed a new literary reputation, since the well-known essay of T. S. Eliot, published in *The Sacred Wood* in 1920, drew attention to the merits of his 'poetry of the surface':

> To deal with the surface of life, as Jonson dealt with it, is to deal so deliberately that we too must be deliberate in order to understand . . . the polished veneer of Jonson reflects only the lazy *reader's* fatuity; unconscious does not respond to unconscious; no swarms of inarticulate feelings are aroused. (My italics)

The elasticity which allows the warp of an old text to be crossed with the woof of a modern rendering is not found in Jonson; and the mere fact that he has anticipated some of the black moods of modern interpretation blocks the way to a more modern treatment. Jonson is *not* our contemporary *because* he is so precise. It has been remarked that Jonson builds whole comic scenes upon obscure contemporary games of challenge and abuse, such as the games of 'club' and 'dor' in *Cynthia's Revels* and the game of 'vapours' in *Bartholomew Fair;* these are too specific to retain the interest of Rosalind's wooing games. The old sweet comedy curdled with modern bitterness now makes a better dish than comedy which has a bitter basis of its own.

A couple of books which may be taken to provide the equivalent to Barber's study of the Shakespearean background are Brian Gibbons's, *The Jacobean City Comedy* (Hart Davis, 1968), and Ian Donaldson's *The World Upside-Down* (Oxford, 1970). The first stresses the dark aspect of these plays, the other their festive gaiety. Gibbons defines a purely literary and limited genre; the plays of Marston, Middleton and Jonson 'are all satiric and have urban settings; they exclude material appropriate to romance, fairy tale, sentimental legend or patriotic chronicle' (p. 24), and derive their style on the one hand from moral satire and on the other from jest books, pamphlets about the underworld of London cheats, with some borrowings from the professional Italian stage. (It is essentially the work discussed in Chapter 9 above). Gibbons would see its flowering between 1597 and 1616, when these plays broke through the conventional providential view of social hierarchy, which joined microcosm and macrocosm in a single system. The older Elizabethan World Picture might have been accepted as a useful frame for discourse, but 'deeds and language such as men do use' revealed that the practical skill of the financial shark, the industrialist and the politician operated in free dissociation from such pieties. As Shakespeare had shattered the old forms of compliment ('My mistress' eyes are nothing like the sun') so the comic satirists released with exhilaration into drama the vigorous figure of the malcontent, the social critic, the outsider, reversing the traditional rôle of a play's Presenter who of old had duly reeled off its 'moral, teaching education'. Gibbons compares the result with the deflationary zest of Bertolt Brecht (but for that reason these comedies were of little use to Brecht himself). At its best, in Middleton's *Michaelmas Term*, Marston's *Dutch Courtesan*, above all in the mature Jonson, City comedy is neither didactic nor antididactic, but a finely balanced mixture of farce and realism, or Aristophanic and Terentian elements. Even if it is well plotted, the action may well consist of a series of jest or *lazzi*, which break away from the old conventions and set up new ones.[14]

An upholder of norms who enjoyed abnormalities (as Harry Levin remarked), Jonson who saw the world as 'a shop of toys and trifles', enjoyed the concourse drawn to the Alchemist's house, or the Fair, yet Donaldson has shewn how this society is dismembered, its action very largely self-defeating, its triumphs mere triumphs of verbiage, of 'noise and nonsense'.[15] The *bravura* style of certain modern productions could no doubt put the lines across, with heavy cutting and a generous filling out of the sub-text. Jonson's Dickensian comedies of the London underworld, *The Alchemist* and *Bartholomew Fair*, have proved much the most popular with modern audiences; these belong to a line that descends recognisably through *The Beggar's Opera* to modern times. In *The World Upside Down*, Donaldson traces the influence of one of Jonson's leading ideas. The 'absurd', however, has become grimmer in modern times and satire of polite brutality and controlled violence (as found in Restoration comedy) is in general far more to the taste of the modern playgoer. It is not the plays of Jonson or Fletcher but of their successors, Etherege, Congreve and Farquhar (even, sometimes of Dryden and Cibber) that invite modern restaging, where a lighter disillusion plays over the social surface not of the City but of High Life. Nevertheless, the literary as distinct from the theatrical popularity of Jonson has grown. In the universities, where in many cases social and interdisciplinary features of literary history are stressed, Jonson's plays take a central place. In most American and some British universities, medieval studies have been dropped from the syllabus, so that Elizabethan drama forms the earliest and toughest historical component in the course. Many new editions of renaissance plays have been issued. Among them, some of the most popular dramas have appeared in four or five editions during the last decade. These have been accompanied by 'casebooks', collections of criticism.[16] It may be that Jonson really is at his greatest in the study; his great density of language asks deliberation, as Eliot remarked; he should, perhaps, have been a novelist. L. C. Knights, whose study *Drama and Society in the Age of Jonson* (1936) helped to establish the modern image of Jonson, has never been deeply interested in live theatre, and like T. S. Eliot, approaches Jonson as a reader.

iv. The Court Masque

It has recently been argued that the mood of the Jacobean first decade was not tragic nor satiric, but rather tragicomic; that the euphoric consequences of a peaceable succession and the foiling of the Gunpowder Plot were reflected in plays that were written by Shakespeare and Jonson with an eye to the royal patronage.[17]. In this period, Jonson himself withdrew from the common stages and concentrated far more on the Court masques, of which kind he was acknowledged master, and whatever happened on the public stages, euphoria is necessary for the masque. These 'offerings' presuppose a different form, based on different social relations from drama; they approach nearer to sports on one hand and to ritual on the other. The presence of the King conferred a special dignity; if he were not present, the performance could not take place. Instead of a plot-line or story, the audience were suddenly confronted, after a period of expectation, by a dazzling spectacle; a group of noble persons, their nobility enhanced by some dignified or even god-like impersonation, were revealed in splendour which aimed at transporting or overwhelming the spectators with 'Wonder' or 'Astonishment'. They were caught up, as it were, into a higher sphere, and as the masquers moved forward, with song and dance, to join the audience, the two worlds met in an act of homage that was also a celebration of unity, concord and harmony. Jonson set out his theory of the masque in *Hymenaei*, where the marriage of two young people symbolizes the unity of James's two kingdoms. The debased theatrical descendant is the 'transformation scene' of modern pantomimes.

Masque, in a much grander way, replaced chronicle history—which suffered an eclipse under King James—as the mythological celebration of social and national virtues.

While the actual event might not live up to this high theory —and as has been indicated in Chapter XI, Jonson's later masques did not maintain the idealism of his earliest ones— he explored in the masque those realms of romance which were excluded from his plays. Prince Henry was compared with Lancelot and the knights of Arthur's court, the god-like powers of James were hymned, even while in *Sejanus* the tragic irony of ill government was exposed in a manner which caused Jonson to be cited before the Privy Council. Taken together, Jonson's satiric comedy and his court masques imply a great capacity for polarising contradictory feelings.

Not only was the masque the predominant and noblest form of entertainment, it involved players, especially the King's Men, who were summoned to Court to help put on the masques, and who took the speaking parts of the anti-masques. Some of these royal shows appeared afterwards on the stage (the dance of satyrs from Jonson's *Oberon* in Act IV of *The Winter's Tale*);[18] and the effect of the masque on the imagery and style of Shakespeare's later plays is clear. Perhaps the famous opposition between Jonson and Shakespeare, of which so little is actually known, developed between the masque writer and the theatre artist. As Levin observed, Shakespeare 'responded to Jonson's brilliant example not through imitation but through sublimation.' Shakespeare was never asked to write a masque, but he transmuted the experience in *The Tempest*.

Closely allied to the later masques is the pastoral romance, which as the polar opposite to black comedy, has been in almost total eclipse recently, except where (as in the case of Marvell's dramatic pastoral lyrics) it has been studied as offering a difficult equilibrium in an age of revolution.

However, in spite of the selective nature of Jacobean revivals on the modern stage, there is no doubt that the whole modern movement in English drama has been strengthened by the power of its Elizabethan and Jacobean inheritance; this has provided both a theatrical model and a social image with which lively interplay could be maintained.

CHRONOLOGICAL TABLE OF PLAYS

(Dates can be approximate only. Where the name is not given, the
performing company is unknown)

1560–1580. Early Elizabethan Drama.

Anon.	*The Pedler's Prophecy*	
	Tom Tyler and his Wife	
Ingelond	*The Disobedient Child*	
Phillip	*Patient and Meek Grissel*	
Edwardes	*Damon and Pithias*	Chapel Boys
Anon.	*Marriage of Wit and Science*	
Fulwell	*Like Will to Like*	
Anon.	*Common Conditions*	
Preston	*Sir Clyomon and Sir Clamydes*	Dudley–Leicester's Men

**1580–1592. The University Wits and Shakespeare: to the closing of the
theatres for plague.**

Anon.	*The Cobbler's Prophecy*	
	Rare Triumphs of Love and For-tune	Derby's Men
	Fair Em	Strange's and Admiral's Men
	Mucedorus	Sussex's and Pembroke's Men
	George-a-Greene	,, ,, ,,
	John of Bordeaux	
	Two Italian Gentlemen	
Greene	*Orlando Furioso*	Queen Elizabeth's Men
	Friar Bacon and Friar Bungay	,, ,, ,,
	James IV	,, ,, ,,
Lyly	*Campaspe*	Chapel and Paul's Boys
	Sapho and Phao	,, ,, ,,
	Endimion	Paul's Boys
	Love's Metamorphosis	,, ,,
	Midas	,, ,,
	Mother Bombie	,, ,,
	Gallathea	,, ,,
	Woman in the Moon	
Munday	*John a Kent and John a Cumber*	Strange's and Admiral's Men
Nashe	*Summer's Last Will and Testament*	
Peele	*Arraignement of Paris*	Chapel Boys
	Orlando Furioso	Queen Elizabeth's Men
	The Old Wives' Tale	,, ,, ,,
Shakespeare	*The Comedy of Errors*	
	The Two Gentlemen of Verona	
	The Taming of the Shrew	

223

1594–1598. From the re-opening of the theatres to the revival of the boys' troupes and the War of the Theatres.

Chapman	*The Blind Beggar of Alexandria*	Admiral's Men
	An Humourous Day's Mirth	,, ,,
Haughton	*Englishmen for My Money*	,, ,,
Jonson	*Tale of a Tub*, first version	Chamberlain's Men
	Every Man in his Humour, first version	,, ,,
Munday	*Downfall and Death of Robert Earl of Huntingdon*	Admiral's Men
Porter	*Two Angry Women of Abingdon*	,, ,,
Shakespeare	*Love's Labour's Lost*	Chamberlain's Men
	A Midsummer Night's Dream	,, ,,
	Merchant of Venice	,, ,,
	I and II *King Henry IV*	,, ,,
	Much Ado About Nothing	,, ,,

1599–1608. From the revival of the boys' troupes to the King's Men's acquisition of the New Blackfriars Theatre.

Anon.	*Look About You*	Admiral's Men
	Merry Devil of Edmonton	Chamberlain's Men
	Trial of Chivalry	Derby's Men
	Weakest Goeth to the Wall	,, ,,
	Fair Maid of Bristowe	King's formerly Chamberlain's Men
	The London Prodigal	,, ,, ,,
	The Maid's Metamorphosis	Paul's Boys
	Wisdom of Doctor Dodypoll	,, ,,
	The Thracian Wonder	
	Grim the Collier of Croydon	
	Wily Beguiled	
	Nobody and Somebody	Queen Anne's formerly Worcester's Men
	The Wit of a Woman	
	Every Woman in her Humour	
	The Puritan	Paul's Boys
Armin	*Two Maids of Moreclacke*	King's Revels Boys
Barry	*Ram Alley*	,, ,, ,,
Beaumont and	*The Woman Hater*	Paul's Boys
Fletcher	*Knight of the Burning Pestle*	Queen's Revels, formerly Chapel Boys
Chapman	*All Fools*	,, ,, ,,
	May Day	,, ,, ,,
	Sir Giles Goosecap	,, ,, ,,
	The Gentleman Usher	,, ,, ,,
	Monsieur d'Olive	Queen's Revels
	Widow's Tears	,, ,,
	Eastward Ho! (with Jonson and Marston)	,, ,,

Day	*Blind Beggar of Bednal Green*	Admiral's Men
	Isle of Gulls	Queen's Revels
	Humour out of Breath	King's Revels
	Law Tricks	„ „
	Travails of Three English Brothers	Queen Anne's Men
	(with Rowley and Wilkins)	
Dekker	*Old Fortunatus*	Admiral's Men
	The Shoemakers' Holiday	„ „
	Patient Grissel (with Chettle and Haughton)	
	Satiromastix	Chamberlain's Men
	I and II *The Honest Whore* (with Middleton)	Prince Henry's, formerly Admiral's Men
	The Whore of Babylon	Queen Anne's Men
	Westward Ho! (with Webster)	Paul's Boys
	Northward Ho! (with Webster)	„ „
Heywood	*Four Prentices of London*	Worcester's Men
	How a Man may choose a Good Wife from a Bad	„ „
	Fair Maid of the Exchange (?)	
	If you know not me you know Nobody	Queen Anne's formerly Worcester's Men
	The Wise Woman of Hogsdon	„ „
Jonson	*Every Man out of his Humour*	Chamberlain's Men
	Cynthia's Revels	Chapel Boys
	Poetaster	„ „
	Volpone	King's Men
	The Satyr	Masque
	Masque of Blackness	„
	Hymenæi	„
	Hue and Cry after Cupid	„
Marston	*Histriomastix*	Paul's Boys
	Jack Drum's Entertainment	„ „
	What You Will	„ „
	Dutch Courtesan	Queen's Revels
	Malcontent	„ and King's Men
	The Fawne	„ „ „
Rowley, S.	*When you see me, you know me*	Prince Henry's Men
Rowley, W.	*A Shoemaker a Gentleman*	Queen Anne's Men
Shakespeare	*As You Like It*	Chamberlains afterwards King's Men
	The Merry Wives of Windsor	„ „ „
	Twelfth Night	„ „ „
	All's Well that Ends Well	„ „ „
	Measure for Measure	„ „ „
	Pericles (with Wilkins?)	„ „ „
Sharpham	*The Fleire*	Queen's Revels

1609–1616. From the opening of the New Blackfriars Theatre to Shakespeare's death and the publication of Jonson's Works.

Beaumont and Fletcher	*Philaster*	King's Men
	The Captain	,, ,,
	The Woman's Prize	,, ,,
	The Scornful Lady	Queen's Revels
	Wit at Several Weapons	,, ,,
Cooke	*Greene's Tu Quoque*	Queen Anne's Men
Dekker	*If it be not good, the devil is in't*	,, ,, ,,
	Match me in London	,, ,, ,,
	The Roaring Girl (with Middleton)	,, ,, ,,
Field	*A Woman is a Weathercock*	Queen's Revels
	Amends for Ladies	,, ,,
Heywood	*Fortune by Land and Sea* (with W. Rowley)	Queen Anne's Men
	I and II, *The Fair Maid of the West*	,, ,, ,,
	The Golden Age, The Silver Age, The Brazen Age, The Iron Age	,, ,, ,,
Jonson	*Epicoene*	Queen's Revels
	The Alchemist	King's Men
	Bartholomew Fair	Lady Elizabeth's Men
	The Devil is an Ass	King's Men
	Masque of Queens	
	Love Restored	
	Irish Masque	
	Masque of Christmas	
Middleton	*Chaste Maid in Cheapside*	Lady Elizabeth's Men
	The Widow	
Shakespeare	*Cymbeline*	King's Men
	The Winter's Tale	,, ,,
	The Tempest	,, ,,
	King Henry VIII (with Fletcher?)	,, ,,

Fletcher died in 1625, Middleton in 1627, Dekker in 1632, Munday in 1633, Jonson in 1637, Heywood in 1641.

NOTES

CHAPTER I

Page Note No.

3 1. F. E. Schelling's *History of Elizabethan Drama*, 2 vols., Boston, 1908; with A. H. Thorndike, *English Comedy*, (New York, 1929), it remains the most complete survey.

3 2. On the Revenge Play, F. T. Bowers, *The English Revenge Tragedy, 1587–1642*, Princeton, 1940; on the English History Play, E. M. W. Tillyard, *Shakespeare's History Plays*, 1944; on domestic tragedy see H. H. Adams, *English Domestic or Homiletic Tragedy, 1575–1642*, New York, 1943. For the masque, Herford and Simpson's edition of Ben Jonson provides the best starting point.

3 3. See especially T. W. Baldwin, *William Shakespeare's Small Latin and Less Greek*, 2 vols., Urbana, 1944. For the application to non-dramatic poetry, see Hallett Smith, *Elizabethan Poetry*, Harvard, 1952; and to drama, Madeleine Doran, *Endeavors of Art*, Wisconsin, 1954.

3 4. See the two articles by C. R. Baskerville in *Modern Philology*, vol. xiv (1916–1917). The recent researches into stage history by Richard Southern and others have emphasized the same connexion.

3 5. Sweet and bitter fools (cf. *King Lear*, 1.4.150 ff.) were two recognized classes of jester: Queen Elizabeth's jester Pace was a bitter fool. For the two kinds of comedy see Nevill Coghill, 'The Basis of Shakespearean Comedy', in *Essays and Studies of the English Association*, New Series, vol. 3, 1950. In *Shakespeare and The Rival Traditions* (New York, 1952), Alfred Harbage develops a theory of contrast between the public and private theatres, which would assign sweet comedy to the former and bitter comedy to the latter. See below, note 13 to Chapter II.

4 6. See Harbage; and cf. below, note 2, Chapter II.

4 7. Cf. below, Chapter IV, p. 44, and Chapter VI, p. 77. Madeleine Doran, *Endeavours of Art*, Chapter 10, deals with the conversion of narrative into drama. Both the cyclic form of miracle plays, and the way in which each actor describes the action as it occurs and records his own feelings, derive from recited narrative.

4 8. Cf. below, Chapter IV, p. 42.

5 9. Cf. below, Chapter IV, pp. 51–53.

6   10. See Gladys Willcock, 'Shakespeare and Elizabethan English', *Shakespeare Survey*, 7, Cambridge, 1954.

6   11. Cf. below, Chapter XI.

7   12. See T. S. Eliot, 'Tradition and the Individual Talent' and 'The Music of Poetry', both reprinted in *Selected Prose*, ed. John Hayward (Penguin Books, 1953).

7   13. This play is completely vindicated by acting. Cf. below, Chapter IX, note 18.

8   14. Cf. Gladys Willcock: and G. E. Bentley, *Shakespeare and Jonson. Their Reputations in the Seventeenth Century Compared*, 2 vols., Cambridge and Chicago, 1945.

8   15. Samuel Johnson, *Preface to Shakespeare. Johnson on Shakespeare*, ed. W. Raleigh, Oxford, 1929, p. 12.

9   16. See Mario Praz, 'Shakespeare and Italy', *Shakespeare Survey*, 7, and below, Chapter II, p. 21.

9   17. Among surviving relics of popular art may be counted sea shanties, country dances, painted farm-carts, roundabouts and old inn signs. The gaudy interior of the Globe Theatre as described by C. Walter Hodges (see note 2 to Chapter II), with the pillars and pilasters gilded and tricked out in colour, the allegorical paintings and zodiacal design for the Heavens, strongly suggests the decorative style of the modern Fun Fair.

9   18. For the last twenty years the appreciation of asyndetic forms of medieval poetry has been growing: it will be sufficient to refer to the Israel Gollancz Memorial Lectures of the British Academy for 1945 (by Nevill Coghill on *Piers Plowman*), and for 1950 (by Dorothy Everett on Chaucer).

10   19. It is useful to compare a few minor plays in the Shakespearean and Jonsonian form, e.g. Cooke's *Greene's Tu Quoque* with Barry's *Ram Alley*, where the story is the same but the treatment is different.

CHAPTER II

12   1. For lost plays on saints, see J. M. Manly, 'The Miracle Play in Medieval England' (*Transactions of the Royal Society of Literature*, 1927). For the Coventry play, see below, Chapter XI, note 8.

13   2. See the revolutionary account of the theatre in C. Walter Hodges, *The Globe Restored*, 1953. The whole relation of actors to audience is that of the street performer to the surrounding crowd. For the actors' use of the yard, see

NOTES

J. W. Saunders, 'Vaulting the Rails', *Shakespeare Survey*, 7, 1954. Leslie Hotson, *The First Night of 'Twelfth Night'* (1954), argues for an arena stage, surrounded by the audience on all sides, which he appears to have proved for the Whitehall performances; it has not been generally accepted for the public stages. R. Southern, *The Open Stage*, 1953, relates the Elizabethan theatre to modern trends in production, and also supplies the best account of modern views upon it.

13   3. In Jonson's *Masque of Augurs*, 1622, there is a reference to country players still 'strolling about in several shires' without licence from the Office of Revels. The quotation is from Professor Harbage, to whom I am indebted for some of the information in the following pages.

13   4. Evidence for the survival of town players is given by C. R. Baskerville (see note 4, Chapter I).

14   5. *Histriomastix or The Player Whipt*: an allusion to the penalty for vagabonds. For further discussion of these plays see below Chapter III, p. 41. Compare the 'players' in Middleton's *Mayor of Queenborough* and *A Trick to Catch the Old One*.

14   6. Henry Crosse, *Virtue's Commonwealth*, 1603. Quoted by K. J. Holzknecht, *The Backgrounds of Shakespeare's Plays* (American Book Co., 1950), p. 167. Holzknecht's chapter on the audience is the best general account of Elizabethan playgoers.

14   7. In his projected Academy. Gresham's College had lecturers in rhetoric: Ben Jonson's *Discoveries* may be the notes for lectures delivered there.

15   8. Edward Gayton, *Pleasant Notes upon Don Quixote*, 1654. Quoted by Holzknecht, p. 173. *The Merry Milkmaids* was a jig.

15   9. See the article by J. W. Saunders (note 2 above).

16   10. See C. R. Baskerville (note 4, Chapter I). Captain Cox, who led the performers of the Coventry Hock Tuesday play before Queen Elizabeth in 1575, had a library of plays and romances which indicates clearly the taste of popular players. A list of his books, beginning with *King Arthur* and *Huon of Bordeaux*, and including some fifty titles, is in Robert Laneham's letter from Kenilworth, reprinted in John Nichols, *The Progresses and Public Processions of Queen Elizabeth*, 2 vols., 1788. I owe some of the information in the next paragraph to Dr. T. W. Craik.

17   11. Perhaps the 'shrewd boy' who was carried off by the devil in *Wisdom* was a stooge. In the Prologue to *The Devil is an*

Ass, a parody of a moral play, Ben Jonson begs the spectators not to

> 'force us act
> In compass of a cheese trencher. This tract
> Will ne'er admit a Vice because of yours.
> Anon who worse than you the fault endures
> That yourselves make? when you will thrust and spurn,
> And knock us on the elbows: and bid turn:
> As if, when we had spoke, we must begone,
> Or till we spake, must all run into one,
> Like the young adders at the old one's mouth!'

17 12. Follywit and his men, disguised as My Lord Owemuch's Players, are acting before Follywit's uncle, a country justice, when a constable brings one of the party in on a charge of theft. They pretend the constable is part of their play, bind and gag him, and rob the audience before escaping. In *The Mayor of Queensborough*, a gang of thieves, disguised as strolling players, rob the Mayor, who, like Sir Thomas More, has insisted on thrusting himself into the play and taking on the clown's part.

17 13. Yet such great ones, being in themselves symbolic, were actors too. In some of his distinctions between Man and Office, Shakespeare does not compare the player with the king, but the king with the player.

18 14. See Alfred Harbage, *Shakespeare and the Rival Traditions*. Though Professor Harbage pushes his argument to extremes, his distinction between the two kinds of drama seems incontrovertible.

18 15. This chorus has parallels in Dekker and Heywood, in *The Whore of Babylon, Four Prentices of London, Old Fortunatus*. The chorus of *Faustus*, which wafts the spectators over the Alps, is easily outdone by the Presenter Fame in *The Travails of Three English Brothers*, who in six lines transports Sir Antony Shirley from England to Persia, and in the final scene discovers with a perspective glass one brother in England, one in Persia and one in Spain, but all on the stage in three dumb shows.

19 16. S. Johnson, *Preface to Shakespeare*, 1765. W. Raleigh, ed.: *Johnson on Shakespeare*, p. 27. Johnson adds: 'A play read, affects the mind like a play acted'. Cf. C. R. Baskerville: 'There is no indication that in the Middle Ages plays were regarded anywhere in Europe as literature for reading'.

19 17. Instead of distancing the audience, such a speech includes them, since, as Donne in a much-quoted passage observes,

NOTES

they are involved in mankind. Compare R. Southern, *The Open Stage*, pp. 24–42, for the actor's point of view. 'There is no possibility of a shallow pretence at forgetting the audience. . . . What is needed is not a stage *before* an audience but a stage *in* an audience'.

19   18. *Jack Drum's Entertainment*, 1601. Act 5. One of Marston's contributions to the Poets' War.

20   19. The following two paragraphs are indebted to the lively work of Marchette Chute, *Shakespeare of London* (1952).

21   20. See C. T. Prouty, 'An Early Elizabethan Playhouse', *Shakespeare Survey*, 6, 1953, which describes a hall belonging to the Church of St. Botolph without Aldersgate, used for acting in the 1560s.

22   21. Henslowe's Diary supplies plenty of evidence. Such plays might be brilliant as well as popular, e.g. *Eastward Ho!* which displays the best qualities of Jonson, Chapman and Marston.

22   22. See Anthony Sampson, in *Signature*, New Series, xv, 1952.

23   23. See Alice Walker, *Textual Problems of the First Folio*, Cambridge, 1953.

23   24. W. W. Greg lists only 186 lost plays against 900 survivors, but those which perished would mostly perish title and all. Thomas Heywood claimed to have had a hand in 220 plays: some twenty-three survive. Schelling thought perhaps half the plays written after 1558 survived.

24   25. A charming account of a popular version of *Richard III*, acted as a folk-play by the coloured people of La Ceiba in Spanish Honduras, is given by Louise Wright George in *Shakespeare Quarterly*, vol. 3, October 1952.

25   26. T. S. Eliot, 'The Music of Poetry', 1942.

26   27. This formula is that of John Matchlock, founder of Hitchin Grammar School.

CHAPTER III

27   1. Aristotle in the *Rhetoric* distinguished *ethos* (fixed temperament) from *pathos* (feeling appropriate to a given situation), and it was generally accepted that comedy imitated *ethos* (cf. Chapter IV, below, p. 43). For the development of medieval views of comedy, see the article by Nevill Coghill (Chapter I, note 5 above).

29   2. The quotation is from John Northbrook, *Treatise wherein Dicing, Dancing, Vain Plays are reproved* (1577). Gosson's *School of Abuse* appeared in 1582.

30   3. Whetstone, preface to *Promos and Cassandra* (before 1578).

Page Note No.

30   4. Sidney, *Defence of Poetry*. The complaint persists as late as Jonson's final plays (cf. Chapter VII, p. 103).

31   5. See Chapter I, note 5. Marston's *Malcontent*, a wholly satiric tragi-comedy, is described in the Induction as 'a bitter play' which is defined as 'satire or moral'. Though made by the foolish Sly, the description is apt. Shakespeare's work was nearly always described as 'sweet'.

31   6. Cicero's definition, as recorded by Donatus. It is not found in the works of Cicero, but was a commonplace of the sixteenth century. See below, Chapter VII, p. 108.

33   7. John Soowthern, *Pandora, the musique of the bewtie of his mistress Diana* (1584).

34   8. See Richard F. Jones, *The Triumph of the English Language* (1953). Latin conferred a special dignity: like splendid garment or golden shrine, it had a natural suitability for lofty subjects. To write learnedly in English laid open the treasures of learning in a dangerous way. Here, however, the reformers could come to the rescue. The translation of the Bible justified all other translations. The plain simplicity of homespun excelled the royal robes of the learned tongue (cf. Chapter VI, note 13).

34   8a. See Gladys Willcock, 'Shakespeare and Elizabeth English', *Shakespeare Survey*, 7 (1954).

34   9. The Reformation had helped to destroy the prestige of Latin: the printing press had brought books within the reach of a large public and created a demand for books in English. The machinery of local government, the growth of trade and technical processes all required the development of the English language. New scientific and technical vocabularies had to be evolved, and the Latin ones replaced by English in the older sciences.

35   10. Thomas Heywood's *Apology for Actors*, written perhaps in 1607, was published in 1612.

37   11. More especially in the work of T. W. Baldwin. In its application to the drama, see Madeleine Doran, *Endeavours of Art*.

37   12. Many of the interludes have proverbs for their titles. Simpler examples of the dialogues which led up to full-scale plays are the Cambridge debates between Ruff, Cuff and Band, and Sword, Rapier and Dagger (*Harleian Miscellany*, x). Professor H. H. Adams (see Chapter I, note 2) connects domestic tragedy closely with the Prodigal Son plays.

38   13. In *Histriomastix* (1599) the poor artificers who form themselves into Sir Oliver Owlet's Men are still acting moralities. Their poet is writing a *Prodigal Child*:

NOTES

Posthaste: 'Enter the Prodigal Child'—fill the pot,
I would say.

'Huffa, huffa, who calls for me?
I play the Prodigal Child in jollity.'

Clout: O detestable good.
Posthaste: 'Enter to him Dame Virtue'
'My son, thou art a lost child.
(This is a passion, note you the passion?)
And hath many poor men of their goods beguiled.
O prodigal child, and child prodigal.'
Read the rest, sirs, I cannot read for tears.

40   14. Cf. also Chapter VI, pp. 88–90, and Chapter VII, pp. 108–110.

41   15. See note 13. The Italian Lord is answered by an obstinate Englishman:

'By'r Lady, sir, I like not of this pride,
Give me the ancient hospitality.
They say tis merry in hall, when beards wag all.
The Italian lord is an ass.'

41   16. This play is itself a translation from the Italian of Luigi Pasqualio, *Il Fidele* (1579). It is reprinted by the Malone Society.

CHAPTER IV

42   1. See the article by Gladys Willcock (Chapter I, note 10). Lyly's letter to Lady Squemish is a parody of the usual letter form (see below p. 46).

42   2. The question of Transubstantiation and the Real Presence in the Sacrament was neatly evaded by Elizabeth herself in the characteristic lines:

'Christ was the Word that spake it,
He took the bread and brake it:
And what that Word doth make it,
That I believe, and take it.'

43   3. Compare the words of Lope de Vega: 'When I have to write a comedy, I lock up the precepts with six keys, cast Terence and Plautus from my study . . . and I write according to the art invented by those who sought the vulgar applause. For, as the common herd pays for them, it is meet to speak to them like an ignoramus in order to please them.'

43   4. T. W. Baldwin has insisted that there is no evidence that plays were written for private performance, and the plays performed at Court were taken from the public repertory. The literary kind is directed towards one sort of *theme* or another, e.g. court plays would appeal to the equivalent of that large public which today enjoys *The Tatler, The Sphere, The Illustrated London News.* The three divisions correspond roughly to the predominant forms in the 1580s, 1590s, 1600s.

44   5. See R. M. Wilson, *Lost Literature of Medieval England* (1952), for the medieval romance. Chaucer was fairly frequently dramatized. Richard Edwards wrote a lost *Palamon and Arcite* in the sixties; *Appius and Virginia* (the Physician's Tale in *The Canterbury Tales*) was printed in the seventies, Phillips' *Meek and Patient Grissel* in the the sixties, *The Thracian Wonder* (the tale of Constance) in the late fifteen-nineties and *The Two Noble Kinsmen* well into the seventeenth century.

44   6. *Every Man out of his Humour.* See G. M. Young, *Shakespeare and the Termers* (British Academy Annual Shakespeare Lecture, 1947), for an account of the influence of the Inns of Court upon the theatre, and cf. below, Chapter IX, pp. 138 ff. Though it is true that younger brothers of these families might be bound 'prentices in the City, and though the 'prentices included all the future Lord Mayors of London, yet the code of behaviour for the two groups was sharply different, and status, not family, determined behaviour. See the play *Fortune by Land and Sea* (below, p. 87) for an illustration.

46   7. For the Jacobean style in compliment see Chapter XI, pp. 188–9. Letter-writing was an important feature of school-training and manuals were common.

46   8. See Hallett Smith, *Elizabethan Poetry*, Chapter I, for an account of the pastoral as depicting the joys of retirement, *otium*: and cf. the soliloquies of King Henry IV and King Henry VI in Shakespeare on the joys of humble life (2 *King Henry IV*, 3.1; 3 *King Henry VI*, 3.5).

47   9. Cf. below, Chapter VII and XI. In *Bartholomew Fair*, the puppet play of Hero and Leander seems in part to recall Edwards's *Damon and Pithias*.

49   10. For Udall, see above, Chapter III, p. 30. Heywood also seems to support Mulcaster (p. 37) when he says plays teach a man 'not to stare with his eyes, draw awry his mouth, confound his voice in the hollow of his throat or tear his words hastily between his teeth: neither to buffet his

desk like a madman nor stand in his place like a lifeless
image, demurely plodding and without any smooth and
formal motion. It instructs him to fit his action to his
phrase and his pronunciation to both.'

50	11.	Cf. above, Chapter III, p. 38.
50	12.	Cf. below, Chapter V, pp. 65–6.
51	13.	Cf. Chapter VII, p. 79.
51	14.	See K. M. Lea, *Italian Popular Comedy* (Oxford, 1934).
51	15.	See above, note 7. The soldier's rough wooing was a comic turn of which Shakespeare made use again in *Henry V*: it persists as late as Fletcher, in *A King and No King, The Bondman, The Mad Lover* and other plays. See below, Chapter X.
52	16.	Sister Miriam Joseph's *Shakespeare and the Arts of Language* (New York, 1947) is difficult to use, since she does not distinguish between earlier and later uses of the same figure, or what might be called degrees of density in the clusters of figures.
52	17.	Cf. Sonnets 33, 34, 35, 36; 69, 70; 82, 83, 84; 93, 94, 95, 96 for the friend; and 130, 131; 137, 138; 141, 144; 152 for the mistress.
52	18.	Gervais of Melkley: quoted by Dorothy Everett, 'Chaucer's Art Poetical' (British Academy Israel Gollancz lecture, 1950), note 9.
53	19.	See Saladin Schmitt 'Shakespeare, Drama and Stage' (*Shakespeare-Jahrbuch*, bd. 89).
54	20.	See A. Sackton, *Rhetoric as a Dramatic Language in Ben Jonson* (Columbia, 1948). For a modern equivalent to Jonson's views on decorum, see T. S. Eliot, *Poetry and Drama* (1950), pp. 11–20.
56	21.	This play ends with a formal contrast between wife and whore: see below, Chapter VIII, p. 133. Timon's speech is found in Act 3, scene 1 (27–40). The last line is repeated in the Bawd's counsel of Marston's *Malcontent* (4.1) and was proverbial.
56	22.	The iteration of a single catchword may become infuriating to the modern ear, but a good clown might have charmed the groundlings with Simon Eyre's 'Prince am I none, yet am I princely born' or his wife's 'Let that Pass'; the Host of *The Merry Devil of Edmonton* iterates, 'I serve the good Duke of Norfolk' and the priest, 'Grass and hay, we are all mortal men'. *Greene's Tu Quoque* was named from the catchphrase of the clown. In *All's Well that Ends Well*, the clown comes to grief through over-trusting his catchwords 'O Lord, sir!' and 'Spare not me'.

57   23. In such passages as these, from *A Defence of Rhyme* (1603), 'Suffer then the world to enjoy that which it knows, and what it likes . . . all our understandings are not to be built by the square of Greece and Italy. We are the children of nature as well as they. . . . Eloquence and gay words are not of the substance of wit, it is but the garnish of a nice time. . . . Perfection is not the portion of man. . . . Plodding on in the plain tract I find beaten by Custom and Time, contenting me with what I see in use.' This work, written against Campion's theory of quantitative verse, provoked Ben Jonson, as he told Drummond, to write a Discourse of Poesy against both.

57   24. See Eugene M. Waith, *The Pattern of Tragicomedy in Beaumont and Fletcher* (Yale, 1952).

CHAPTER V

61   1. *Campaspe* has been beautifully produced at Redlands School, Bristol.

61   2. Enid Welsford, *The Court Masque* (1927), p. 281.

61   3. Alfred Harbage, *Shakespeare and the Rival Traditions* (New York, 1952), p. 81.

62   4. Cf. below, Chapter VI, p. 79. On the physical level, Lyly clearly made full use of the resources of his stage. See, for examples, Richard Southern, *The Open Stage*, p. 110.

64   5. In this way, the sonnet form replaced the medieval religious allegory, in which almost *any* subject social, personal, or theoretical could be incorporated. It could also, of course, decorously conceal a particular story which might be far from decorous. The interpretations of Lyly's *Endimion* includes possible stories of bloodshed and adultery; my own interpretation of *The Woman in the Moon* would link it with the story of Sir Henry Lee and his beautiful but flighty mistress, Anne Vere.

65   6. These three authors represent the purest artificial comedy of the English stage: it will be noticed that each of their three speeches comes from a woman, and that in Congreve and Wilde, while the romantic values are permitted ostensibly to triumph, neither the sermons of the reformed Angelica nor of the equally angelic Woman of No Importance can be compared with the tartness and vitality with which love is mocked.

65   7. For *Humour out of Breath*, see below, p. 170: it is about ten years later than Lyly and from Whitefriars. *The Wit of a*

Woman is an early Jacobean play: the company is unknown. Its symmetry is of a much simpler kind: a quartet of girls, a quartet of young lovers, and a quartet of amorous old fathers, on the Plautine model. 'It is plotted like a catch', as K. M. Lea observes.

66   8. Compare the immaturity of *Campaspe*:

> *Sylvius:* Dost thou believe that there are any gods, that thou art so dogged?
> *Diogenes:* I needs must believe there are gods: for I think thee an enemy to them.
> *Sylvius:* Why so?
> *Diogenes:* Because thou has taught one of thy sons to rule his legs and not to follow learning; the other to bend his body every way and his mind no way.
> *Perim:* Thou dost nothing but snarl and bite like a dog.
> *Diogenes:* It is the next way to drive away a thief.
> 5.1.18–29.

66   9. Cf. below, Chapter VI, p. 78, and above, Chapter IV, p. 47. Lyly is the only English comic writer mentioned by Ben Jonson in his tribute to Shakespeare prefixed to the First Folio—except Chaucer.

66   10. T. S. Eliot, 'Tradition and the Individual Talent' (*Selected Prose*, ed. Hayward, p. 25).

67   11. For tales of wandering knights, cf. Chapter II, note 1. The list of lost plays of the seventies and early eighties in Alfred Harbage, *Shakespeare and the Rival Traditions*, pp. 61–62, contains many names which suggest such themes. See also the reading of Captain Cox (Chapter II, note 10).

67   12. Nashe, son of a clergyman, was at St. John's College, Cambridge, with the other East Anglian, Greene. Lodge was the son of a Lord Mayor of London, and eventually became a landed squire himself. Only one drama by Nashe survives, and none entirely by Lodge; both collaborated in one or two other plays, but their dramatic gifts were negligible.

68   12a. The plot is that of Italian tragi-comedy; it is roughly the same as that of W. Taylor, *The Hog hath lost his Pearl*.

69   13. See the Life of Peele by R. Horne, *Works*, ed. C. T. Prouty, Yale, 1952, vol. I, p. 90.

69   14. Peele's city pageants with the nymphs, soldiers, etc., resemble nothing so much as an animated Albert Memorial. The collection of Merry Jests of George Peele, most of which are old stories, may be compared with the more famous Hundred Merry Tales (cf. Benedick's taunt, *Much*

Ado About Nothing, 2.1.134), or the Book of Riddles (*Merry Wives of Windsor*, 1.1.229), both aids to conversation much favoured by dull wooers.

72   15. *Mucedorus* was first issued in 1598, but belongs to the earlier decade. The third Quarto contains the addition at the end of the final exchange of Comedy and Envy which forms part of the War of the Theatres, and seems to be directed against Jonson. Since it emanated from Shakespeare's company, and Shakespeare's name was first associated with the enlarged play, this could have been the purge which he is said to have administered to Jonson. See below, Chapter VII, p. 101.

75   16. The thrice three Muses mourning for the death of Learning late deceased in Beggary (*Midsummer Night's Dream*, 5.2.52–53) appear in this play mourning for the imminent death of Pithias. See Chapter IV, p. 50. Egeon's adventures with his two sons remind me faintly of the story of that lost play of 'Placy Dacy' (St. Eustace) which Manly discusses (see note 11 above) and which was given at Braintree, where Udall was vicar in 1534. Egeon is, however, derived from that medieval storehouse, Gower's *Confessio Amantis*.

75   17. For the idea that Shakespeare invented the English History see F. P. Wilson, *Marlowe and the Early Shakespeare*, Oxford 1953, pp. 106–108.

75   18. Cf. above, Chapter IV, p. 53. For Schmidt see note 19 to Chapter IV. Shakespeare lived in lodgings throughout his London career, whereas all the other established actors led highly domestic lives. Indeed, without a household in which a boy could be received, it was impossible for an actor to take a 'prentice.

76   19. Janet Spens, *Elizabethan Drama*, 1922, p. 32. Miss Spens lays great stress on Shakespeare's debt to festival games and the popular tradition in general. See the chapter 'Munday and the Apocrypha'. Munday wrote for the rival company, the Admiral's.

CHAPTER VI

77   1. Behind Sidney for instance are Minturno and Castelvetro.

77   2. See Valentina Capocchi, *Genio e Mesteire: Shakespeare e la commedie dell' Arte* (Bari, 1950).

78   3. See above, Chapter IV, pp. 43–45.

78   4. See above, Chapter IV, pp. 50–51.

79   5. The young man who becomes a bear in *The Old Wives'*

Tale and the disdainful nymphs of *Love's Metamorphosis* are given a metamorphosis in the full Ovidian sense: there is a change of sex in *Gallathea* and a double change of sex in *The Maid's Metamorphosis*. But the memory of Ovid's convenient, or inconvenient trickeries rapidly faded. Compare, however, Jonson's masque, *Lovers Made Men*, Drayton's poem *The Owl* and *The Strange Metamorphosis of Man* (1634), a collection of sketches, half Character, half Emblem.

80   6. In Act I of Dekker's *Wonder of a Kingdom* 'You play the constable wisely' evokes 'The constable wisely! he calls me fool by craft': in *A Mad World, my Masters* the foolish jester says of the players: 'They put all their fools to the constables part always'. Other foolish constables occur in *The Famous Victories of Henry V, Love's Labour's Lost, Tale of a Tub* and *Blurt Master Constable*.

81   7. B. L. Joseph, *Elizabethan Acting*, Oxford, 1951, states the extreme case for formal theory.

81   8. Richard Flecknoe, quoted by J. Isaacs, 'Shakespeare as man of the Theatre', reprinted in *Shakespeare Criticism 1919–35*, ed. Anne Bradby, Oxford, 1936.

82   9. This is the formula of Geoffrey de Vinsauf, which, however, was in his case applied to verbal variation.

85 10. The Proem to *The House of Fame* discusses and classifies dreams, daydreams and visions, the intervals between them, and the relative weight of physiological and psychological causes, gravely refusing to come to any conclusion and leaving the matter to 'grete clerkes' to decide. Chantecleer and Pertelote take sides, the former voting for precognition and the latter for indigestion as the cause of dreams. In *Troilus*, Book V, the question is left open once more.

86 11. He is in fact wearing the sort of costume that a country mummer might do.

86 12. See below, Chapter VII, pp. 110–112. *Disguise* sometimes meant *deceit*. There is no dramatic parallel for the corresponding disguise, the heavenly humility of the Incarnation, though claims have been made for Vincentio of whom Angelo says:

> 'I perceive your Grace like power divine
> Hath looked upon my passes.'

In his poem on the Passion, Milton compared Christ in the flesh to a player:

> 'O what a mask was there, what a disguise!'

87   13. The morality play, *Cloth Breeches and Velvet Hose*, Greene's *Quip for an Upstart Courtier*, and the roles of Clay and Tub in Jonson's *Tale of a Tub* all depend on this antithesis. The Elizabethans still associated different clothes with different ranks, and the jests about courtiers who spend all their money in buying a fine wardrobe were probably based on fact. In religion, of course, fine vestments were associated with Rome, and the Vestarian controversy provoked bitter quarrels throughout Elizabeth's reign.

88   14. Armin's play was *The Two Maids of Moreclacke* (1605). For this and other matters pertaining to the fool see Leslie Hotson, *Shakespeare's Motley* (1952). For disguise plots in general see V. O. Freeburg, *Disguise Plots in Elizabethan Drama* (New York, 1915). He cites five main sorts of disguise: the heroines as page, the boy-bride, the disguised ruler, the spy, and the thief.

90   15. Does this final contest of the birds—the contemplative owl and the mocking cuckoo—owe anything to Chaucer's *Parliament of Fowls*, that courtly, mocking, and inconclusive debate on a lover's duties, in which all the wooers, like the King of Navarre and the followers, are banished from felicity for a year?

92   16. Disguised rulers appear in *George-a-Greene*, Heywood's *King Edward IV*, and *When You See Me, You Know Me*: disguised princes include Mucedorus, and the heroes of *Fair Em*, and *Humour out of Breath*. In satiric comedy Duke Hercules in *The Fawne* and Duke Altifront in *The Fleire* play highly ambiguous parts; the most extraordinary of all is the hero of *The Malcontent*.

93   17. Hamlet's use of the pun and of ironic quibbles is a development of Shakespeare's own interest, but it is peculiarly suited to the display of an unbalanced mind. It may be that the quite new and startling capacity to depict imbalance which several of the dramatists possessed was due to their linguistic inheritance, rather than to a psychological interest. The variety of speech between the Fool, Lear and Poor Tom a Bedlam, which makes up the storm music of *King Lear*, is a poetic achievement, not a clinical one.

93   18. In the final plays there is the same bewildering multiplicity of possible sources as in the earlier comedies. Miss K. M. Lea sees *The Tempest* a model Italian Arcadian pastoral (*Italian Popular Comedy*, vol. 2, pp. 443–453). It is generally taken as a wedding masque; Ben Jonson, in his scornful reference to 'Tales, Tempests and such drolleries', appears to class it with popular romances.

NOTES

CHAPTER VII

94   1. The quotation is from Dekker's preface to *Satiromastix*. In the Second Part of the *Return from Parnassus* (4.3) Kempe the actor says:

> 'O that Ben Jonson is a pestilent fellow, he brought up Horace giving the Poets a pill, but our fellow Shakespeare hath given him a purge that hath made him bewray his credit.'

Shakespeare's one reference to the War (*Hamlet*, 2.2) has no reference to Jonson.

94   2. See Gerald Bentley, *Shakespeare and Jonson: their Reputations in the Seventeenth Century Compared*.

95   3. Marston's notorious *Metamorphosis of Pygmalion's Image* (1598) marks the transition: it is an Ovidian poem, which he published with a prefatory verse describing it as a satire upon erotic poetry.

96   4. See J. B. Leishman's edition of *The Pilgrimage to Parnassus* (1949), pp. 45–50, and Hallett Smith, *Elizabethan Poetry* (Harvard, 1952), Chapter IV. In general, satire failed as an art; its barking, snarling and railing, and its licensed obscurity (the decorum required such poems to be canine and dark) produced a barbarous eloquence, which too often reminds the modern reader of the popular sports of bear and bull baiting, which Shakespeare used for comparison—'The nation holds it no sin to tarre them to controversy'.

96   5. In the native tradition there were such flytings as that of Dunbar and Kennedy; in the academic, the quarrel of Harvey and Nashe, or, more decorous, of Gosson and Sidney: in the ecclesiastical, the Marprelate controversy, and the polemics of Parsons and Jewel.

97   6. The connexion of this satiric poetry with the opposition of Artsman and Villanist in *Love's Labour's Lost*, where the scholar's melancholy humour of contemplation is replaced by the jovial humour of the sanguine lover must await the further elucidation of Miss Frances Yates, who has collected much material on this subject since her last published study of *Love's Labour's Lost* in 1936.

97   7. The secular morality was a familiar type: see the introduction to A. P. Rossiter's edition of *Woodstock* (1946). *Respublica* was the title of a Marian moral *Histriomastix* play. The use of Queen Elizabeth as Goddess is repeated by Jonson. The ending of *Every Man out of his Humour* had to be altered, but is restored from Jonson's note to the Quarto.

98   8. For a discussion of the traditional figure of Envy see C. R. Baskerville, *English Elements in Jonson's early Comedy* (Austin, Texas, 1911), Chapter 7. Envy was to the poet what Danger was to the courtly lover.

99   9. I cannot see more than a touch of Ben Jonson in the figure of Brabant Senior in Marston's *Jack Drum's Entertainment* (1601): Lampatho Doria, in *What You Will* (1601), is also supposed to be Jonson. These portraits have really no interest: whereas the depicting of the country players in *Histriomastix*, crying their simple prologue among the turmoil of the market, has the same sort of value as Captain Tucca's rehearsal of old plays in *Poetaster* or the scene with Kempe and Burbage in *The Return from Parnassus*.

99   10. Marston is depicted under the name of Crispinus, who appears in Horace, *Satires*, I.1, I.3, and as a challenger to the poet in I.4. Fannius (the name given to Dekker) also appears in this satire.

102   11. This is a quotation from the Players' Song in *Histriomastix*, which seems to infer, as Shakespeare does in *Hamlet*, that the popularity of the boy players had forced one of the men's companies at least to take to the road.

> 'Some up, some down, there's Players in the town,
>   Ye wot well who they be:
> The sum doth arise, to three companies.
>   One, two, three, four make we.
> Besides we that travel, with pumps full of gravel,
>   Made all of such running leather:
> That once in a week, new masters we seek,
>   And never can hold together.'

103   12. The action is based on four students and two morality characters, Furor Poeticus and Phantasma, who come on in turn, and whose attempts to gain employment range from posing as French physicians (at a fee of fourpence with eightpenny tip) to fiddling. Such a character as Amoretto with his sonneting and his hunting terms is a cross between Master Stephen and Fastidious Brisk; and the other satirized characters could all be paralleled from Jonson's plays. See Leishman, pp. 59–60, for the writer's adherence to Jonson. There is a fierce attack on the wealth of players (ed. cit., p. 350).

106   13. There is undoubtedly an element of compensation in the stoic indifference of Chapman as displayed for instance in *Ovid's Banquet of Sense* (1595), a 'correction' of the usual Ovidian poem, which Jonson may be parodying in Ovid's

farewell to Julia in *Poetaster*—a scene that also has obvious affinities with the orchard scene in *Romeo and Juliet*. Phantasy's defence by Quadratus in Marston's *What You Will* (2.1) is probably the frankest example of compensation. It is

> 'a function
> Even of the bright immortal part of man . . .
> By it th'inamorate
> Most lively thinks he sees the absent beauties
> Of his lov'd mistress.
> By it we shape a new creation
> Of things as yet unborn, by it we feed
> Our ravenous memory, our intentions feast:
> Slid, he that's not Phantastical's a beast.'

109   14. It has been contended by Marjorie Nicholson that the death of Queen Elizabeth as well as of Elizabeth Drury is the theme of this poem, the two being related as macrocosm and microcosm.

109   15. Madeleine Doran in *Endeavors of Art*, Chapter XII, compares the narrative technique in Renaissance painting, whereby a series of events might be represented within the same framework, with the use of contrasted plot and sub-plot in the drama, and the presentation of legendary material such as that of *Pericles* covering a span of years.

110   16. L. C. Knights, *Drama and Society in the Age of Jonson* (1937), p. 188. The structure of the old moral play is most closely reflected in the later comedies, especially *The Devil is an Ass* and *The Magnetic Lady*; but it is most powerfully and successfully present in the characterization of *Volpone*.

110   17. Amorphus, the fantastic traveller, for instance might be classed with the social types in Wilson's *Art of Rhetoric*, where the soldier is described as a braggart, the scholar as simple, a russet coat as sad and sometimes crafty, a courtier flattering, a citizen gentle: so here in a much more special-ized way, such character represents a separate Vice of courtship, as the dedication in the Folio 'To the Special Fountain of Manners' makes very clear. Jonson warns the Court of James that the satire may still apply, although 'In thee the whole Kingdom dresseth itself and is ambitious to use thee as her glass'.

112   18. In the preface to the original conclusion in the Quarto. Jonson's original ending had to be cancelled, as the personal appearance of Queen Elizabeth was apparently not favoured, but part of the old ending is preserved in the

special epilogue for performance at court, which is addressed to the Queen.

113   19. In the play written as a sequel and correction to this, *Amends for Ladies*, Field uses the old medieval contrast between the faith of a maid, a wife and a widow, which Dekker used in *Patient Grissel*. A real devil emerges in a natural character when Giles Overreach becomes possessed at the end of Massinger's *A New Way to Pay Old Debts*.

114   20. *The Late Lancashire Witches. The Old Joiner of Aldgate*, Chapman's lost play, also staged a recent lawcase. Moll Frith, *The Roaring Girl* of Middleton's play, may have made a personal appearance on the stage when it was performed. His *Game at Chess* is the most famous example of a comment on contemporary affairs of state: although allegorical in form, its references were so exclusively directed towards the Spanish Marriage proposed for Prince Charles that its staging was an unbelievable audacity.

CHAPTER VIII

119   1. E.g. the dance concludes *Much Ado About Nothing*, the judgement scene *Measure for Measure*. Dekker's *Shoemakers' Holiday* has both kingly judgement and a wedding march, like Marston's *The Fawne*.

119   2. *Elizabethan and Jacobean* (Oxford, 1945), pp. 92–97. This period is also dealt with by Patrick Cruttwell in *The Shakespearean Moment* (1954). 'The 1590s are the crucial years ... which led directly to the greatest moment in English poetry: the "Shakespearean moment", the opening years of the seventeenth century ... brought about that deep change of sensibility which marks off the earlier from the later Elizabethans, which alters the climate from that of *Arcadia* and *The Faerie Queen* to that which welcomed *Hamlet*'—or, it may be added from that which welcomed *Mucedorus* to that which welcomed *Volpone*.

120   3. His *Patient Grissel* has an analogue in Phillip's play, *The Pleasant History of Patient Grissel* (c. 1565). The second part of *The Honest Whore* is based on the old Schools tradition of the Prodigal Son (see p. 127). Prodigal Sons also appear in *The Wonder of a Kingdom* and *The Sun's Darling*. Morality figures appear in the inductions to *The Whore of Babylon*, *Old Fortunatus* and throughout *The Sun's Darling*, a moral masque.

122   4. In *Old Fortunatus*, the opening scene where Fortunatus is offered a choice of wisdom, strength, health, beauty, long

life or riches, and chooses riches, recalls the choice of Faust. In this play Fortune is shown triumphing over kings whom she makes her footstools—including Bajazet, whom Tamburlaine treated in like fashion. In *If it be not a good play*, the false choice made by the young king, the shows presented to him by the devils his servants, and the mocking of the friar all recall *Faustus*.

122 5. 'The Labours of writers are as unhappy as the children of a beautiful woman, being spoiled by nurses, within a month after they came into the world'. He adds that he did not see the play acted: 'my ears stood not within reach of their 'larums'. It suggests some dramatic poem butchered to meet a popular demand.

123 6. This play, based on Deloney's popular story, strongly recalls Greene's *Friar Bacon and Friar Bungay*. The word 'frolic' which recurs in both sets the key. Both have the same roles for the King, the prince or noble, the faithful 'fair maid' and the lively omnipotent old man, though one is magician and the other shoemaker. Sim Eyre in his turn produced Hob the Tanner of Tamworth in Heywood's *Edward IV*, and Hobson in *When you see Me, you Know Me*. (Yet the dialogue between Rose, Sybil and the Huntsman in *The Shoemakers' Holiday* is almost in the manner of the hunting scene in *Love's Labour's Lost*.)

123 7. The Welshmen appear in *Patient Grissel*, *Satiromastix* and presumably the lost *Wars of Henry I* and *The Welshman's Prize*; Dutchmen in *The Shoemakers' Holiday*, *Northward Ho!* and the anonymous *Weakest Goeth to the Wall*.

123 8. Hazlitt for instance talks of the 'precision of nature, truth and purity of tone' with which, when the disguised Orlando says to his daughter 'You'll forgive me', she replies, 'I am not made of marble: I forgive you'. But he does not add Orlando's smutty rejoinder: 'Nay, if you were made of marble, a good stone cutter might cut you'.

124 9. E.g. Celestine in *Satiromastix*, Mistress Justiano in *Westward Ho!* Dekker wrote plays on popular religious subjects: including a *Jephthah* and a *Pontius Pilate*. The *Whore of Babylon* is antipapal, and the original version of *The Virgin Martyr* may have been written early.

125 10. Even this is more tolerable than the outrage to which Dorothea is subjected in *The Virgin Martyr*, equalled only by Heywood's *Rape of Lucrece*. Lamb's remarks about the 'raciness' and 'glow' of the impurities setting off the rest 'as Caliban serves to show Miranda' is a glaring example of misapplied comparison.

127 11. Popular plays abound in familiar characters. The cripple of Fenchurch in *The Fair Maid of the Exchange* was probably a real person. Heywood wrote a play on Cutting Dick, a highwayman of Wiltshire, and Armin depicted a well-known 'natural' of Christ's Hospital. Dekker, besides his contributions to the Poets' War, is thought to have put Chapman into *Northward Ho!* as Bellfort.

At the same time he uses *literary* models—e.g. Bellafront's reception of her suitors in *The Honest Whore* is based on Imperia's in Middleton's *Blurt, Master Constable*, and Candido has a resemblance to Quilto in Middleton's *Phoenix*, and to Water Camblet in *Anything for a Quiet Life*: his humour of patience, however, is familiar in Dekker. He was so popular evidently that he had to be put into Part II, and provided with a new wife, more shrewish than the first.

128 12. The vogue was begun by *How a Man may Choose a Good Wife from a Bad*, generally attributed to Heywood. The pedant Aminadab is certainly close to Boniface of *The Wise Woman of Hogsden*, but the general treatment is more serious and nearer to a morality. See below.

128 13. The doughty heroines of Heywood's *Johan Johan*, and *Tom Tyler and his Wife*: the general situation of course stretches back to Mrs. Noah in the miracle plays, and to the Wyf of Bath.

130 14. For example, the account of the muster at Tilbury in *The Whore of Babylon* clearly owes something to *Henry V*:

'The drum that gave the call could not be heard
For justling armour! ere the call was done
It was so ring'd about with groves of pikes
That when they broke on both sides to give way,
The beating of the drum was thunder's noise,
While coats of steel clashed so on coats of steel,
Helmets on helmets that they struck out fire. . . .
Men faster came to fight than to a feast,
Nay, women sued to us they might be pressed.'

Dekker may have contemplated a historical series like Shakespeare's: *Sir Thomas Wiat*, with the first part of *If you See Me, you Know Me*, may be the *disjecta membra* of the lost first and second parts of *Lady Jane*, which story immediately precedes the events of *The Whore of Babylon* (see A. M. Clark, *Thomas Heywood*).

130 15. In *Every Man out of his Humour*, 3.6: '. . . as of a duke to be in love with a countess, and that countess to be in love with the duke's son, and the son to love the waiting maid:

some such cross-wooing, with a clown to their serving man. . . .'

131   16.   The dedication of *Match me in London*, addressed to Lodo-wick Carlell, a young musician. This play is set in Seville, but contains some very English citizens. It is closely re-lated to the plot of Middleton's *Women Beware Women*, with a happy end instead of a tragic one.

132   17.   A rather jingoistic little play, in which the piteous cries of the poor little Dutchman, suspended in a basket between Heaven and earth, are mirth for the callous young lovers. (This play depends on the opposition of youth and age, as well as Englishmen and foreigners.) 'O vater, vater,' he cries, 'here be such cruel daughterkins, ic bin all so weary, all so weary, all so cold, forbe in dit little basket. Ic pray de help me.' To which even the cheated old usurer, the girls' father, replies mockingly:

> 'Why, how now, son! what have your adamants
> Drawn you up so far, and then left you hanging
> Twixt heaven and earth, like Mahomet's sepulchre?'

This anti-refugee play from the Admiral's may be com-pared with the well-known plea for foreigners in *Sir Thomas More*, attributed to Shakespeare.

133   18.   Lovers who feign death include Celestina (*Satiromastix*), Infelice (*The Honest Whore*), Mrs. Arthur (*How a man may Choose*), Mrs. Justiniano (*Westward Ho!*), the Countess (*Law Tricks*), Hero (*Much Ado about Nothing*) among the heroines. Among the heroes there are Freevill (*Dutch Courtesan*), Pasquil (*Jack Drum's Entertainment*), Geraldine (*Greene's Tu Quoque*), Touchwood Junior (*A Chaste Maid in Cheapside*) and Polydore (*The Mad Lover*). Husbands are falsely reported dead in *The Weakest Goeth to the Wall*, *The Shoemakers' Holiday* and *The Two Maids of Moreclacke*. Madness is feigned in *The Roaring Girl* and *Match Me in London*, deafness in *The Wild Goose Chace* and blindness in *Fair Em*. The heroine smears herself with disfiguring ointment in *The Trial of Chivalry*, *The Gentle-man Usher* and *Jack Drum's Entertainment* to escape the unwanted attentions of a false lover.

133   19.   *A Maidenhead Well Lost* and *The Changeling* have the first: *All's Lost By Lust* and *The Hog hath lost his Pearl* have the second.

133   20.   1573–1641. His non-dramatic work, unlike Dekker's, is less interesting than his plays. Heywood showed some

power of dramatic development, though he failed to adapt himself to the Caroline mood, and his last plays though efficient are lifeless. Heywood was happier than Dekker: after a few years' bondage to Henslowe, he escaped and joined Worcester's (later Queen Anne's) Men, for whom he wrote regularly thereafter. They played at the Rose and after 1606 at the Red Bull in Clerkenwell.

134 21. This was during the period when both worked for Henslowe.

134 22. Dick of Devonshire was a real pirate: Heywood also wrote a play about a highwayman. Even when his characters are not historical, they are always assimilated to the popular types of the broadsheet ballads.

135 23. The play was imitated in *The Travails of Three English Brothers* (a 'true' story) by John Day; and by many others. It is the kind of play which could hardly have been written earlier, yet which seems timeless.

135 24. See above, p. 86.

136 25. Besides his plays he wrote an encyclopædic *History of Women*.

137 26. The conventional expectation might be indicated by *Arden of Feversham*. The underplot is copied in *A Fair Quarrel* by Middleton, with a Fletcherian treatment.

CHAPTER IX

138 1. For the connexion of this Christmas revel, *Gesta Grayorum*, with the stage, see Frances M. Yates, *Love's Labour's Lost* (Cambridge, 1936). In Dekker's comedy *If this be not a good play the devil is in it*, six counsellors advise the young king in terms not unlike those of *Gesta Grayorum*—which is reprinted in John Nichols, *Progresses and Public Processions of Queen Elizabeth* (1778) and by the Malone Society.

139 2. See W. Rowley's *A Shoemaker a Gentleman* for the legend of the royal shoemakers, Crispin and Crispianus; and Heywood, *Four Prentices of London*. A defence of the 'flatcap' is set out by Candido the linen draper in Dekker, 2nd Part of *The Honest Whore* (1.3).

140 3. The effect is similar to that of the royal procession in Shakespeare's *King Henry VIII* (cf. J. T. Saunders, 'Vaulting the Rails', *Shakespeare Survey*, 7 (1954)). It also provides the kind of glide into epilogue that the private theatres liked.

NOTES

144   4. For the hermetic doctrine of Chapman's poetry, see Miss Yates; and Jean Jacquot, *George Chapman* (Paris, 1951). The language of this passage of Jonson is that of Chapman, and as the whole play resembles his work, which was better known than might be expected (his *Blind Beggar of Alexandria* was a success), it seems probable that Jonson meant the debt to be noticed. Momford, in Fletcher's *Elder Brother*, has a similar speech which may be modelled on Jonson's.

144   5. I have used the names from the later version exclusively, to avoid confusion. In the early version, the names were Italian. Simpson would place the revision about 1612: others place it earlier.

144   6. See Chapter VII for a discussion of these plays. Jonson began with concentrating on the events of the plays, then he concentrated on the characters: then he withdrew for an interval and composed his tragedy of *Sejanus*. The progress is typical of his deliberate method.

145   7. Jonson has only a limited range of characters which he tends to repeat. The well-born wife and her doting husband reappear in Puntarvolo and his wife, Albius and Chloe, Sir Politick and Lady Would-be, Captain Otter and his 'princess'. The pairs of gulls, from Stephen and Matthew onwards, appear in nearly every play; and two witty conspirators are frequent.

146   8. A number of plays in which the devil gets the worst of it appeared on the popular stages, such as Haughton's *The Devil and his Dam*, and Dekker's *If this be not a good play, the devil is in it. Wily Beguiled* and various other plays with Grim the Collier of Croydon in them treat of the cheated devil: hence perhaps the proverb 'Like will to like, quoth the devil to the collier'. The black-faced collier seems to have strayed from some Plow Monday play.

        Plays of mock conjuring, of the kind practised by Jonson's Fitzdottrel, were also popular: e.g. *The Puritan*, and Fletcher's *The Chances*. But Jonson is also indebted to Boccaccio for his plot.

147   9. Cf. below, p. 181. Wittipol does not actually seduce Mrs. Fitzdottrel but he courts her before her husband's face: he has much in common with the more gentlemanly kind of Restoration hero.

147 10. Compare the very different and goodnatured dedication of Day's *Humour out of Breath* to 'Signior Nobody'.

149 11. Cf. Asper-Macilente, the envious hero of *Every Man out of his Humour*. The role played by Malevole is followed

almost exactly by Vindice the hero of Tourneur's *The Revenger's Tragedy*. For Elizabethan melancholy and the malcontent type, see Lawrence Babb, *The Elizabethan Malady* (Michigan, 1951).

149 12. This of course recalls Hamlet's wish to kill his uncle body and soul: Malevole however does not plan to kill, but to torture his victim into crime; yet his magnanimity in finally sparing Mendoza's life has been seriously commended by critics! This is only possible if it is argued that as Malevole he tortures Pietro Jacomo, but as Altofront spares Pietro Jacomo's life and also Mendoza's.

150 13. These 'stabbing similes' are very characteristic of Webster, who wrote the Induction to *The Malcontent*, but they are a recognized rhetorical device. Webster must have imitated Marston rather than Marston Webster.

151 14. Compare Portia's characterization of her wooers, *The Merchant of Venice*, 1.2.

151 15. Compare again both Hamlet, 'What a piece of work is man', and the Duke in *Measure for Measure*. All three passages draw on the medieval tradition of the contempt of the world, *De Contemptu Mundi*, as embodied in the work of Pope Innocent III. It is not surprising, in view of the final sentence, that Marston found it necessary to explain his innocence of any political disaffection.

153 16. Compare Middleton's play *The Widow*, where a pocket is picked while the victim has a tooth drawn or an eye-bath: after which the thief observes

> 'O tell me not, I have known purses gone
> And the thief stand and look one full i' the face
> As I may do your worship and your man now.'

In the same play Martia is robbed and then arrested for robbery. The tricks were commonplace on the Italian stage. Jonson's example of Edgeworth the cutpurse of *Bartholomew Fair*, though later than Marston, is earlier than Middleton.

154 17. The effect of this final scene recalls *Measure for Measure*, and Franceschina would not be entirely out of place among the Overdo household. Her power to fascinate Malheureux against his will distinguishes her from the courtesans of such popular plays as *How a Man may Choose a Good Wife*, though the argument of Marston's play is identical with Heywood's. In his tragedy, *The Insatiate Countess*, Marston drew an equally horrible but much less convincing temptress.

155 18. The unity of *The Changeling* was first pointed out by William Empson in *Some Versions of Pastoral* (1936). The apparent dislocation of the story by the mad scenes, the development of the principal character, and the two parallel plots are all Shakespearean in style.

157 19. The Widow-hunt occurs in *Michaelmas Term, No Wit, no Help like a Woman's* and *The Widow*: in *Your Five Gallants* there is an heiress, Katherine; and courtesans pose as heiresses in *A Trick to Catch the Old One*, *A Mad World my Masters* and *A Chaste Maid in Cheapside* (also in Rowley's *A Match at Midnight*). Law terms are exploited in *The Widow*, *Michaelmas Term*, and *The Phoenix*: gangs of cheats appear in *Blurt, Master Constable*, *The Widow*, *Your Five Gallants*, *A Mad World, My Masters*, *The Phoenix*, and Quomodo's servants in *Michaelmas Term* work in the same manner.

158 20. *Blurt, Master Constable* (1602), *Michaelmas Term* (1607), *The Phoenix* (1607), *Your Five Gallants* (1608), *A Mad World, My Masters* (1608), *A Trick to Catch the Old One* (1608). *The Roaring Girl* and *A Chaste Maid in Cheapside*, both for the public stages, appeared after an interval, and the later Fletcherian group, *The Witch*, *A Fair Quarrel*, *The Mayor of Queenborough*, *The Spanish Gipsy* between 1616 and 1623.

159 21. This passage, which appeared some two years later than the publication of *The Revenger's Tragedy*, has an obvious connexion with Vindice's great speech 'Doth the silk worm expend her yellow labours . . .'. Markedly as this most Jonsonian tragedy differs from *The Changeling*, it is very difficult, after reading Middleton's comedies of this period, not to feel that the many echoes—some of a very slight kind, and not like ordinary borrowings—indicate the presence of a common hand in these plays.

160 22. Lazarillo de Tormes, the hero of the first Spanish picaresque novel, began his career as cheat by stealing from the blind beggar whom he led about. Middleton is prepared to mix times and customs as well as races: in *The Mayor of Queenborough*, Hengist and Horsa share the stage with Elizabethan rustics. But the difference between Middleton's and Dekker's Londoners may be seen by comparing the woollen draper Quomodo of *Michaelmas Term* with the linen-draper Candido of *The Honest Whore*; or the goldsmith Touchstone of *Eastward Ho!* may be compared with Yellowhammer of *A Chaste Maid in Cheapside*.

160 23. See Chapter VI, note 13. For the general tradition of the honest plain man, such a figure as Thomas of Woodstock

in his frieze coat (in the play of that name) may be taken as typical. The corresponding antithesis between the gorgeous whore and the threadbare poverty of virtue is perhaps most fully expressed by Castiza of *The Revenger's Tragedy.* Marston, Jonson and Webster have an almost identical vocabulary to describe the painting of diseased women which perhaps derives from Roman satire (compare Maquerelle in *The Malcontent*, the empress in *Sejanus* and the old lady in *The Duchess of Malfi*).

161   24. See above Chapter IV, p. 48, the lines of Weever.

161   25. See Chapter VIII, note 18.

163   26. 'When you shall hear
  Gallants void from sergeants' fear,
  Honesty and truth unslandered,
  Woman manned but never pandered,
  Cheats booted but not coached,
  Vessels older ere they're broached;
  If my mind be then not varied,
  Next day following I'll be married.'   5.2.

CHAPTER X

166   1. Madeleine Doran, *Endeavours of Art*, p. 174.

167   2. The Parnassus plays have been so attributed perhaps only because of Day's prose tract, *Peregrinatio Scholastica*, which was never published (MS. Sloane, 3150). But the theme is a commonplace. Other reasons are dismissed by J. B. Leishmann in his edition of *The Three Parnassus Plays*, pp. 31–32.

167   3. He was the son of a husbandman, born at Cawston in Norfolk. His work lies in the pastoral tradition of Peele, Drayton, Jonson, Herrick: he has perhaps most affinity with Drayton (cf. *Nymphidia*).

168   4. The Messianic Eclogue was the basis of much pastoral poetry celebrating Elizabeth's reign, e.g. Shakespeare's, or, as some would say, Fletcher's encomium at the end of *King Henry VIII.*

168   5. See above, Chapter II, p. 24, for the continuing popularity of *Mucedorus*.

169   6. Sir Edward's letter, March 7, 1606, was written within a month of the production of the play. See the preface to G. B. Harrison's edition (*Shakespeare Association Facsimiles*, No. 12). The title of *The Isle of Gulls* might recall *The Isle of Dogs* to the Elizabethan playgoer: this play, by Nashe, when produced in 1597, had led to the suspension of

NOTES

all playing for two months, and to the imprisonment of the actors concerned.

171   7. Bullen noted echoes of *Pericles* in this play, and other examples of Day's direct borrowing will be found in the notes to his edition of the *Works*. Day seems to have associated with Dekker very closely: passages from *The Parliament of Bees* are almost identically reproduced in *The Wonder of a Kingdom*, and others in *The Noble Soldier*, which Dekker wrote with Rowley.

171   8. Irus has three separate disguises in *The Blind Beggar of Alexandria*. For an account of the other plays see V. O. Freeburg, *Disguise Plots in Elizabethan Drama* (see above, Chapter VI, note 14).

171   9. Preface to *The Revenge of Bussy d'Ambois*. Chapman's heroes are dramatically conceived, but in his tragedies they are too dominant to allow complete drama to develop.

173   10. Dowsecar appears in *An Humourous Day's Mirth* and Clarence in *Sir Giles Goosecap*. Compare the character of Charles in Fletcher's *The Elder Brother*. In all these cases melancholy is expelled by the sanguine humour of love. Chapman's characters often served as model: Poggio of *The Gentleman Usher* reappears in Middleton's *Women beware Women* and Ford's *'Tis Pity she's a Whore*. Monsieur d'Olive is probably the original of Mont Marine in Fletcher's *Noble Gentleman*.

173   11. For example the wounding of Strozza by the poisoned arrow is anticipated by the masque scene in which the Duke enters 'bound' and claims to have been wounded by a boar which turned into a lady and shot him, under the figure of Diana. This allegory is explained, it provides the material for a show, but it does not really relate with the subsequent scene. In *Monsieur d'Olive* two embassies—d'Olive's and St. Anne's—have nothing in common and nothing to contrast but make up the plot and subplot.

174   12. The device of the disfiguring ointment occurs in *The Trial of Chivalry* and in Marston's *Jack Drum's Entertainment*. Vincentio's rivalry with his father for the hand of Margaret recalls *The Wisdom of Dr. Dodypoll*, Marston's *The Fawne*, and Fletcher's *Monsieur Thomas*.

175   13. Compare the judgement scene at the end of *Bartholomew Fair*. Perhaps the nearest thing to *The Widow's Tears* in matrimonial cynicism is Chaucer's *Merchant's Tale*.

176   14. *The Puritan*, written five years earlier for one of the children's companies, contains a widow and her two daughters who all make protestations against matrimony

and all succumb; but the play is chiefly devoted to the conjuring tricks of an Oxford scholar, in the manner of those of *The Merry Devil of Edmonton*. Dekker, Middleton and Fletcher all use the theme of the widow-hunt. *Keep the Widow Waking*, a lost play, depicted a recent public scandal, in which a wealthy old woman was trapped into matrimony by a schemer.

177   15. A study of the problems of authorship is being undertaken by Cyrus Hoy, of the University of Virginia. Some consideration is given in the work of A. C. Partridge.

178   16. See above, Chapter VI, p. 91. The lady protests throughout that she loves Petruchio:

> 'Were I yet unmarried, free to choose
> Through all the tribes of men, I'll take Petruchio,
> In's shirt, with one ten groats to pay the priest,
> Before the best man living. . . .'

179   17. Many of these disguises are in common form: the man who disguises himself as a woman to achieve a conquest of his mistress appears in Haughton's play, *Englishmen for My Money*, as well as *Monsieur Thomas* and *The Wild Goose Chace*. See Chapter VIII, note 18, for other examples.

180   18. On the other hand, Fletcher's lyrics are often the clinching statement of a main theme. Such for example is the beautiful lyric of Charles in *The Elder Brother*, 3.5, where this scholarly Morose is converted to love.

182   19. This is the doctrine of *Le Cid* or *Don Sebastian*, rather than of *Much Ado About Nothing* or *All's Well that Ends Well*. Of the point of honour and the duel, apart from this play and *The Little French Lawyer*, not much is heard: but compare *A Fair Quarrel*, a play which has given rise to some sentimental vaporizings, but which is remarkably inconsistent in its view.

183   20. Monsieur Thomas, the soldier lover of *The Wild Goose Chace*, Wittipate and his brother in *Wit at Several Weapons*, all achieve advanced intoxication.

184   21. In tragi-comedy and tragedy a peculiar cumulative style is developed with all the marks of rhetorical inflation upon it. See above, Chapter IV, p. 56.

185   22. See John Danby, *Poets on Fortune's Hill* (1952), for an account of this play; and for a general account of lovemelancholy, Lawrence Babb, *The Elizabethan Malady*, Chapters VI and VII.

NOTES

CHAPTER XI

187   1. The marriage of Hymen and Eucharis in the Tale of Teras forms part of the Fifth Sestiad of *Hero and Leander*, and is a gorgeous celebration of the public and ceremonial nature of the contract. Ironically the Jonsonian marriage was that of the Earl of Essex and Lady Frances Howard, which led to the Overbury murder five years later, a scandal in which even royalty was implicated.

188   2. The traditional garment for Nobody, who appears in Jonson's first masque, *The Satyr* (June, 1603): compare the morality *Nobody and Somebody*. The four ancient poets appear in *The Golden Age Restored* (1616) and Skelton and Scogan in *The Fortunate Isles* (1626), 'in their habits as they lived'. They lead in the antemasque of Howleglass, the four knaves of cards, two ruffians, Elinor Rumming, Mary Ambree, Long Meg of Westminster, Tom Thumb and Dr. Rat. Skelton speaks Latin and English.

188   3. In the antemasques to *Love Restored* and *The Masque of Augurs*.

188   4. Compare the mistaken letter of the Rycote masque (Chapter IV, p. 46).

189   5. Felons were burnt in the hand. Jonson had himself been branded on the thumb for killing a fellow actor, Gabriel Spencer, in a duel.

190   6. The somewhat presumptuous, not to say, reckless classifying of Jonson as an anal-erotic psychological type by Edmund Wilson in *The Triple Thinkers* (1948) ignores the revels and the full dramatic implications of the acted play. He is treating Jonson simply as a lettered writer.

190   7. *Pleasure Reconciled to Virtue* is a masque to which Milton was deeply indebted. It includes the figure of 'Comus ye god of cheer or ye belly', leading in a rout of bottles and tuns. The basic idea is of course that of the Choice of Hercules between pleasure and virtue. This masque caused a quarrel with the ambassadors who were to see it. Hence the jest in *The Masque of Augurs* (see p. 193) about the Welsh ambassador (a common name for the cuckoo).

192   8. An account of Captain Cox's entertainment will be found in Robert Laneham's letter reprinted with the account of the Kenilworth entertainment in John Nichols, *Progresses and Public Processions of Queen Elizabeth* (2 vols., 1788). The play celebrated a local victory of English over the Danes, supposed to have occurred in 1012. 'The thing they said is grounded on story and for pastime wont to be

plaid in our city yearly: without ill example of papistry or any superstition.'

194   9. For the pun, cf. *Hamlet*, 2.2.174. The ten children of Christmas are Misrule, Carol, Mincepie, Gambol, Post-and-Pair, New Year's Gift, Mumming, Wassail, Offering and Baby-Cake, each dressed in character and attended with a torch bearer bearing emblems of his state.

194   10. Such as those of *The Hue and Cry after Cupid*, where Venus descends crowned, attended by the Graces, to the music of a song:

> 'Beauties, have you seen this toy,
> Called Love, a little boy?
> Almost naked, wanton, blind,
> Cruel now, and then as kind?
> If he be among you, say?
> He is Venus' runaway.'

195   11. Michael Drayton was left almost alone to write in the fashion of the earlier day. The first part of his Polyolbion came out in 1612, the second in 1622, and *Nymphidia* in 1627. Jonson's failure as a dramatist, culminating in the fiasco of *The New Inn*, provoked his furious *Ode to Himself*, for which he was taunted by some of the younger writers.

195   12. See note 2. Scogan was Henry VIII's jester, and a popular collection of jests was attributed to him. He is a comparable figure to Will Summers.

195   13. See above, Chapter VII, p. 104, and Chapter II, p. 15. Chapman also uses the comparison (Chapter IX, p. 165). The original is Martial, Book IX, lxxxi:

> 'Cenae fercula nostra
> malim convivis quam placuisse cocis.'

195   14. Compare the mock-praise of the antemasque by Vangoose in *The Masque of Augurs*: 'de more absurd it be, ever all de better. If it go from de nature of de ting, it is de more art: for dere is art, and dere is nature, you shall see.'

196   15. Compare the masque at the end of *Cynthia's Revels*, where Cupid enters disguised as Anteros, leading various disguised characters. When they are unmasked, and Cupid also appears in his true colours, he is banished by Cynthia and the masquers punished. The masque here then turns out to be a mockery: it becomes instead a moral stripping of the vices and a Judgement scene.

196   16. Various works by Wilson Knight; E. M. W. Tillyard, *Shakespeare's Last Plays* (1951), S. L. Bethell, *The*

NOTES

Winter's Tale (1947), may be cited. Perhaps the finest commentary is T. S. Eliot's poem 'Marina' based upon *Pericles*.

197   17. George Wilkins, *The Painful Adventures of Pericles, Prince of Tyre, being the true History of the Play of Pericles, as it was lately presented by the worthy and ancient poet, John Gower*, 1608. The relation of this work to the play is complex, as it appears to rely upon a drama substantially different from the text which now survives. *Pericles*, like *Mucedorus* and *Hamlet*, must have existed in several forms. Tatham, in lines prefixed to Brome's *Jovial Crew*, thinks it Shakespeare's: 'But Shakespeare, the plebean driller, was Founder'd in *Pericles*'.

197   18. These include symmetrical reduplication of all the characters: Hippolito, the 'man who has never seen a woman', being the most disagreeably salacious, and the new Miranda, in the guise of a Restoration prude, the most unrecognizable of the originals.

198   19. Cf. above, p. 115, for other examples. The play of *The Clown and the Cheats*, in Middleton's *Mayor of Queenborough*, is strongly reminiscent of the cheats of Autolycus in *The Winter's Tale*.

198   20. See J. M. S. Tompkins, 'Why Pericles?' (*Review of English Studies*, New Series, Vol. III, pp. 315–324), and John Danby, *Poets on Fortune's Hill*. There is a significant difference as well as a likeness in comparison with the theme of submission to an earthly ruler. A kind of masculine Patient Grissel emerges in Heywood's *Royal King and Loyal Subject*, Chapman's *Chabot*, and the tragi-comedies of Fletcher, quite devoid of Pericles' prowess.

200   21. Granville Barker's appreciation in his *Prefaces to Shakespeare*, Second Series (1930), emphasizes this quality, and is the best introduction to the play.

201   22. 3.4, 38 ff. 'False to his bed? What is it to be false? . . .' Imogen's feelings, a mixture of Desdemona's and Hermione's, are confused but quickly brought under control.

202   23. Shaw's views on the play are well known. Dr. Johnson's are even more entertaining:

> 'To remark the folly of the fiction, the absurdity of the conduct, the confusion of names and manners of different times, and the impossibility of the events in any system of life, were to waste criticism upon unresisting imbecillity, upon faults too evident for detection and too gross for aggravation.'

202   24. The chief correspondences are between *Cymbeline* and *Philaster*. Arethusa is Imogen; Bellario, Fidele; Philaster, Posthumus; and Pharamond, Cloten. Arethusa loves without her father's consent, runs away, is falsely accused and wounded, and rescued by a countryman. Bellario in her page's attire wandering in the woods, and seeking death, is, like Arethusa, a creature of absolute fidelity: both are ready to die at Philaster's hand. But there are echoes of other plays of Shakespeare: the King's prayer (*Philaster*, 2.4) recalls Claudius, and Philaster in situation resembles Hamlet; Dion's speech following is in the tradition of Malvolio; Arethusa's defence of Bellario recalls Desdemona's of Cassio. It seems unlikely that the more complex indebtedness should occur in the earlier play.

202   25. See Lawrence Babb, *The Elizabethan Malady*. Sir John Gielgud's production gave this interpretation to the part: i.e. Leontes was treated sympathetically.

204   26. See note 19 above for a parallel to Autolycus. The idyll of Act IV represents The Triumph of Time (the sub-title of Greene's original romance). Perdita as a re-embodiment of Hermione—the likeness is stressed when she meets Leontes —was in Gielgud's production dressed in a replica of her mother's costume for the final scene. It is perhaps worth noting that in this play the rediscovery of Hermione is directly staged, and that of Perdita played down; whereas in the corresponding scenes of *Pericles*, it is the daughter's discovery which is stressed, and the reunion of husband and wife becomes a more or less formal pageant.

204   27. See Paul N. Siegal, 'Leontes a Jealous Tyrant' (*Review of English Studies*, New Series, Vol. I, pp. 302–307).

CHAPTER XII

207   1. See e.g. Robert Speaight, *William Poel and the Elizabethan Revival* (London 1954), Peter Arnott, *Greek Scenic Conventions in the fifth century* B.C. (Oxford, 1962), Chapters 1—2.

209   2. This in itself revives the Elizabethan courtly habit of 'exploding the play' at the end by such a device as Paris's delivering the ball of gold to Queen Elizabeth at the end of Peele's *Arraignment of Paris*; or the more popular habit of the clowns in improvising jests on themes supplied by the audience.

211   3. Philip Stubbes, *An Anatomy of Abuses* . . . 1583, ed. F. J. Furnivall (London, 1877), p. 147. He continues:
Against May, Whitsunday or other time all the young men and maids, old men and wives run gadding overnight to the woods . . . where they spend all the night in pleasant pastimes . . .

NOTES

I have heard it credibly reported . . . that of forty, three-
score or a hundred maids going to the wood over night, there
have scarcely the third part of them returned home again
undefiled (p. 149).

In *Two Noble Kinsmen*, the Jailor's Daughter certainly expects
that after a night in the greenwood, she will have enjoyed Palamon.
For a consideration of ambivalence and the sinister element in
A Midsummer Night's Dream, see Herbert S. Weil Jr., 'Comic
Structure and Tonal Manipulation in Shakespeare and Some
Modern Plays', *Shakespeare Survey* 22 (Cambridge, 1969).

212   4. See David M. Bergeron, *English Civic Pageantry*, 1558-1642
(London, 1971) p. 126. Sir William Harper, of the Merchant
Taylors, was inaugurated in 1561.

212   5. Glynne Wickham, *Early English Stages* (London, 1959, 1963,
1972) discusses at length the game or playhouses, which he
derives from the ancient playing place, while distinguishing
plég stow and *plég hus*, vol. 2, Pt. 2, 1972 (chapter XI).

212   6. See William Ingram, 'The Playhouse at Newington Butts',
Shakespeare Quarterly vo. XXI, No. 4 (Autumn, 1970) pp. 385-
298. The playhouse at first belonged to Jerome Savage, of the
Earl of Warwick's Men; Strange's Men played there as late as
1592 and Henslowe arranged for the Admiral's and the Chamberlain's Men to open there after the long closure for plague of all
London threatres, in 1594. It was taken down in 1597.

213   7. Glynne Wickham, *loc. cit.*

214   8. David Reisman, *The Lonely Crowd* (Yale, 1950); Daniel J.
Boorstin, *The Image* (New York, 1962). These are cited as famous
examples of a whole flourishing literature of sociology. Boorstin's
discussion of the pseudo-event and his chapter on 'Dissolving
Forms' are particularly relevant.

214   9. Theseus and Hippolita doubled with Oberon and Titania, at one
point very ostentationsly exchanging rôles; Puck doubled with
Philostrate; Egeus doubled with Peter Quince because Quince
originally cast himself as Thisbe's father, although he does not
actually appear in the Play within the play.

216 10. The work of Jean Jacquot and his colleagues at the *Centre
Nationale de la Récherche Scientifique* includes such central
collections as *Le Lieu Théâtral à la Renaissances* (Paris, 1964)
and *Dramaturgie et Société* (Paris, 1968).

216 11. The following paragraphs summarise an argument I have put
forward in an article, 'Shakespeare and the Transformation of
Tudor Society', *Review of National Literature*: 'Shakespeare and
England', ed. Anne Paolucci (New York, Fall, 1972). I have
made use for the purposes of definition there of the work of Jean
Piaget, *Le Structuralisme* (Presses Universitaire de France,
No. 1311, collection *Que sais-je?* Paris, 1968).

216 12. See especially Sydney Anglo, *Spectacle, Pageantry and Early*

Page *Note No.*

Tudor Politics (London, 1969); the work of David M. Bergeron (note 4 above); for the iconography of Queen Elizabeth, see Roy Strong, *Portraits of Queen Elizabeth I* (Oxford, 1963).

217   13. For Glynne Wickham, see the reference in note 5 above, and for the decline of provincial theatre, see L. G. Salingar, in *Dramaturgie et Société* (note 10 above).

219   14. For the plot of *The Silent Woman*, long considered a classic unity see Ray L. Heffner in *Elizabethan Drama*, ed. Ralph J. Kaufman (Oxford, 1961). Ian Donaldson published a rejoinder in *The World Upside Down*, Chapter 2.

219   15. Harry Levin, '*The Tempest* and *The Alchemist*' in *Shakespeare Survey* 22 (Cambridge, 1969), a volume devoted to aspects of Comedy. Ian Donaldson, 'Language, Noise and Nonsense: *The Alchemist*' in *Seventeenth Century Imagery*, ed. Earl Miner (California University Press Berkeley and London, 1971). Cf. also his article in *The Sphere History of Literature*, ed. Christopher Ricks, vol. 3 (London, 1971).

220   16. The Revels Plays, the Regent Renaissance Drama Series, the New Mermaids have all produced a good deal of Jonson in their single-play volumes; as for the volume of commentary, the annual Shakespeare bibliography in *Shakespeare Quarterly* now contains over a thousand items each year.

220   17. Glynne Wickham in a paper read at Stratford in 1972, to be published in *Shakespeare Survey* for 1973.

222   18. I have dealt with *Two Noble Kinsmen* from this point of view (*Shakespeare* 1971 (Proceedings of the World Shakespeare Congress, Vancouver, August 1971) ed. Clifford Leech and J. M. R. Margeson (Toronto, 1972), pp. 21-36.) In the same volume, Bernard Beckerman writes on the role of the theatre director, in combining a modern 'frame' with Shakespeare's text.

INDEX

INDEX

262

INDEX

263

INDEX